RIVERS IN HINDU MYTHOLOGY AND RITUAL

RIVERS IN HINDU MYTHOLOGY AND RITUAL

By

Dr. S.K LAL

BKP

BHARATIYA KALA PRAKASHAN
DELHI (INDIA)

First Edition : 2007

Published by **C.P. Gautam**
BHARATIYA KALA PRAKASHAN
3421-A, IInd Floor, Narang Colony, Tri Nagar,
Delhi-110035. Phone : 27393083, 32967505 (O), 32492129 (R)
E-Mail : bkp 3421@yahoo.co.in

ISBN : 81-8090-147-5

Laser Type Setting by
A-ONE GRAPHICS
JD-18C, IInd Floor, Pitampura, Delhi-110088

Printed By :
BDH Printer at Salasar Imaging Systems
Delhi.

Dedicated
To
My Father
Ramapati Prasad Lal

CONTENTS

	Transliteration	...	*ix*
	Introduction	...	*xi*
1.	Rivers	...	1-156
2.	Abbreviations & Bibliography	...	157-159
3.	List of Mountains	...	160-162
4.	Index of Rivers	...	163-175
5.	Index of Tīrthas & Temples	...	176-179
6.	General Index	...	180-188

TRANSLITERATION

अ	आ	इ	ई	उ	ऊ	ऋ
a	ā	i	ī	u	ū	ṛ
लृ	ए	ऐ	ओ	औ	अं	अः
lṛ	ē	ai	ō	au	aṁ	aḥ
क	ख	ग	घ	ङ		
ka	kha	ga	gha	ṅa		
च	छ	ज	झ	ञ		
ca	cha	ja	jha	ña		
ट	ठ	ड	ढ	ण		
ṭa	ṭha	ḍa	ḍha	ṇa		
त	थ	द	ध	न		
ta	tha	da	dha	na		
प	फ	ब	भ	म		
pa	pha	ba	bha	ma		
य	र	ल	व	श	ष	
ya	ra	la	va	śa	ṣa	
स	ह	क्ष	त्र	ज्ञ		
sa	ha	kṣa	tra	jña		

INTRODUCTION

गङ्गे च यमुने चैव गोदावरि सरस्वति।
नर्मदे सिन्धो कावेरि जलेऽस्मिन् सन्निधिंकुरु॥

आह्निक सूत्रावलि: १०६

Such is the attitude of a pious Hindu towards his rivers. He invokes the seven holy rivers, in different parts of our country, to be present in the water for his morning bath. He believes that the presence of these rivers in the water makes it as holy and sacred as the rivers themselves are. *Medhyā vā āpah* (*waters are indeed sacred*, ŚB 1.1.1.1), and *amṛtā hyāpḥ* (waters are in fact nectar, ŚB 3,9,4,16). And so, he believes, they will bring him purity and immortality.

The rivers had attracted the attention of even the Ṛṣi-poets of the Vedas. Right from the Ṛgvedic times downwards to the post-Vedic and Purāṇic periods, Sanskrit literature is replete with vivid descriptions and perspicuous portrayals of the rivers and the venerations the poets had for them. The rivers are not regarded as merely a flowing mass of waters, but as life-bestowing, life-nurturing, and life-protecting divine mothers. They are implored for protection (*avantu mā sindhavaḥ pinvamānāh*, ṚV 6.52.4). They are the very breaths of people (*āpo vai prāṇāḥ*, ŚB 3. 8. 2. 4). They are sources of plenitude (*te sindhavo varivo dhātana*, ṚV 7.47.4) and they are prayed to grant people nourishment and delight (ṚV 10.9.1).

Banks of the rivers are regarded as suitable sites for performing sacrifices (Gopatha Brāhmaṇa 1.2.14). Offerings are made to the rivers in sacrifices (*ṚV* 1.23.18; 7.47.3). The river Sarasvatī is particualaly urged to accept the sacrifice (*ṚV*

1.3.10; 11). She is worshipped while the sacrifice is in progress (*ṚV 10*.17.7).

It may be pointed out that in the Purāṇic literature all the seven streams of the river Sarasvatī are linked with one or the other sacrifices (Vāmanp., SM, 16. 17; 18; 36. 54). The absence of the Sarasvatī in a sacrifice was considered a deficiency (Vāmanp., SM, 16. 19; 20).

Once Brahmā performed a great sacrifice. Many Ṛṣis arrived there, but they did not see the river Sarasvatī there. They told Brahmā that the sacrifice would not bear fruits unless Sarasvatī was present. Brahmā thought of her and she appeared there under the name Suprabhā.

Many kings of yore had performed great sacrifices on the rivers. King Matināra performed a twelve-year long sacrifice on the bank of the river Sarasvatī. After the completion of the sacrifice, Sarasvatī married the king and begot a son named Taṁsu. King Daśaratha (of the Rāmāyaṇa) had performed the Putreṣṭi on the bank of the Sarayū and obtained four sons: Rāma, Lakṣmaṇa, Bharata, and Śatrughna. King Drupada had performed a sacrifice on the bank of the river Kalmāṣī for getting a child. Draupadī was born as a result of that sacrifice. Dharma had performed a sacrifice on the bank of the Vaitaraṇī. The river Manoramā has risen from the sacrifice of Uddālaka in the north of Kośala. At the confluence of the rivers Jalā and Upajalā, the king Uśīnara had performed the sacrifice and thereby had surpassed Indra in greatness. It is said that Dakṣa had performed the sacrifice in a village Dhulkhed on the bank of the river Bhīmā.

This close associaton of the rivers with the sacrifices was carried on, albeit in a transformed way, in the post-Vedic particularly Purāṇic literature. It is found in the Purāṇic texts that the rivers and their connection with the sacrifices have, as it were, merged into one. The rivers themselves have become so holy and sacred that they yield fruits and bring rewards of the Vedic sacrifices like the Agṇiṣṭoma, the Vājapeya, and the Rājasūya. What is required is a dip in their waters.

Thus, if a person bathes in the river Āpagā and the river Sarasvatī, he reaps the fruits of the Agniṣṭoma sacrifice. A person who offers ablutions to gods and manes at the confluence of the Śoṇa and the Jyotirathā obtains the merit of the Agniṣṭoma. The rewards of the Agniṣṭona and Atirātra sacrifices are gained if one observes fast on the banks of the river Aruṇā. A bath in the river Dṛṣadvatī and ablutions to gods and manes on her banks brings the benefits of the Agniṣ ṭoma and Atirātra sacrifices, and a bath in the confluence of the river Aruṇā and the Sarasvatī brings the fruits of the same sacrifices.

Whoever takes a bath on the twelth of the bright half of Māgha in the Urvaśī-Kuṇḍa on the Bhasmācala, which is a hill in the river Brahmaputra, obtains the merit of performing the Aśvamedha sacrifice. A dip in the river Jayantī earns a person the fruits of the Rājasūya sacrifice. The river Kauśikī grants the rewards of the Rājasūya sacrifice to a person who resorts to her.

The river Gaṇḍakī and the river Veṇṇā bestow the merits of the Vājyapeya sacrifice to a person who bathes in them. A dip in the river Bāhudā yields the benefits of a sacrifice. A bath in the confluence of the Payoṣṇī with the river Mahā brings the rewards of performing one hundred sacrifices.

A person who offers ablutions to gods and manes on the banks of the Veṇṇā obtains a chariot drawn by peacocks and swans.

One of the inherent abilities of the rivers in the early literatures which continued to be further emphasized in the Purāṇic literaure is their capability of washing away sins. In ṚV 10.17.10, the rivers have been regarded as destroyers of sins and defilements, and it is solicited that the mother rivers purify and brighten the worshippers by their holy waters. This aspect of holiness of the rivers in removing sins has found ample expression in the post-Vedic Purāṇic literature where it is patently said that almost all important rivers are capable of removing sins (MBh 3.82. 113; 135; 8.3.55; Matsyp., 185.11;

Padmp., Ādikhaṇḍa, 41.4; Vāmanp., SM, 15.47; Varāhp., 144.9; etc.).

If a person observes fast on the banks of the river Aruṇā and bathes in her water, he is absolved of even the greatest sins like brahmahatyā, and his family up to the seventh generation is purified. Even the demons became free from demonhood after drinking the water of the Aruṇā.

King Bhīmaratha of Ayodhyā had once killed, unknowingly, a Brāhmaṇa couple. To get rid of the sin, the king practised penance and propitiated Śiva. Śiva, being pleased, asked the king to seek a boon. The king saw that Śiva was full of fatigue and three were drops of sweat on his forehead. (Śiva, after killing the demon Tripura, had come to Bhīmāśaṅkara for rest). Bhīmaratha requested Śiva to turn his drops of sweat into a river. Śiva did so. This became the river Bhīmā. The king bathed in the river and was condoned of the sin. The confluence of the Dṛṣadvatī with the Kauśikī is so sacred that when a person bathes there he is freed from all sins. By merely seeing the water of the Gaṇḍakī one's sins of mind (*mānasa-pāpa*), by touching her water one's sins of bad deeds (*duṣkarma*), and by drinking her water one's sins of speech (*vācika-pāpa*) are burnt. A person who bathes in the *Saṅgama* of the rivers Kālikā and Sarayū is absolved of all sins. One who keeps fast on the banks of the river Kumāradhārā and bathes in her is forgiven even for the sin of brahmahatyā. One who takes a dip in the river Śālunkinī gets his sins remitted and he obtains his desired *loka*. Indra had killed Vṛtra who was a Brāhmaṇa. Due to his this sin, Śrī deserted him. He bathed in the river Samaṅgā and was pardoned of the sin and he regained his lost glory. He bathed in the river Aruṇā and became free from the sin of killing Namuci. A person who fasts for three nights and bathes in the confluence of the Aruṇā and the Sarasvatī is freed from the sin of brahmahatyā and his family up to the seventh generation is cleansed of all defilements. Bathing on the Paurṇamāsī of the month of Māgha at Galiteśvara on the river Tāpī brings virtues equal to donating ten lakhs gold coins at Puṣkara.

The rivers are regarded as an effective source of removing ugliness and bringing lustre to one who bathes in them. Even the gods resort to the rivers.

Skanda repented because he had pierced the mt. Krauñca who was his own brother where Mahiṣāsura had been hiding. Skanda thereupon lost his lustre. Viṣṇu advised him to go to the tīrtha Pṛthūdaka and bathe in the river Oghavatī. Skanda did so, and regained his splendour. The king Purūravas practised penance on the banks of the river Haimavatī to get rid of his ugliness (Matsyp. 115) and regained his handsomeness. (See under Airāvatī for the story). Kubera became the lord of wealth after bathing in the Godāvarī. Indra once lost his positon of the king of gods. He regained it after he was sprinkled with the water of the Godāvarī. When the lustre of Ṛṣi Paraśurāma had dimmed by the arrow of Rāma, the Ṛṣi secured it only after bathing in the river Vadhūsarā.

From the above details, a pertinent purpose of Sanskrit writers emerges. They may have intended to prescribe baths in a river with a view to aiming at and emphasizing on a person's physical hygiene under the garb of religion, and also preventing him from polluting the rivers.

The rivers are deemed to have the power of removing the harmful effects of poison and curing snake bite. The river Sarasvatī makes poison flow away (ṚV 6.61.3) and in ṚV 6.61.4 she is invoked to eliminate the effects of poison. The rivers are prayed to wash off the poison of snakes (AV 10.4.20). In Viṣṇu p.4.3.10, it is said that the very name of Narmadā blots out the fear of snakes. The same Purāṇa (*ibid*) mentions a story wherein the Narmadā is empowered with such a boon. (See under Narmadā).

The rivers are also regarded as capable of curing diseases. The waters are regarded as physicians (AV 6.24.2). The rivers are invoked to cure diseases named *Śipada* and *Śimida* (ṚV 7.50.4). Kauśikasūtra 30.13 employs AV 6.24, which is a prayer to the river, for removing heart ailments (*hṛdaya-doṣa*), dropsy (*jalodara*) and jaundice (*kāmala*). A person who bathes in the river Aṁbuvaśyā gets cured of all diseases. The water of the river Śatadru also cures diseases.

The waters of some of the rivers are regarded medicinal. The water of the Śatadru is appetising (*pācanam*). The water of the Yamunā produces heat and wind in the body, and it is also digestive. The water of the Godāvarī cures leprosy, consumption, blood-pressure and indigestion. The water of the Gaṅgā is cool, sweet, appetizing and digestive. It enhances intelligence. The water of the Narmadā is light and cool, and it pacifies heat and bile.

There is a practice among the village folk. If a person suffers from a particular neck-disease (*gaṇḍamāla* in Hindi), a vow is made to the river Gaṅgā that if the person is cured, the river would be worshipped with a rite known as *gaṅgā māī kī mālā* (garland for mother Gaṅgā). After the initial rites are performed on the bank of the river, the performer with other participants goes to the other bank of the Gaṅgā meausring the entire breadth of the river with a huge garland. The remaining rites are performed on reaching the other bank.

It is efficacious to take bath in a river daily. It is more efficacious on certain auspicious days of a month. A bath in Gaṅgā on the full-moon days of Āṣāḍha, Kārtika, Māgha, and Vaiśākha brings great merit (*puṇya*). One acquires holiness after a bath in the Gaṅgā on the seventh of the bright-half of Māgha, on a Akṣayatithi, on the Amāvāsyā days, on the day of Saṅkrānti and on the days of solar and lunar eclipses. A dip in the water of Kāverī accrues the fruit of donating one thousand cows. Bathing in the confluence of the rivers Veda and the Kṛṣṇā produces merit equal to donating ten thousand cows, or donating land. One who bathes in the river Payoṣṇī at Koṭitīrtha and has *darśana* of Koṭeśvara there, gets the benefits of giving away a hundred thousand kapilā cows. A bath in the river Varadā brings rewards of donating one thousand cows.

A person, desirous of a son, should bathe in the Yamunā on each Śrāvaṇa-nakṣatra for a year. He would get a son like Parāśara.

A bath in the Tāpī-sāgara-saṅgama on the Amāvāsyā of the month of Mārgaśīrṣa yields great rewards. Bathing at Galiteśvara on the Tāpī on the Paurṇamāsī of Māgha brings benefits equal to donating ten million gold coins at Puṣkara.

The rivers are imbued with purity, sanctity, and divine powers. They are efficient means to bring salvation and also to enable one to go to the imperishable world (Akṣaya-loka) and to the abodes of gods, such as, Brahmaloka, Indraloka, Viṣṇuloka, Rudraloka, Sūryaloka, and Soma (Candra) loka, etc.

An offering of Śyāmāka grains into the river Āpagā to gods and manes brings great religious merits, and an offering of cooked rice balls (*piṇḍas*) to the maneṣ in the month of Bhādrapada in that river brings salvation. A person who bathes in the Narmadā and fasts there for a night liberates himself and his one hundred ancestors. A bath in the river Tāmraparṇī frees a person from the cycle of births and deaths.

One who observes fast, consuming only air, on the banks of the river Kauśikī goes to the heaven in twenty-one days. It is enjoined in MBh, Āraṇyakaparva, 85.94 and many Purāṇas that the charred bones and ashes of the burnt body of a dead person should be cast in the river Gaṅgā. It enables the person not only to go to the heaven but also stay there as long as the bones remain in the water of the Gaṅgā.

An ablution of water to the manes in the Mahānadī entitles a person to secure Akṣaya-loka. A person who bathes in the river Aṁbuvaśyā goes to the Brahmaloka. A dip in the river Gaṇḍakī and also in the river Kaṁpanā enables one to go to the Sūryaloka. Somaloka is gained by bathing in the river Candrabhāgā. The river Sakṛnnandā makes one's soul pious and he attains Indraloka. One who stays on the banks of the river Viśalyā obtains Rudraloka. The river Narmadā enables a person to secure Rudraloka.

The rivers are venerated as divine beings, so much so that many important gods of Hinduism are associated with them, or they actually dwell in them in one form or the other. Thus,

Vāmana lives in the river Airāvatī in the form of Rūpadhara. Brahmvp, Prakṛtikhaṇḍa, 11.12 mentions that Gaṅgā is the beloved of Kṛṣṇa. She is regarded as a portion *(aṁśa)* of Rādhā. Gaṅgā married Kṛṣṇa (*Ibid*., 10.114). However, it is Śiva who is more prominently associated with Gaṅgā.

Viṣṇu lives in most of the rivers in different forms. It may be pointed out that in the Vedic literature, it is Indra who is mostly associated with the rivers. The rivers are wives of Indra (ṚV 5.42.12) and he is their lord (ṚV 10.180.1.). The rivers obey Indra's commands (ṚV 1. 109.3) and never violate his authority (ṚV 7.47.3). Indra, however, has never been associated with any particualr river. In the post-Vedic Purāṇic literature, that place has been taken by Viṣṇu. Gaṅgā is Viṣṇu's wife (BrahmVP, Prakṛtikhaṇḍa, 6.17). The rivers Varaṇā and Asi have risen from the two toes of Yogaśāyī (Viṣ ṇu) (Vāmanp, 3.27.28).

Vāmanp., 63.7 mentions different forms of Viṣṇu who live in the rivers. A few of them may be metioned here.

Viṣṇu lives in the river Bhīmā in the form of Śaṅkukarṇa, and in the river Devikā as Bhūdhara. The river Gaṇḍakī once practised penance and pleased Viṣṇu for a boon. She chose to become his mother. Viṣṇu granted and said that he would remain in the form of Śālagrāmas (stones in a special shape found in the bed of the Gaṇḍakī) with her and would be worshipped in that form as her son. (For the importance of Śālagrāma, see Padmp., Pātālakhaṇḍa, 4.20.16 ff). Viṣṇu lives in the river Mahākośī as a *haṁsa*. He lives in the river Mahodakī as Kuśapriya, as Akhaṇḍa in the river Payoṣṇī, as Śambhu in the Sarayū, as Rukmakavaca in the Śoṇa, as Dvijapriya in the river Vipāśā, as Kumārila in the Vitastā, and as Śrīkaṇṭha in the river Yamunā. In fact, it is said in the Padmp., Bhūmikhaṇḍa, 39.46-47 that all rivers, whether flowing through a village or a forest, are holy and that if no name of a tīrtha on rivers is known, it should be called Viṣṇutīrtha.

ग्रामे वा यदि वाऽरण्ये नद्यः सर्वत्र पावनाः।
तत्र तत्र प्रकर्तव्याः स्नानदानादिकाः क्रियाः।।
यदा न ज्ञायते नाम तासां तीर्थस्य सत्तम।
नाम चैव प्रकर्तव्यं विष्णुतीर्थमिदं नृप।।

Some of the incarnatious of Viṣṇu had taken place on the rivers. Agnip. 2.4 mentons that Manu had found the fish (of the Matsyāvatāra of Viṣṇu) in the river Kṛtamālā. The ship sailed up to the Satīdeśa which is now known as Kashmir. In the legend of Deluge, Viṣṇu had become Matsya. The ship (*nau*) in which the creatures were carried was in fact goodess Durgā. The ship was carried to the west of the Banhal Pass in the Pir Pantsal range to the highest peak called Nau-bandhana-tīrtha.

Viṣṇu's Varāhāvatāra took place on the right bank of the river Vitastā at Varāhamūla (now called Baramula) on the Śūkara-kṣetra situated about fifty kms from Śrīnagar.

There was a demon named Guha. He practised penance to propitiate Brahmā. Guha sought a boon that neither Viṣṇu nor Śiva could be able to kill him. Brahmā granted the boon. Puffed up with the boon, Guha started persecuting gods and men. Because of the boon, it was necessary for Viṣṇu and Śiva to have a combined form to kill the demon. They became Harihara. It is stated that the Harihara incarnaton had taken place at Kudlur where the river Tuṅgabhadrā meets the river Haridrā.

Aśvakrānta is a tīrtha on the northern bank of the river Brahmaputra. It is said that when Kṛṣṇa came to Pragjyotiṣa (modern Assam), he rested on this hill with his horse. This is a tīrtha sacred to Janārdana. To the south of Aśvakrānta is situated the lake Aśvītīrtha. The tīrtha is also associated with the Kalkī incarnation of Viṣṇu.

Besides gods, the rivers are associated with the humans also as their spouses and wives. The story of the marriage of Gaṅgā with king Śantanu is well-known (MBh, Ādiparva, 1.91; 92 and Devībhp. 2.3;4). King Matināra performed a twelve-year long *sattra* on the bank of the river Sarasvatīī. After the completion of the sacrifice, she married the king. Taṁsu was born out of this marriage. The river Śuktimatī flowed by the capital city of king Uparicara. The mount Kolāhala sought the river Śuktimatī who was in deep love with her. The king did not like this, and struck the mountain with his foot. The river came out of the embrace of Kolāhala. But by that time she had already conceived. In due course, she gave birth to a twins. The river gave both the children to the king. He appointed the male child as the General of his army, and married the female named Girikā. The river Tāpī, daughter of Vivasvān, married kịng Saṁvaraṇa and begot a son named Kuru.

Kuntī (of the Mahābhārata) is said to have left the infant Karṇa in a casket (*manjūṣā*) in the river Aśvanadī.

Many *tīthas* (holy places of pilgrimage) are situated near or on the banks of the rivers. These tīrthas have been mentioned, in this work, along with the descriptions of the individual rivers. An Index of the tīrthas has also been added.

Some of the Jyotirlingas are found on the banks of the rivers and their sources. At Bhīmāśaṅkara, the source of the river Bhīmā, there is the famous Jyotirliṅga. At the village Tryaṁbaka, which is the source of the Godāvarī, there is the Jyotirlinga called Tryaṁbakeśvara. On the island of Māndhātā, in the river Narmadā, stands the famous temple of Omkāranātha which is one of the twelve Jyotirlingas. The famous Jyotirlinga of Mahākāla is found in Ujjayini (Ujjain) on the bank of the river Śiprā.

Many Āśramas (hermitages) of the Ṛṣis and Munis were situated on the banks of the rivers. The hermitage of Ṛṣi Ārṣṭaṣ eṇa was situated on the bank of the river Aśvarathā. Ṛṣi Bhāradvāja had his Āśrama on the confluence of the Gaṅgā and the Yamunā. Kuśadhvaja, brother of king Janaka, lived in the city Saṅkāśya on the bank of the river Ikṣumatī. The Āśrama of sage Kapila was situated on the river Kapiladhārā. (This Kapila is different from Ṛṣi Kapila of Sagaropākhyāna). The holy Naimiṣāraṇya of the Mahābhārata and the Purāṇa fame was situated on the bank of the river Dṛṣadvatī. The famous Pañcavaṭī where Rāma, Sītā, and Lakṣmaṇa had spent their exile is situated on the bank of the Godāvarī near Nashik. The town Wai (in Maharashtra) is situated on the river Kṛṣṇā. Wai is identified with Virāṭanagarī where Pāṇḍavas had spent the 13th year of their exile incognito (*ajñātavāsa*). Ṛṣi Uśanas, the preceptor of the Asuras, practised penance on the bank of the river Oghavatī and there he secured the knowledge of Sañjīvanī (a kind of elixir which can restore the dead to life) from Śiva. Ṛṣi Dachīci practised penance on the bank of the Sarasvatī.

It is believed that Brahmā meditated at the tīrtha Pṛthūdaka (present Pehoa) on the Sarasvatī at the time of the creation of the universe. Śrī Kṛṣṇa with Baladeva and Sudāmā, had his education in the Āśrama of sage Sandīpanī on the bank of the river Śiprā. The famous Śriṅgerīmaṭha is on the left bank of the river Tuṅgā (a branch of the river Tuṅgabhadrā).

According to tradition, the fight between *gaja* (elephant) and *grāha* (alligator) had taken place at Sonapur on the river Śoṇa (Bhāgp. 8.2.3). However, according to Varāhp. 144. 116f, the fight had taken place at the confluence of the Devikā, the Gaṇḍakī and the Gaṅgā.

It was on the bank of the river Tamasā where Vālmīki had witnessed the *Krauñca-vadha* (shooting of the bird krauñca by a fowler) and where the Ṛṣi cursed the fowler in a verse in the Anuṣṭubh metre which became the first verse of its kind. Vālmīki later composed the great epic Rāmāyaṇa.

Many demons were killed on the banks of the rivers. The demons Madhu and Kaiṭabha were killed by Viṣṇu on the hill Bhasmakūṭa (or Bhasmācala) in the river Brahmaputra. It is said that Kāmadeva was burnt into ashes on this hill by the fire of the third eye of Śiva.

The demon Dhundu practised penance and obtained a boon from Brahmā that he would not be killed by anyone including gods. The boon was granted. Dhundu went to the

Svargaloka and declared himself Indra. The gods repaired to the Brahmaloka. He wanted also to capture Brahmaloka. Śukrācārya, preceptor of demons, advised him to perform a hundred Aśvamedha sacrifices to be able to go to the Brahmaloka. The bank of the river Devikā was selected as the site for the yajña. The gods were alarmed and approached Viṣṇu for succour. Viṣṇu took the form of a dwarf (*vāmana*), left his body in the river Devikā and began drowning. Dhundu left the sacrifice and rushed to rescue Viṣṇu. On being enquired, the Brāhmaṇa said that he was kicked out of his house penniless by his brother. Dhundu offered him money but the Brāhmaṇa wanted only three steps of land. Dhundu granted. The Brāhmaṇa (Vāmana) measured the entire universe in his three steps. Dhundu was humbled.

It is held that near the mouth of the river Mahī, god Śiva had killed the demon Andhaka. It is also believed that Skanda had killed Tārakāsura at the Stambha-tīrtha (present Cambay or Khambhat) which is situated on the confluence of the Mahī with the sea. Narmadā issued forth from the tears of joy that Śiva shed after killing Andhaka. As mentioned earlier, the Harihara incarnaton of Viṣṇu and Śiva had taken place at Kudlur where the river Tuṅgabhadrā meets the river Haridrā.

Sanskrit works dealing with rites and rituals enjoin that Śrāddha (rites for ancestors) should be performed and *dāna* should be given on the banks of the rivers. The performance of Śrāddha, Homa, and Japa on the river Daśārṇā brings great rewards. The river Gandhakālī is regarded as the daughter of the Pitṛs. Hence, it is beneficial to perform Śrāddha on her banks. Narmadā is also regarded as the mind-born daughter of the Pitṛs named Somapās. Śrāddha performed on her banks brings great rewards to the performer. It is very efficacious to give Dāna and perform Śrāddha on the banks of the river Kauśikī. The performance of Śrāddha on the river Phalgu in Gaya accrues to the performer great *puṇya*.

One marvels at the ingenious creative powers of the Purāṇic and post-Purāṇic Sanskrit authors who have shown unique and extra-ordinary imaginations in inventing sources of the origin and rise of the rivers, other than mountains and lakes, although they knew very well the actual and natural sources of the rivers. But in mythological parlance, Sanskrit authors have brought out many stories and legends as sources for the rivers to appear on the earth and thus they have enriched Hindu mythoogy enormously.

Bhīmaratha was the king of Ayodhyā. Once, while hunting, he unknowingly shot an arrow at a Brāhmaṇa couple who were sporting in the form of a doe and a dear. To expiate the sin, the king was advised to get the river Bhīmā on the earth. Lord Śiva, after defeating the demon Tripura, had come down to Bhīmāśaṅkara for rest. The king came from Ayodhyā to Bhīmāśaṅkara to practise penance and to propitiate Śiva. Śiva was pleased, and asked the king to seek a boon. The king saw that Śiva was very tired and drops of sweat had appeared on his fore-head. Bhīmaratha requested Śiva to turn the drops into a river. Śiva did so. This became the river Bhīmā named after the king. The king bathed in the river and was absolved of the sin.

Viṣṇu once practised penance for the welfare of the mankind. A stream of perspiration dripped from his *gaṇḍa* (cheek). It became the river Gaṇḍakī. The river Mahī had her source in the sweat running down from the body of king Indradyumna of Ujjain. There is another source for the origin of the river Mahī.

A young Gurjar girl used to churn curds. A young man used to gaze at her. The Gurjar girl could not bear this and out of embarrasement threw herself into the pot of curds. The pot overflowed and a river came out. That is the river Mahī.

Once Śiva with Umā practised penance on the mt. Ṛkṣa. Sweat dripped from his body which turned into a river. That river is Narmadā, also called Rudriyā.

Viṣṇu, as Varāha, killed the demon Hiraṇyākṣa who had seized the earth and plunged it into the water. Viṣṇu fought with the demon with his tusk and lifted the earth. In the fight, Varāha had perspiration trickling down from his high (*tuṅga*) left tusk. That became the river Tuṅgā. The sweat dripping from his right tusk which was firm and steady (*bhadra*) became the river Bhadrā. And the stream coming down from his eye became the river Netravatī.

Śiva went to the site of the sacrifice of Dakṣa where Pārvatī had burnt herself. Śiva was furious. Seeing his wrath, the Vasus melted out of fear, and a river flowed. It became the river Sītā. Śiva was very much agrieved at the death of Pārvatī, and he sighed so heavily that a cloud of vapour rose in the sky from his body and flowed down. It became the river Vaitaraṇī.

It is also said that the river Vaitaraṇī rose from the tears of Rāma when he wept for Sītā after her abduction.

Pulomā was the wife of Ṛṣi Bhṛgu. Once Bhṛgu went out for his morning ablutions. A demon came in the guise of a Varāha and kidnapped her. Pulomā was pregnant at the time, the foetus fell on the ground and a boy was born who later became Ṛṣi Cyavana. The lustre of the fallen *garbha* killed the demon. Pulomā wept for her misfortune and a great river rose from her tears. Brahmā named it as the river Vadhūsarā.

The river Payoṣṇī rose from a huge quantity of milk. The legend tells :

Once 70,000 ascetics came to the king, Gaya, and asked him for milk. The king searched all over the world for such an enormous quantity of milk but in vain. Even the celestial cow Kāmadhenu and the Kṣīrasāgara (sea of milk) were unable to provide so much milk. Finally, Gaya approached Śiva. Śiva gave the king a digit of the moon on his forehead who is actually the daughter of the moon. She served each one of the ascetics a hundred cups filled with milk at a time, and filled their cups again and again, so much so that the ascetics could not drink any more, and the milk started overflowing. That became the river Payoṣṇī.

The river Karatoyā flowed out of the water that was poured

on the hands of Śiva at the time of his wedding with Pārvatī. Similarly, at the time of the marriage of Arundhatī with Vasiṣṭha, the water used in the nuptial and the Avabhṛtha-baths flowed in seven streams. The river Sarayū is one of them.

Sarasvatī appeared whenever the river was remembered. Thus for instance:

Once some holy Munis took up their residences in the Naimiṣāraṇya. They thought of the Sarasvatī there. She appeared before them and was named Kāñcanākṣī. Once Ṛṣi Uddālaka meditated upon Sarasvatī. She appeared before him in Kośala where she is known as Manoramā.

Brahmā performed a sacrifice. Many sages came to attend. They did not see Sarasvatī there. They told Brahmā that the sacrifice would not become perfect unless the river Sarasvatī was present there. Brahmā thought of Sarasvatī and she appeared there instantly. She was named Suprabhā. Once king Gaya, while performing a sacrifice at Gayā, thought of Sarasvatī. The river appeared before him and was named Viśālā.

After the death of Pārvatī, Brahmā went to the mt. Kailāsa to console Śiva. After sometime, both of them came down to the lake Śipra. Śiva stared at the lake and a river flowed from it. The river was named Śiprā. Once Ṛṣi Vasiṣṭha sat in meditation and in that state, with his powerful and penetrating gaze, looked at the sage Visvāmitra. This powerful gaze pierced two holes in the earth and from both the holes two rivers came out, one was Sarasvatī and the other was Sābhramatī (Sabarmati).

Śiva had cut off one of the five heads of Brahmā. In order to atone for the sin, Śiva practised a severe penance on the Varadamūla hill. The penance was so severe that it would have consumed the entire universe with the rising heat of *tapasa*. Viṣṇu therefore poured the water of the Bhāgīrathī from his conch over the head of Śiva. As the water flowed, it became the river Varadā.

The rivers Varaṇā and Asi flowed from the right and left

foot of Yogaśāyī Viṣṇu. Gaṅgā issued from the foot of Viṣṇu when, in his Vāmanāvatāra, he had stretched out his leg upward to measure the three worlds. The Brahmakaṭāha of the nail of his left toe broke and a stream issued forth which was named as Viṣṇupadī Gaṅgā.

The river Acchodā is the mind-born daughter of the Pitṛs named Agnisvāttas who dwell in the Somapatha-loka. The Narmadā is also the mind born daughter of the Pitṛs named Somapās who dwell in the Sumānasa-loka above Brahmaloka.

The river Sarasvatī has risen from the root of the Plakṣa (fig) tree, therefore she is also called Plakṣajā.

The common folks believe that the river Karmanāśā issued forth from the saliva of king Triśaṅku who is still hanging (now as a constellation) between the heaven and the earth.

There was a pious king named Rantideva.He used to perform great many sacrifices in which animals were offered. The number of animals was so large that a river flowed out of the secretions of the heaps of hides (*carman*). That is the river Carmaṇvatī (modern Chambal).

It is also believed that some goddesses, Apasarases, and even mortal women have turned into rivers due to one reason or the other.

The river Vitastā is deemed to be an incarnation of Pārvatī.

Satyavatī, the mother of sage Jamadagni and elder sister of sage Viśvāmitra, followed her husband to the heaven after his death, and the legend says that she was then transformed into a river flowing from the Himālaya, now known as the river Kauśikī.

There was a king named Rājānaka who practised penance on the bank of the river Bhīmā. This worried Indra. He sent Apasarases Mūḷā and Mūṭhā to seduce the king. The king cursed them to become rivers. They are today the rivers Mūḷā and Mūṭhā, tributaries of the Bhīmā. Similar is the case with the origin of the river Nīrā. There was a king named Śyāvāśva who practised penance in order to attain Brahmahood. This worried Indra who sent Apsaras Nīrā to Bhīmāśaṅkara to disturb the king. The king cursed the Apsaras to turn into a river. That is the river Nīrā today.

Once a Brahmaṇa lady was going on a pilgrimage. The Aśvins saw her on the way, and, in spite of her protestations, violated her. She dropped the foetus in a garden and reported the matter to her husband. He suspected her fidelity and forsook her. By her power of *yoga*, the lady transformed herself into a river. That is the river Godāvarī.

Once Brahmā wished to perform a sacrifice. Viṣṇu, Śiva, gods, Ṛṣis, and Gandharvas attended the sacrifice. The auspicious time for the sacrifice approached. But Sāvitrī, Brahmā's wife, forgot the time and was delayed. In the meantime, Brahmā took the Yajña-dīkṣā with his other wife, Gāyatrī. When Sāvitrī finally arrived and saw that the sacrifice had already commenced, she became enraged and cursed Brahmā, Viṣṇu and Śiva, as also Gāyatrī to become rivers. Angered by this, Viṣṇu also cursed Sāvitrī to become a river. So all the five became rivers. Viṣṇu became the river Kṛṣṇā, Śiva Veṇyā or Veṇṇā, and Brahmā Kakudmatī (the present Koynā), and Sāvitrī and Gāyatrī by the same names. These five rivers rise in the Sahyādri.

[Note: All the above details have been summarized from the rivers that are mentioned in this work.]

Geographical Details of Rivers

Although Sanskrit writers have woven many a mythological web as the sources of the rivers, it is not that they did not know the actual sources of the rivers, viz., mountains, hills and lakes. Sanskrit literature provides fairly correct informations about the origin of the rivers. The rivers can be grouped under the following heads:

Rivers rising in the mountains:

1. *The Himālayas*

Alakanandā, Bāhudā, Brahmaputra, Chandrabhāgā,

Devikā, Dhūtapāpā, Dṛṣadvatī, Gaṅgā, Gomatī, Irāvatī, Kauśikī, Kuhū, Mandākinī, Sarasvatī, Sarayū, Yamunā, etc.

2. *The Vindhyas*

Antaḥsīlā, Durgā, Kumudvatī, Mahāgaurī, Payoṣṇī, Veṇṇā, etc.

3. *The Ṛkṣa* (Eastern part of the Vindhya)

Citrakūṭā, Citrotpalā, Daśārṇā, Karamodā, Karatoyā, Mahānadī, Mañjulā, Narmadā, Nirvindhyā, Śoṇa, Śuktimatī, Surasā, Tamasā, Tāpī, Vaitaraṇī, Vāluvāhinī, Viśālā, etc.

4. *The Pāriyātra* (Western part of the Vindhya)

Candanā, Carmaṇvatī, Kuntī, Lūpī, Mahī, Varṇāśā, Vedasmṛti, Vedavatī, Vetravatī, Vṛtraghnī, etc.

5. *The Sahya* (Northern part of the Western Ghats)

Bhīmā, Godāvarī, Kāverī, Kṛṣṇā, Kṛṣṇāveṇī, Tuṅgabhadnā, Veṇā, etc.

6. *The Malaya* (Southern part of the Western Ghats)

Kṛtamālā, Tāmraparṇī, Utpalāvatī, etc.

7. *The Śuktimat* (Southern part of the Eastern Ghats)

Kumārī, Kūpā, Palāśiṇī, Ṛṣikulyā, Sukumārī, Trisāmā, Vaṁśadharā, etc.

Rivers rising in the lakes

Acchodā (from the lake Acchoda),

Brahmaputra (from the Mānasarovara),

Lūpī (or Lūnī) from the Bisal lake on the Pāṅyātra), Sarayū (from the Mānasarovara), Śiprā from the lake Śipra).

[Note : The above list is not exhaustive. Refer to the individual rivers also.]

The contributions of the rivers as motifs to the art, literature, and sculpture is immense. The descent of Gaṅgā (*Gaṅgāvataraṇa*) and Śiva bearing Gaṅgā on his head (*Gaṅgādhara-mūrti*) have provided ample ideas to the artists, poets, painters, and sculptors of the Gupta and post-Gupta periods.

For the Purāṇic authors the episodes Gaṅgāvataraṇa and Gaṅgādhara Śiva have provided grand themes and for the medieval artists and sculptors the incidents served as an inspiration for depicting, on the one hand, the love between Śiva and Gaṅgā and, on the other, the displeasure and dejection of Pārvatī who feared that her husband's love would be shared by another woman. (For a detaild study of Gaṅgadhara-mūrtis, see M.-E. Adicean, "Les Images de Śiva dans L'Inde du Sud," *Arts Asiatique,* Tom 32, 1976 and C. Sivaramamurti, *Gaṅgā*, Orient Longman, 1976.

Another important motif is Gaṅgā-Yamunā-Saṅgama. In the famous Udayagiri caves (District Vidisa, Madhya Pradesh), the scene of the confluence of the Gaṅgā and Yamunā has been beautifully carved (cave No. 5). Two streams (suggested by means of wavy lines) from two opposite directions have been shown flowing, and the two godesses, Gaṅgā and Yamunā, are shown standing on their *vāhanas*, *makara*, and *kūrma*. Each of them holds a pitcher in her hand. At the junction of the two streams, Varuṇa is depicted in a standing pose.

The rivers are usually depicted as young, beautiful and charming damsels on the door jambs as door-keepers and decorative figurines. (C. Sivaramamurti, *ibid.*, has collected a good number of them).

It is now my great pleasure to acknowledge the help that I have received from many a person in the preparation of this work.

First and foremost, I am greatly indebted and profoundly grateful to the late lamented Professor Dr. R.N. Dandekar who has alwasys been a beacon in all my research activities during the last more than thirty years of my association with him first as a Ph.D. student, and then as a collaborator to his Vedic Bibliography. Though he is no more, I continue to derive inspiraton from his sacred memory.

Professor Dr. V.S. Datye of the Department of Geography, University of Pune, Pune, has kindly provided geographical details of the rivers which are mentioned with each river under the heading Geographical Details. My great thanks to him.

I am also thankful to Shri C.P. Gautam, Bharatiya Kala Prakashan, Delhi, for acccepting this work in his scheme of publications, and executing it in a short time and satisfactory manner.

Finally, I pray to the waters, the mothers:

आपो अस्मान्मातरः शुन्धयन्तु घृतेन नो घृतप्वः पुनन्तु।

Ṛ V 10.17.10

[Waters, our mothers, the purifiers, may they purify us and brighten us with their waters].

Vijayā Daśamī,
October 2, 2006.
Pune.

S.K. Lal

RIVERS IN HINDU MYTHOLOGY AND RITUAL

Acchodā

The celestial river Acchodā is also known by the names of Acchodakā and Acchodikā. The river rises from the lake Acchoda which is situated near the mountain Candraprabha (Matsyp. 121.6-7). The mt. Candraprabha is situated to the north-east of the mt. Kailāsa in the middle of the Himālayas. Vāyup. 47.5-8 also mentions the same. It adds that from the lake Acchoda two rivers, Acchodikā and Mandākinī, flow.

The forest Citraratha (Rām. Ayodhyā-Kāṇḍa, 2.65.3) is situated on the bank of the Acchodikā (Matsyp. 121.3). Maṇibhadra, the General of the army of the Yakṣas and the Guhyakas, lived there (Matsyp. 121.9).

Padmp, Sṛṣṭi-khaṇḍa, 5.9.11ff mentions the following legend about Acchodā:

There are *lokas* known as the Somapatha where Pitṛs named Agniṣvāttas dwell. Acchodā is their mind-born daughter. There is also a lake, named Achhoda, created by the Pitṛs where the maiden Acchodā performed penance for a husband for a thousand celestial years. The Pitṛs were pleased and asked her to seek a boon from them. She asked for Amāvasu, who is one amongst them, to be her husband. On account of her this improper desire, the Pitṛs were angered and cursed her. On account of the curse, she fell on the earth and became Amāvāsyā. She begged of the Pitṛs for their pardon and deliverance from the curse. The Pitṛs said that in the Dvāpara age she would be born from the womb of a fish and become the daughter of king Vasu. She would obtain a son from Ṛṣi Parāśara, then she would be married to Śantanu and get two sons from him named Vicitravīrya and Citrāṅgada. After giving briths to these two sons, she would become Proṣṭhapadī Aṣṭakā in the Pitṛloka, Satyavatī in the Bhūloka (mortal world), and a river by the name of Svacchodā on the earth.

The Mārkp. 56, describing the course of the river Gaṅgā, says that the eastern course of the Gaṅgā from the mountain Meru is known as Sītā which also flows through the forest Caitraratha (Mārkp. 56.6). The Matsyp. 121.9 also mentions that the river Accchodakā is another name of the river Mandākinī. Hence the Sītā and the Acchodā may be regarded as the same river both being indentical.

Geographical Details

The mt. Candraprabha, near which is the lake Acchoda, and from which the Acchodā rises, is identified with the Surange La (a range of the mt. Kailāsa to its north-east), from which a number of streams and their tributaries discharge their waters in the lake Kongys Tso (also called lake Gounche). The fact that Maṇibhadra, the General of the Yakṣas, lives there with his retinue of Guhyakas, refers to the ancient settlement of Thokchan which is an important centre of this region (S.M. Ali).

Adrijā

The river Adrijā rises from the mountain Vindhya (Mārkp. 57.21; MBh, Anuśāsanaparva, 13.151.17). According to the Śabdakalpadruma (s.v.), Adrijā is another name of the river Durgā. That river may therefore be identified with the river Durgā. (See also under Durgā below).

The Kūrmp. 46.31 speaks of a river Adṛryā which rises from the mt. Pāriyātra (western part of the Vindhyas). From the context, it seems that the Adṛryā is identical with Adrijā.

Airāvatī

The river Airāvatī rises from the Himālayas. She is also known by the name of Irāvatī (Kūrmp. I. 46.29). She is identified with the modern river Ravi in Panjab. The river Airāvatī was known to the Vedic people as Paruṣṇī. (See under Paruṣṇī also). The river Airāvatī is also known as Haimavatī (Matsyp. 116.1).

The Matsyp. 115 narrates the following legend regarding Airāvatī:

King Purūravas was a Brāhmaṇa in his previous birth. He once observed the *Dvādaśī-vrata* and worshipped lord Janārdana with a view to obtaining a kingdom. However, during the observance of the *vrata* he bathed with his body rubbed with oil. That was a mistake. When on fast, one should not rub his body with oil before bath. As a result, although by the virtue of his *vrata*, the king obtained the kingdom of the Madras, he became ugly due to the mistake. In order to get rid of his ugliness, he practised penance on the bank of the river Airāvatī. (Cf. also Vāmanp. 53).

God Vāmana lives in the river Airāvatī in the form of Rūpadhara (Vāmanp. 63.5).

Geographical Details

The Airāvatī rises from the Barabangahal as a joint streem formed by the glacier fed Bhadal and Taut-Gari, and flows north-westward. Then she turns to the south-west, and flows along the Indo-Pak border for some length and finally joins the river Chenab from the right.

The Airāvatī appears first at the south-west corner of Chamb in Himachal Pradesh as the confluence of two streams, one flowing from north-east and the other from south-east.

From Chamb, she flows past Lohal taking a south-westerly course and meets the river Chenab between Ahmedpur and Saraisindhu in Pakistan.

Alakanandā

The river Alakanandā is one of the seven streams of the Gaṅgā (Mārkp. 56.8; Kūrmp. I.46.31; Vāyup. 14.18). The course of the river Gaṅgā from the mountain Meru to the mountain Himavat is known as Alakanandā. Alakanandā flows southward towards the mt. Gandhamādana through the forest Nandana. It is also said that the river Gaṅgā is known among the gods and the Gandharvas as Alakanandā (MBh, Ādiparva, 1.158.18). According to Bhāgp. 4.6.24; 5.17.5, the river Bhāgīrathī is joined by the Alakanandā at Devaprayāga. The combined stream is then called Gangā. According to Nāradp. II. 67.72.73, the Bhāgīrathī and Alakanandā meet near Badarikāśrama.

The modern river Alakanandā is a major tributary of the Gaṅgā in her upper course. The river Alakanandā rises from the twin glaciers named as Bhagīratha Kharak and Santopantha. She combines in her the waters of the Khīrā Gaṅgā, Bhiundar Gaṅgā, Dhavli Gaṅgā, Nandākinī, Pindar Gaṅgā, and Mandākinī, and then joins the river Bhāgīrathī at Devaprayāga. From Devaprayāga she is known as Gaṅgā in her onward journey. The holy shrine of Badarīnātha (also Badarikāśrama) is situated on the bank of the Alakanandā.

Geographical Details

Alakanandā rises from the eastern side of the Chaukhamba peaks. She flows south-south-east up to Joshimath (Viṣṇuprayāga) where Dhavalīgaṅgā joins her from the left bank. Thereafter, the river Alakanandā flows towards south-west up to Karṇaprayāga where she is joined by the river Pindar on the left bank. Then she flows towards west, and at Rudraprayāga she is joined by the river Mandākinī on the right bank. Still flowing west-south-west she meets the Bhāgīrathī on the right bank at Devaprayāga, and then they acquire the name of Gaṅgā.

Tributaries of Alakanandā

1. Sarasvatī on the left bank near Māna.
2. Khīragaṅgā on the right bank near Hanumān Chatti. The holy shrine of Badarīnātha is between Māna and Hanumān Chatti.
3. Bhiundhar Gaṅgā on the left bank near Govinda ghat.
4. Dhavalī Gaṅgā from the left bank. Viṣṇuprayāga is situated there.
5. Birahī Gaṅgā from the left.
6. Nandākinī from the left. Nandaprayāga is on the junction.
7. Pindar from the left. Karṇaprayāga is situated there.
8. Mandākinī on the right. Rudraprayāga is situated there.
9. Bhāgīrathī from the right bank. Devaprayāga is situated there.

Aṁbuvaśyā

In reply to a query of Bhīṣma about the benefits of visiting *tīrthas*, Ṛṣi Pulastya enumerates the rivers of Bhāratavarṣa. The river Aṁbuvaśyā is one of them. It is said that a person who bathes in this river gets rid of all diseases and goes to the Brahmaloka (MBh, Āraṇyakaparva, 3.81.46).

Aṁbumatī is avariant of Aṁbuvaśyā. (Mbh., Āraṇyaka-parva, 3.81.46fn).

The tīrtha Kośeśvara is situated there.

Aṁśumatī

Aṁśumatī is a Ṛgvedic river (ṚV 8.96.13-15; AV 20.137.7-9). The Bṛhaddevatā narrates a story about this river:

Soma was once struck by the fear of Vṛtra. He ran

away from the gods and hid himself in the river Aṁśumatī which flowed in the country of the Kurus. Indra and Bṛhaspati went to plead with him to return. In the meantime, Indra along with the Maruts was also preparing to attack Vṛtra. Seeing Indra approaching him, Soma arrayed himself against Indra with his army thinking that it was Vṛtra who was approaching him to attack with his army. Bṛhaspati told Soma that it was Indra and not Vṛtra, but Soma did not believe. Indra then used his force and took him back to the gods.

The Ṛks (ṚV 8.96.13-15) are employed in the Brāhmaṇācchansin Śastra during the third pressing of Soma (ĀśŚS 8.3; VaitŚS 32.33).

Sometimes, the river Yamunā is also called Aṁśumatī (Rām., Ayodhyākāṇḍa, 2.49.11).

Anitabhā

The river Anitabhā is a Ṛgvedic river (ṚV 5.53.9). She was an affluent of the river Sindhu. However, Sāyaṇa understands the word *antitabhā* as an adjective qualifying the river Rasā which is also mentoined in the same Rk. P.L. Bhargava opines that it is probably the river Alingar, a tributary of the river Kabul (Vedic Kubhā).

Antaḥśilā

The river antaḥśilā rises from the mountain Vindhya (Kūrmp. I.46.35.). Vāyup. 45.103 has the variant Antaśilā.

Antaḥśilā is the same river as Antaḥsirā below.

Antaḥsirā

The river Antaḥsirā rises from the mountain Ṛksa, the eastern range of the Vindhyas (Mārkp. 57.25). According to Pargiter (Mārkp. 57.25 fn), this river is one of the northern tributaries of the Mahānadī.

The Varāhp. 85 reads Antyāgirā for Antaḥsirā.

The river Antaḥsirā has been identified also with the river Tikkira. (See also under the river Brāhamaṇī).

Āpagā

The sacred river (Vāmanp, SM, 13.7) Āpagā rises from the mountain Sahya (Vāyup. 45.104). The Holy tīrtha Mānuṣa is situated at a distance of a *kroṣa* (about three kms) from that river (MBh, Āraṇyakaparva, 3.81.55). This river is frequented by the Siddhas. An offering of Śyāmāka grains into the river to gods and Pitṛs brings great religious merit. And even if one Brāhmaṇa is fed on the bank of the river, it is equal to feeding ten million Brāhmaṇas. A person obtains the fruits of the Agniṣṭoma sacrifice when he bathes in this river, stays there for a night, and worships gods and Pitṛs (MBh, Āraṇyakaparva, 3.81.55-59). An offering of rice balls (piṇḍas) to the manes in the months of Nabhasya (Bhādrapada, September-October) on the bank of the river Āpagā brings salvation (Vāmanp. 15.6).

The river Āpagā is identified with the modern river Ayuk which flows along the west of the river Ravi in Panjab. Sometimes the Ṛgvedic river Āpayā is identified with Āpagā (Pargiter, Mārkp. 57.57 fn under Madrakas; and Nandu lal Dey, s.v.). (See also Āpayā below).

Aparanandā

The river Aparanandā rises from the mountain Hemakūṭa which lies between the sources of the Gaṅgā and the Kauśikī (MBh, Āraṇyakaparva, 3.109.1). The mt. Hemakūṭa is encircled by another river called Nandā. Both the rivers Aparanandā and Nandā have the virtue of removing the fear of sin (MBh, Āraṇyakaparva, 3.109.1-2). The Aparanandā may be the same river as the Alakanandā mentoined above. (See also Nandā below).

Āpayā

The river Āpayā is a Ṛgvedic river (ṚV 3.23.4) which

flows between the rivers Dṛṣadvatī and Sarasvatī. She is a small tributary of the Sarasvatī and flows past Thaneswar. She is identified with the modern river Indramatī.

Ārjikīyā

Ārjikīyā is a river in the region of Kuruksetra (Max Müller, *Vedic Hymns*, I. 399). In ṚV 8.7.29 Ārjīka is said to be a place which was well populated. Sāyaṇa explains the term *ārjikīyā* as: *rijikā nāma deśaḥ tatsambandhinī* (belonging to a place named Ārjīka). The place is also famous for Soma (ṚV. 8.64.11; 9.65.23). Soma is entreated to flow from the land of Ārjīka (ṚV 9.113.2). She is also mentioned in Nadī-stuti-sūkta (ṚV 10.75.5) with other Vedic rivers.

The Nirukta (9.26), however, regards Ārjikīyā as just another name of the river Vipāś.

Geographical Details

The river Ārjikīyā is the modern river Vipāśā (=Beas). She rises from the Pirpanjal range near the Rohtang Pass. She flows to the west up to Dinanagar in Panjab and then turns to the south-west, and joins the river Sutlej from the left side.

Tributaries:

1. River Pārvatī on the left.
2. Hurla on the left.
3. Sainja on the left.
4. Tirthan on the left.
5. Uhl on the right.
6. Suketi on the right.

The other tributaries of Ārjikīyā are: Luni, Awa, Baṅgaṅgā, Manuni, Gaj, and Chaki.

Aruṇā

The river Aruṇā is a tributary of the river Sarasvatī in

Kurukṣetra (MBh, Āraṇyakaparva, 3.81.131). She flows between Sarasvatī and Dṛṣadvatī near Pṛthūdaka (modern Pehoa). Aruṇā is a very sacred river (Vāmanp, SM, 19.30). It is said that if a person observes fast on the bank of the Aruṇā and bathes in her water, he is freed from the greatest sins like Brahmahatyā, and gains the merit of the Agniṣṭoma and Atirātra sacrifices. Also his family up to seventh generation is purified (MBh, Āraṇyakaparva, 3.81.131-132). Indra bathed in the river Aruṇā and became free from the sin of killing Namuci (MBh, Śalyaparva, 9.42).

MBh, Śalyaparva, 9.41;42 relates the following story about the origin of the river Aruṇā:

Ṛṣi Viśvāmitra had a grudge against the growing popularity of Ṛṣi Vasiṣṭha. (For the rivalry between Viśvāmitra and Vasiṣṭha see MBh, Ādiparva, 1.166; 167). Their hermitages were situated on the opposite banks of the river Sarasvatī. Once Viśvāmitra asked Sarasvatī to bring Vasiṣṭha to him. Sarasvatī sensed the sinister motive of Viśvāmitra. She was in a dilemma. If she brought Vasiṣṭha, Viśvāmitra would definitely harm him, and thus she would become an accessory in the crime. If, on the other hand, she did not bring Vasiśṭha to him as asked by the latter, she would be incurring the wrath and consequent curse from the wrathful Viśvāmitra. Vasiṣṭha, however, asked Sarasvatī to obey Viśvāmitra. When she came to Viśvāmitra with Vasiṣṭha, the sage was engaged in a sacrifice. She took advantage of that situation and carried Vasiṣṭha back to his Āśrama thinking that she had already obeyed Viśvāmitra. But Viśvāmitra was not to be fooled like this. When he came to know the trick played by Sarasvatī, he was wroth and cursed the river that her stream would be filled with blood in place of water.

This provided the demons with a veritable feast. They gathered on the banks of the Sarasvatī and indulged in drinking blood.

One day some Ṛṣis came to the river Sarasvatī and saw the great river's sad plight. They took pity on her, and by the power of their penance, they redeemed her of her curse. But now the demons were in trouble. All their enjoyments was stopped. They, therefore, complained to the Ṛṣis. The Ṛṣis, for the sake of the Rākṣasas, brought forth another river and named her Aruṇā. But the river proved to be so sacred that the moment the Rākṣasas drank her water, they became free from their demonhood because the river Aruṇā had the power of cleansing a person of his even greatest sins like Brahmahatyā (cf. also Vāmanp. 19).

According to MBh, Āraṇyakaparva, 3.82.135, Aruṇā is a branch of the river Kauśikī. The *saṅgama* of Aruṇā and Sarasvatī is situated about five kms north-east of Pṛthūdaka.

Asi

The river Asi rises from the left foot of Yogaśāyī who is regarded as being a portion *(aṁśa)* of Viṣṇu and as living in Prayāga. From his right foot flows the river Varaṇā. The city Vārāṇasī is situated between these two rivers (Vāmanp. 3.25 29). They form the northern and southern boundaries of Vārāṇasī (Kūrmp. I.31.63).

Asiknī

Asiknī means black in colour. The river Asiknī is a Vedic river (ṚV 8.20.25; 10.75.5). She is known as Candrabhāgā in the Purāṇas (Bhāgp. 5.19.18), and as Chenab at present. This river is, at her source, a combination of two streams, namely, Candrā and Bhāgā. The river rises in the state of Himachal Pradesh and, flowing through Kashmir, enters Pakistan where she joins the river Sutlej (Vedic Śutudri).

Geographical Details

The river Chenab (Vedic Asiknī) has her source in the

Himālayan canton of Lahul in Panjab. She flows in two streams. The stream of Candrā issues forth from a snow bed by the side of Bara Lacha. The other stream called Bhāgā rises from the north-western side of that Pass. The two streams meet at Tandi (in Himachal Pradesh). The combined streams are known as Chandrabhāgā (Chenab). She flows through Panjab and Himachal Pradesh, and Jammu and Kashmir above Kishtwar. From Kishtwar to Jangalwar her course is southerly. She flows westward from Jangalwar up to Arnas. Thereafter, she flows in the southerly direction and from Akhnur she flows in the south-western direction through Pakistan.

The chief tributaries of Candrabhāgā (Vedic Asiknī, modern Chenab) are:

Uniar, Shudi, Bhutna, Maruvardwan, Golan Lar, Lidar Kol, Bichlari, Ans, and Tawi.

The river Jhelam joins the Chenab at Trimmu. This combined stream is joined by the river Ravi. The Chenab is further on joined by the river Sutlej at Madwala. This combined stream then flows further on as Panjnad and joins the river Sindhu at Mithankot.

Aśmanvatī

Aśmanvatī is a Ṛgvedic river (ṚV 10.53.8). She is mentioned in a rite in the marriage ceremony. If a bride, while going to her husband's home, has to cross a river, this Ṛk (ṚV 10.53.8) is recited when the bride boards a boat (ĀśvGS 1.8.2-3).

Dey indentifies the Aśmanvatī with the river Oxus.

Aśvanadī

The river Aśvanadī is a tributary of the river Carmaṇvatī (MBh, Āraṇyakaparva, 3.292.7-9;22;25). Carmaṇvatī is the modern river Chambal. Kuntī (of the Mahābhārata) is said to have left the infant Karṇa in a *mañjūṣā* in this river. (See under the river Kuntī below).

Aśvarathā

The river Aśvarathā flows near the mountain Gandhamādana. The hermitage of Ṛṣi Ārṣṭaṣeṇa was situated on the bank of this river (MBh, Āraṇyakaparva, 3.157.11-19).

Ātreyī

The river Ātreyī is one of the three streams which together form the river Trisrotā (modern Tista) (Mbh, Sabhāparva, 2.9.20 fn). The combined waters of the river Tista pour into the Gaṅgā near Goalundo in north-west Bengal. The base of the Tista delta is the river Padmā.

The Ātreyī is the modern river Atrai. The Atrai flows down from the terrain below Darjeeling. She receives on her way the lesser Yamunā below Santahar, and three other rivers in the district of Rajsahi.

Avantī

The river Avantī rises from the mt. Pāriyātra near Mhow in Madhya Pradesh and flows into the river Chambal (ancient Carmaṇvatī). (Matsyp. 114.24; Vāyup. 45.98; Vāmanp. 13.24).

Avarṇī

Mārkp. 57.20 reads Avarṇī in place of Avantī. The same Purāṇa mentions a people named Avantis who were the inhabitants of the country Avantī. The capital of that country was Ujjayini (Mārkp. 57.52; 55).

Baḍavā

Mārkp. 58.30 mentions a people named Baḍavāmukhas. Baḍavāmukha means 'sub-marine fire' or 'having faces like mares'. A people called Aśvamukhas are mentioned in the Matsyp. 121.58 as dwelling north of the Himālayas.

A Tīrtha named Baḍavā (now know also as Jvālāmukhī

Devī) is situated in Jammu (MBh, Āraṇyakaparva, 3.80.105 fn).

Bāhudā

The river Bāhudā rises from the Himālayas (MBh, Bhīṣmaparva, 6.10.13; Anuśāsanaparva, 13.20.3; 151.22; Kūrmp. I.46.27; Vāyup. 45.95). She flows near the river Sarasvatī. Bāhudā is a very sacred river. A dip in her water gives the benefits of a sacrifice (MBh, Āraṇyakaparva, 3.82.60).

MBh, Śāntiparva, 12.24 relates a story about this river:

There were two brothers named Śaṅkha and Likhita who lived on the bank of the river Bāhudā in separate hermitages. Once Likhita went to visit his brother Śaṅkha. Śaṅkha had gone out. The Āśrama of Śaṅkha was full of ripe and sweet fruits. Likhita could not resist his temptation of plucking and tasting some of them. While he was eating the fruits, Śaṅkha returned. Śaṅkha did not like his brother's this act, and reproached him by saying that he was a thief as he plucked the fruits and ate them in the absence of the owner. Likhita, therefore, must go to the king of the land, named Sudyumna, own his guilt, and ask for a suitable punishment. Likhita did so. But the king forgave him and asked him if he had any wish to be fulfilled. Likhita had no other wish and did not ask for any. This irked the king. He ordered that both hands of Likhita be cut off. Thus maimed Likhita went back to his brother Śaṅkha. The latter advised him to bathe and offer ablutions in the adjacent river. The moment Likhita bathed in the river and tried to raise his hands for offering ablutions, he got two lotus flowers on the extremities of the stumps of his hands. Since then, that river came to be known as Bāhudā.

According to Pargiter (Mārkp. 57.17 fn), the river Bāhudā flows between the rivers Gomatī and the Gaṅgā near

Ayodhyā. He identifies Bāhudā with the Rāmagaṅgā which joins the Gaṅgā on the left bank near Kannauj (Uttar Pradesh). Dey and Sircar disagree. According to them, Bāhudā should be identified with the river Dhabalā (or Dhumalā, or Burhī Rāptī) which is a feeder of the Rāptī in Uttar Pradesh.

Geographical Details

Bāhudā is identified with the river Rāptī. She rises from the Nepal Himālayas and flows in the westerly direction. After crossing the Indian border, she flows in south-easterly direction. She receives the river Bhakla from the right bank to the north of Śrāvastī and Burhī Rāptī from the left bank. Rāptī then turns to south and receives a tributary named Ghonghi on the left bank. Near Gorakhpur (in Uttar Pradesh) she turns south-eastward and receives the river Rohin from the left. Further down stream a tributary, Ami, joins her from the right bank. Rāptī joins the river Ghaghra from the left bank near Dohrighat (Bihar).

Bāluvāhinī

The river Bāluvāhinī rises from the Ṛkṣa part of the Vindhyas (Kūrmp. I.46.35; Vāyup. 45.100; Vāmanp. 13.27 has Balavāhinī). According to Dey, she is the river Bagin in Bundelkhand.

Bhadrā

According to Bhāgp. 5.17.7;8, Bhadrā is one of the four branches of the heavenly river Gaṅgā. Bhadrā flows through the land of the Uttara Kurus and empties herself into the north sea (Kūrmp. I.46.33). Dey identifies this river with the river Yarkand on which the town of Yarkand is situated.

Bhāradvājī

The hermitage of Ṛṣi Bharadvāja was situated on the confluence of the Gaṅgā and the Yamunā (Rām.,

Ayodhyākāṇḍa, 3.83.22). MBh, Bhīṣmaparva 6.10.28 enumerates the river Bhāradvājī along with the rivers Kauśikī, Śoṇa, and Candanā.

Bhīmā

Bhīmā rises from the Western Ghats of the mountain Sahya. Her source is at Bhīmāśaṅkara in the district of Pune. She flows south-eastwards through the districts of Pune, Solapur and Bijapur, and joins the river Kṛṣṇā from the left bank to the north of Raichur in Karnataka.

At the source of the Bhīmā, there is the famous Jyotirliṅga which is one of the twelve ancient and most sacred Jyotirliṅgas. Below Bhīmāśaṅkara, there is the temple of Sākṣa Gopāla.

Bhīmā Māhātmya 4.6-57 narrates a legend about the origin of the river Bhīmā.

There was a king in Ayodhyā named Bhīmaratha. Once while hunting, he shot a Brāhmaṇa couple who were sporting in the form of a doe and a deer. In order to get rid of the sin of killing a Brāhmaṇa couple, the king was advised to get the river Bhīmā on the earth. Lord Śiva, after defeating the demon Tripurāsura, had also come down to Bhīmāśaṅkara for taking rest. The king came from Ayodhyā to Bhīmāśaṅkara to practise penance and propitiate Śiva. Śiva was pleased at his penance and asked him to seek a boon. The king saw that Śiva was full of fatigue and there were drops of perspiration on his forehead. Bhīmaratha requested Śiva to turn his drops of sweat into a river. Śiva did so. This became the river Bhīmā named after the king.

The king bathed in the river, got rid of the sin and returned to Ayodhyā. Therefore, Bhīmā is also known by the name of Bhīmarathā (Mārkp. 57.26) and also as Bhīmarathī (Matsyp. 114.29; Vāyup. 45.104; Varāhp. 85; Viṣṇup. 2.3.11).

Viṣṇu lives in the river Bhīmā in the form of Śaṅkukarṇa (Vāmanp. 63.22).

Bhīmā is called Candrabhāgā in the vicinity of the town Paṇḍharpur (Maharashtra). Paṇḍharpur is situated on the right bank of the Bhīmā. There are eleven ghats on the river Bhīmā in Paṇḍharpur.

Paṇḍharpur is a celebrated place of pilgrimage. There is the famous temple of Viṭhobā where the *Pālakhis* (palanquins) of Sant Jñāneśvara and Sant Tukārāma reach on the Ekādaśī (11th day) of Āṣāḍha (July-August) followed by a large number of devotees called Wārkaris. Great fairs are held there and pilgrims from different parts of the country congregate there. As a tradition, the Chief Minister of the State performs *Pūjā* on that day.

There is a village named Dhulkhed on the bank of the Bhīmā. It is said that Dakṣa had performed the sacrifice at this place. It is here that Pārvatī immolated herself in the sacrificial fire. Vīrabhadra, a *gaṇa* of Śiva, had destroyed the sacrifice and cut off the head of Dakṣa (which was later replaced by a goat's) (Bhīmā Māhātmya 19.18-59).

Tributaries

1. The Bhīmā receives the river Bhāmā near Pimpalgaon. Bhāmā also rises from the Sahyādri range, about ten kms. south of Bhīmāśaṅkara. The valley from which the river Bhāmā moves is called Bhammer.
2. Another tributary of the river Bhīmā is Indrāyaṇī which rises from the Sahya mountain near Kurvande and meets Bhīmā near Tulpur. The famous temple of Sant Jñāneśvara is on the Indrāyaṇī at Alandi near Pune.
3. Bhīmā receives the river Vel a few kilometers from Talegaon-Dhamdhere.
4. Bhīmā receives Muḷā-Mūṭhā near the village of

Ranjangaon. Muḷā-Mūṭhā is the name given to a river composed of seven streams rising from different parts of the Sahyādri range. The stream flows past Pune. At Pune it also receives Mūṭhā. The joint name Muḷā-Mūṭhā is given to this united stream after it receives the river Muḷā at Pune. Bhīmā-Māhātmya 26.33 relates a story about the origin of Muḷā-Mūṭhā.

There was a king named Rājānaka who practised penance on the bank of the Bhīmā. This worried Indra. Indra sent many Apsarases to seduce the king. Muḷā and Mūṭhā were the two among them. The king cursed them to become rivers. When the Apsarases placated him, he modified the curse and said that they would be freed from the curse after meeting the river Bhīmā. Bhīmā receives Muḷā-Mūṭhā near Ranjangaon.

5. Flowing further east from Ranjangaon, Bhīmā meets the river Ghod, to the west of Dhond, from the right bank. The river Ghod also rises in the Sahyādri range about fifteen kms north of Bhīmā.

6. Another river Nīrā meets Bhīmā about ten kms south-west of Temburni in Karmala at Nīrānarsiṁhpur. There is a beautiful temple of Narasiṁha at their confluence.

   The Bhīmā Māhātmya (34.7-19) narrates the following legend about Nīrā:

   There was a king named Śyāvāśva who practised penance in order to attain Brahmahood. This worried Indra who sent Apsaras Nīrā to go to Bhīmāśaṅkara and disturb the king. The king cursed her to become a river.

7. Bhīmā receives another tributary called Mānagaṅgā (modern Māna). The Māna flows southward to meet Bhīmā at Sarkoli from the right bank to the north of Mangalavedha.

8. Near Kudal, about thirty kms south of Solapur, the Bhīmā receives the river Sina from the left bank to the west of Tadwal. The river Sina herself has a tributary called Bhogavatī which meets Sina near Mohol.
9. The river Bhīmā is joined by the river Kagnā near Wadi to the west.
10. The river Bori joins Bhīmā from the left to the west of Afzalpur.
11. The river Amarju joins Bhīmā from the left to the east of Afzalpur.

Bhogavatī

Bhogavatī is one of the streams of the Sarasvatī (MBh, Āraṇyakaparva, 3.25.20). Dvaitavana where the Pāṇḍavas had spent twelve years of their exile was situated on the bank of the Bhogavatī. (See also Oghavatī below).

There is another river named Bhogavatī which is a tributary of the river Sina. The Sina herself is the Tributary of the Bhīmā. (See under Bhīmā).

Brāhmaṇī

During the course of his pilgrimage Prahlāda had visited the river Brāhmaṇī. MBh, Bhīṣmaparva, 6.10.32 reads Brahmāṇī. The Brāhmaṇī flows to the north of the river Godāvarī. The temple of Tridaśeśvara Mahādeva is situated on the bank of this river (Vāmanp. 57.56).

The river Brāhmaṇī flows through the district of Balasore from the north-west to the south-east. She is constituted of two combined hill streams called Śaṅkha and South Koel, both of which rise from Chotanagpur hills. From Rourkela onwards the combined stream is known as Brāhmaṇī. First she flows southwards and then eastwards and then empties herself into the Bay of Bengal to the south of the river Vaitaraṇī.

The Brāhmaṇī is joined by the river Tikkira which rises from the Mandara hills of Sambalapur and flows from north-west to the south-west.

Brahmaputra

The river Brahmaputra is sometimes also called Brahmaputrā (Fem.; Bhaviṣyottarp. 77.58&59). This river is not only one of the biggest rivers of India but of the world. The river is about 2900 kms in length.

The river Brahmaputra rises from the Mānasarovara in the western part of Tibet. The source of this river is near that of the Indus and the Sutlej to the east of the Mānasarovara.

The Brahamaputra runs for about 1300 kms in Tibet in the eastern direction and there it is called Tsango. While entering into India it takes a southward turn. It is joined by two other rivers called Dibang and Luhit. The joint river is then known as Brahmaputra.

Brahmaputra enters Assam through the Mishmi hills. At Goalundo, the river takes a south-western turn and is joined by the river Padmā which is the easternmost and the main stream of the Gaṅgā. This combined stream of the Padmā and the Brahmaputra joins the river Meghnā in Bangladesh which is one of the most important estuaries of the Gaṅgā.

Kālikp. Ch. 85 gives the following legend about the origin of Brahmaputra :

There was a sage named Śantanu in Harivarṣa. He had a wife by the name Amoghā. Brahmā created a son in her. Sage Śantanu placed this son in the midst of four mountains, namely, Kailāsa, Gandhamādana, Jarudhi, and Sambaka. This son of Brahmā assumed the form of a big mass of water and occupied a large area. Gods and heavenly damsels used to bathe in its pure waters.

Once Paraśurāma came there. He had killed his mother

as ordered by his father Jamadagni. The father was pleased with his son's obedience and awarded him with several boons. One of them was the revival of his mother and the other was the removal of the sin of killing his mother. Jamadagni said that the sin of killing one's own mother could not be atoned only by obtaining a boon. He must therefore go to the Brahmakuṇḍa and have bath there. Paraśurāma went to the Brahmakuṇḍa on the Himālayas. With his axe he made way for the son of Brahmā (Brahma-putra) from this Brahmakuṇḍa. From there, the stream came to the lake of Lohit in the valley of Kailāsa. Then Paraśurāma carried this Brahmaputra in the eastern direction digging the way for its stream with his axe. He thus brought it to the land of Kāmarūpa, i.e., Assam.

The famous temple of Kāmākhyā Devī is situated on the Nīlācala hill on the Brahmaputra river at a little distance from Gauhati (Guwahati).

Bhasmakūṭa or Bhasmācala is a hill in the midst of the river Brahmaputra opposite Guwahati. It is stated that Śiva sprinkled ashes before imparting knowledge to Pārvatī at this place. It is also said that Kāmadeva was burnt into ashes at this place by the fire of the third eye of Śiva.

On this Bhasmācala is situated the Urvaśīkuṇḍa. It is stated that the heavenly damsel Urvaśī brought *amṛta* from heaven for goddess Kāmākhyā. Whoever takes a bath in this *kuṇḍa* on the 12th of the bright half of Māgha (February-March) obtains the merit of performing Aśvamedha.

On the north-east of Bhasmakūṭa is situated the temple of Maṇikarṇeśvara. About eight kms from Gauhati is a place called Pāṇḍinātha hill. It is said that the demons Madhu and Kaiṭabha were killed on this mountain.

Aśvakrānta is another tīrtha situated on the northern bank of the Brahmaputra. It is said that when Kṛṣṇa came to Prāgjyotiṣa (Assam), he rested on this hill with his horse.

This is a tīrthạ sacred to lord Janārdana. To the south of Aśvakrānta is situated the lake of Aśvītīrtha. This tīrtha is also associated with the Kalki incarnation of Viṣṇu.

Geographical Details

The upper course of the Brahmaputra lies in Tibet where it is known as Tsangpo. It rises in the Kailāsa range at an elevation of about 5150 metres. This river is called Dihang when it enters Arunachal Pradesh in a south-westerly course near Sadiya. It is joined by the river Dibang from the north and the Lohita from the east. It is from this point that the waters of three streams flow as the mighty Brahmaputra. It flows west-south-westwards up to Dubhri and then southward round the spurs of the Garo hills. The river then enters the plains of Bangladesh and joins the Padmā, a branch of the Gaṅgā, a little above the Goalundo Ghat. The river finally empties herself in the Bay of Bengal.

In the rainy season, the river becomes very large as wide as eight kms from bank to bank and resembles a slow moving lake. (See also Lauhitā below).

Tributaries

There are about thrity-five major tributaries of the Brahmaputra. Some of them are:

1. From the right bank:

   Subansiri, Bhareli, Dhansiri, Barudi, Pagladia, Manas, and Sankosh.

2. From the left bank:

   Lohita, Dibang, Noa-Dihing, Burhi Dihing, Disang, Dikhow, Jhanji, Kapili, Digaru, Kulsi, Singra, Jiniram, Dudhnai, and Krishnai.

Cakṣuṣmatī

The river Cakṣuṣmatī rises from the mountain Himavat

(Varāhp. 85). The Matsyp. 121.22-23 mentions a river named Cakṣuṣī and takes it to be another name of the river Śailodā or Śailodakā. According to Dey, Cakṣuṣmatī is the river Ikṣumatī which is identified with the river Kālīnadī which flows through Kumaun, Rohilkhand, and Kannauj.

Candanā

In MBh, Bhīṣmaparava, 6.10.28 Candanā is mentioned along with the rivers Śīghrā, Picchilā, Bhāradvājī, Kauśikī, Śoṇā, and Bāhudā. Vāyup. 45.95-106 also enumerates a number of rivers among them Candanā is one (vs. 97).

The river Candanā rises from the mountain Pāriyātra. Sircar opines that it is another name of the river Sābarmatī in Gujarat. Dey agrees. But he refers to another river named Candanā in the Santal Pargana in West Bengal which falls into the Gaṅgā.

Candrabhāgā

The river Candrabhāgā was known to the Vedic people as Asiknī. She is the modern river Chenab in Panjab. Candrabhāgī and Candrikā are other names of Candrabhāgā (Śabdakalpadruma, s.v.).

The river Candrabhāgā is connected with the moon. In this connection Kālikp. 20;21 narrates the following legend :

The moon had married twenty-seven daughters of Dakṣa. But he was partial to Rohiṇī. The other sisters, therefore, complained to their father Dakṣa, who thereupon cursed the moon that he would suffer from Yakṣmā (a pulmonary disease). The moon gradually lost his lustre. Later, on the plea of the gods in favour of the moon, Dakṣa advised him to take bath in the river Sītā. When the moon bathed in the river Sītā, she overflowed and a new river rose up. This latter river was named Candrabhāgā.

It may be pointed out that the river Aṁśumatī is also associated with the moon. He is said to have taken refuge in her. (See also under Aṁśumatī and Asiknī above).

The Candrabhāgā rises from the Himālayas in two streams: one called Candrā on the south-west side of Bara Lach, and the other called Bhāgā, on the north-west slope of the Pass. They join at Tandi and the united stream is known as Candrabhāgā (modern Chenab).

Padmp., Ādikhaṇḍa, 1.18.61 and Kūrmp. II.41.35-36 say that Somaloka is gained by bathing in the river Candrabhāgā.

The river Bhīmā at Pandharpur (Maharashtra) is also called Candrabhāgā. She joins the river Kṛṣṇā.

Candrikā

The river Candrikā rises from the Himavat (Vāman p. 13.20). According to the Śabdakalpadruma and Dey, the river Candrikā is another name of Candrabhāgā.

Carmaṇvatī

The river Carmaṇvatī rises from the mountain Pāriyātra (Kūrmp. I.46.31; Mārkp. 57.20; Vāmanp. 13.24; Vāyup. 45.98). She is the same as the modern river Chambal which is a tributary of the Yamunā.

MBh, Droṇaparva, 7.67 narrates a story about the origin of the river Carmaṇvatī. There was a pious king named Rantideva (Bhāgp. 9.21). He was always engaged in sacrifices. Countless animals, who were eager to go to heaven, used to come to him for being immolated in the sacrifices of the king. The number of animals who were thus sacrificed was so large that a river flowed out from the secretions of the heaps of the accumulated hides *(carman)*. That river was named as Carmaṇvatī.

In Meghadūta I. 55, Carmaṇvatī is described by Kālidāsa as the daughter of the cow Surabhi who is the daughter of the celestial cow Kāmadhenu.

Geographical Details

The Carmaṇvatī (Chambal) has her source in the Janpao range of the Vindhyas near Mhow which is about 2020 feet above sea level. She flows in a northerly direction up to Chaurasigarh where she drops to about 1660 feet from her source. After Kota, she enters the plains and runs in north-easterly direction, and flows through Madhya Pradesh and Rajasthan. Flowing in north-easterly direction she enters Uttar Pradesh and joins the river Yamunā at a place about forty kms south-east of Etawah.

Chambal flows in the areas of Gwalior, Indore, Sitamau, and Jhalwar. In Rajasthan, she passes through the Patar Plateau. The river forms a boundary between Bundi and Kotah.

Tributaries

1. The river Chambla joins from the left bank to the south of Nagda.
2. The Maleni from the left bank.
3. Śiprā from the right bank.
4. Choṭi Kālīsindha from the right bank.
5. Gandhi-Sagar reservoir is built on this river.
6. The river Gujatī joins from the left.
7. Bamani joins from the left.
8. Kālīsind joins from the right to the west of Etawah.
9. Mej from the left to the east of Lakheri.
10. Parbati (Pārvatī) from the right near Pali.
11. Banas from the left bank to the south-west of Khandhar.

12. Kuni from the right to the east of Nadigam and north of Udgar.

Citrakūṭā

The river Citrakūṭā is a small stream which rises from the mountain Citrakūṭa (a range of the mt. Ṛkṣa) (Kūrmp. I.46.32; Matsyp. 114.25; Vāyup. 45.99). Running along the south-east of the mt. Citrakūṭa, she meets the Yamunā a little ahead of Karvi (Pargiter, Mārkp. 57.21 fn). According to Sircar, she is the same as the river Mandākin, or a part of her.

Citrakūṭā is also identified with the river Payasvinī (or Paisuni or Pasani), a tributary of Yamunā between the river Ken and Tons near mt. Citrakūṭa.

Citrā

The river Citrā rises from the Himavat (Vāmanp. 13.22). MBh, Bhīṣmaparva, 6.9.30 mentions one Citraśilā. The river Citraśilā flowed in upper Assam according to the Paschimbhag plate of Sricandra (Sircar).

Citrotpalā

The river Citrotpalā rises from the mountain Ṛkṣa (MBh, Bhīṣmaparva, 6.10.32; Kūrmp. I.46.32). She is also known as Citrarathā. Rām., Ayodhyākāṇḍa 2.65.3 mentions a forest named Citraratha through which Bharata passed while returning from Kekaya to Ayodhyā. According to Sircar, Citrotpalā is a branch of the Mahānadī in Orissa, or Mahānadī herself, below her junction with the Pyri (or Pairi) (Mārkp. 57.22). Dey identifies her with the Cittutola, a branch of the Mahānadī.

Dāmodara

The river Dāmodara is one of the western tributaries of the Gaṅgā. It flows through the states of Bihar and West Bengal. It has its source in the Chota Nagpur Hills. After flowing about 600 kms, this river ultimately empties itself into the river Hooghly.

In its upper reaches, it is joined by two major tributaries, the Barakar and the Konar. The river Kana is the principal branch of the Dāmodara.

This river is very sacred to the Santals.

Daśārṇā

Daśārṇā rises from the mountain Ṛkṣa. She is a holy river where performance of *śrāddha, homa, japa,* etc. brings great merit (Kūrmp. I. 47.32; II.37..5-36; Brahmāṇḍp. I.16.30).

She is the modern river Dhasan which rises from the Sagar Plateau near Bhopal. She flows north-eastward, then from Galganj she flows northwards to join the Betwa from the right bank to the south of Orai.

Devikā

There are two rivers by the name Devikā.

1. The First one flows from the Himālayas (Mārkp. 57.18; Matsyp. 114.21; Vāyup. 45.95). There is a tīrtha by the name Vṛṣa on this river. By bathing there one attains Yogasiddhi (Kūrmp. II.37.25). Pargiter identifies this river with the modern river Deog (or Deeg), a tributary of the Ravi on her right bank (Mārkp. 57.18 fn). B.C. Law opines that it is just another name of the lower course of the river Sarayū.

Devikā meets the river Gaṇḍakī, (Varāhp. 144.83; 112). The confluence of the Gaṇḍakī, the Sarayū (i.e. Devikā) and the Gaṅgā forms the Triveṇī. It is said that the fight between the elephant and the crocodile (*gaja-grāha* combat) had taken place there (Varāhp. 144.116f).

2. The second Devikā rises from the mt. Pāriyātra (Kūrmp. I.46.29) which, according to Pargiter, may be in

the Deccan. Devikā is a very sacred river (MBh, Āraṇyakaparva, 3.80.115) and a dip in her water and worship of Maheśvara there fulfills all desires, and brings the fruits of a sacrifice (MBh, Āraṇyakaparva, 3.80.111-112).

Vāmanp. 52.13ff relates the following legend about Devikā:

Once the demon Dhundu, son of Kaśyapa and Danu, practised penanace and obtained a boon from Brahmā that he would not be killed by any one, not even by any god. Dhundu went to Svargaloka and declared himself Indra. The gods repaired to the Brahmaloka. Dhundu wanted also to capture Brahmaloka but there were too many difficulties on the way. Śukrācārya advised Dhundu to perform one hundred Aśvamedha sacrifices which might enable him to go to the Brahmaloka. The arrangements for the sacrifice were duly made and the bank of the river Devikā was chosen as the site for the sacrifice because that sacred river was the fulfiller of all desires (Vāmanp. 52.36). The gods were alarmed and approached Viṣṇu for succour. Visnu took the form of a dwarf (Vāmana), left his body floating in the river Devikā, and began drowning. Dhundu saw the poor Brāhmaṇa, left the sacrifice, and rushed to rescue him. On being asked, the Brāhmaṇa said that he was kicked out by his brother and ousted penniless from his house. Dhundu offered him money but the Brāhmaṇa wanted only three steps of land. The Brāhmaṇa measured the entire universe in his three steps, and thus Dhundu was humbled.

Viṣṇu lives in the river Devikā in the form of Bhūdhara (Vāmanp. 63.30).

Dhūtapāpā

The river Dhūtapāpā rises from the mountain Himālaya (Kūrmp. I.26.29; Matsyp. 114.22). Pargiter (Mārkp. 57.17 fn) points out that she is a tributary of the river Gomatī.

Sircar opines that Dhūtapāpā is a tributary of the Gaṅgā

near Vārāṇasī. The name has been associated with Dhopāpā on the Gomatī, south-west of Sultanpur in Uttar Pradesh.

Ali identifies Dhūtapāpā with the Sharada. (For Sharada, see under Ikṣu).

Dṛṣadvatī

Dṛṣadvatī is a Ṛgvedic river (ṚV 3.23.4). She rises from the Himālayas (Kūrmp. I.46.29; Mārkp. 57.18: Matsyp. 114.22; Vāmanp. 13.21; Varāhp. 85; Vāyup. 45.95). In ancient times, Dṛṣadvatī, which means full of stones, flowed between the rivers Sarasvatī and Yamunā and formed the boundary of Āryāvarta in the east and the south (ManuS 2.17; Vāmanp, SM, 12.9).

According to the present opinion, the river Dṛṣadvatī rises from the hills of Sirmur and flows in the district of Ambala. She meets the Sarasvatī at Sirsa, the place below which both the rivers disappear. The town of Pehoa (ancient Pṛthūdaka) is situated on the Dṛṣadvatī.

Sircar identifies her with the river Rakṣī which flows by the south-east of Thaneswar.

B.C. Law identifies her with the Chautang, a river which rises near Mugalwali and flows to the south-west and finally disappears below Mundh. Chautang flows in between the Yamunā in the east and Markand in the west.

Dṛṣadvatī is a very sacred river (MBh, Āraṇyakaparva, 3.88.10). A person who bathes in her water and offers ablution to gods and manes obtains the merit of the Agniṣṭoma and Atirātra sacrifices (MBh, Āraṇyakaparva, 3.81.73; Vāmanp, SM, 15.46).

According to Vāmanp, SM, 15.57, the river Kauśikī joins the Dṛṣadvatī. The confluence has a special sanctity which redeems one from all the sins.

Naimiṣāaraṇya of the Purāṇic fame was situated on her bank (Vāyup. 14.15).

Dugdhodā

This river rises from the Sahya mountain (Vāmanp. 13.31). She may be indentified with the river Dūdhagaṅgā, a tributary of the river Kṛṣṇā.

Durgā

The river Durgā rises from the mountain Vindhya (Kūrmp. I.46.35; Mārkp. 57.25; Vāyup. 45.103). Pargiter opines that Durgā is another name of the river Brāhmaṇī which flows through the Murshidabad district into the right bank of the Bhāgīrathī branch of the Gaṅgā (Mārkp. 57.25 fn). But Dey says that Durgā is a tributary of the river Sābarmatī in Gujarat.

Durgamā

She rises from the mt. Vindhya (Matsyp. 114.28). She may be the same as Durgā mentioned above.

Durgandhā

She rises from the mt. Vindhya (Vāmanp. 13.29). Durgandhā is another name of the river Vaitaraṇī (Garuḍp. II.35.3). (See also under Vaitaraṇī below).

Gambhīrā

Meghadūta I.40 mentions the river Gambhīrā. She is a river in Malwa. Her water is pure and clear as crystal, and full of fishes.

Gaṇḍakī

The river Gaṇḍakī rises from the Himālayas (Mārkp. 58.18; Matsyp. 114.22; Vāmanp. 13.22; Vāyup. 45.96). She is a very sacred river because, it is said that, she has her source in the combined waters of all tīrthas. A person who takes a dip in her water obtains the merit of the Vājapeya sacrifice and goes to the Sūryaloka (MBh, Ānraṇyakaparva,

3.82.97). One who breathes his last in this river goes to Viṣṇuloka (Varāhp. 114.58). Bathing in Gaṇḍakī in the month of Kārtika (November) brings much merit. It frees a person from all sins and he obtains salvation (Varāhp. 144.109).

Viṣṇu once practised penance for the welfare of mankind. A stream of perspiration flowed from his *gaṇḍa* (cheek). It later turned into a river which is named Gaṇḍakī (Varāhp. 144.94).

Padmp, Pātālakhaṇḍa, 4.20.12ff mentions that Prajāpati felt sad seeing all his creatures *(prajā)* full of sin. He created the river Gaṇḍakī from his *gaṇḍa* so that his *prajās* may atone their sins by taking bath in that river. She is resorted to by gods and demons alike. Simply by seeing her one's sins of mind, by touching her water one's sins of bad deeds, and by drinking her water one's sins of bad speech are burnt.

The river Gaṇḍakī herself once practised austere penance and pleased Viṣṇu thereby. Viṣṇu asked her to seek a boon. She aspired to become his mother. Viṣṇu granted that he would always remain in the form of Śālagrāmas (stones in a special shape found in the bed of the Gaṇḍakī) with her and would be worshipped in that form as her son (Varāhp. 144.35ff). (For the importance of Śālagrāma, see Padmp, Pātālakhaṇḍa, 4.20.16ff).

The river Gaṇḍakī along with the rivers Devikā and Aparā (i.e. Gaṅgā in this context) forms a *triveṇī* which is regarded very sacred (Varāhp. 144.83-84).

Geographical Details

Gaṇḍakī is the modern river Gaṇḍaka. She originates in the hills of south Tibet. Passing through Nepal, she receives four tributaries on the left side and two on the right. Those on the left are 1. Buriā Gaṇḍaka, 2. Madi, 3. Seti, and 4. Kālī. The upper tributary of the Gaṇḍaka on her side joins her at a place north-west of Nayakot in Nepal, and the lower tributary called Rāptī joins her above the district of Champaran.

The Gaṇḍakī enters in India in between the districts of Gorakhpur and Champaran. Her main stream flows into the Gaṅgā between Sonapur in the Chapra district and Hazipur in the district of Muzzafarpur.

There is another Gaṇḍaka known as Burhī Gaṇḍaka which rises from the hills of Hariharpur in Nepal. It flows parallel to the river Gaṇḍaka and joins the Gaṅgā west of Gogri.

For Gaṇḍakī Mahatmya, see Padmp, Pātālakhaṇḍa, 4.4.20.

The Bhṛgutuṅga tīrtha (Varāhp. 146.51-52) and the Śālagrāma tīrtha where the Goddess lives in the form of Mahādevī are situated on the bank of Gaṇḍakī (Matsyp. 13.33; 22.62; Brahmp. II.13.89).

Gandhakālī

The river Gandhakālī is regarded as the daughter of the Pitṛs, hence it is beneficial to perform *śrāddha* on her banks (Kūrmp. II.37.30-31). (Cf. also Brahmāṇḍp. II.13.76-79).

Gandhavatī

Meghadūta I. 33 mentions the river Gandhavatī. She abounds in lotus flowers. She is a river in Malwa (Madhya Pradesh). She is a tributary of the river Śiprā.

Gaṅgā

The holiest river Gaṅgā is mentioned in the Ṛgveda also (ṚV 10.75.5). In ṚV 6.45.31, the word *Gāṅgyaḥ* occurs. Her valley was inhabited by the Paṇis.

The river Gaṅgā is regarded as the mixture of holy waters of all the tīrthas and is therefore regarded as supreme among all the rivers (MBh, Ādiparva, 1.92.49; Śāntiparva, 12.274.16; Anuśāsanaparva, 13.14.37). She is very efficacious in removing sins. Padmp, Ādikhaṇḍa 1.41.14 says:

yojanānāṁ sahasreṣu gaṅgā smarati yo naraḥ/
api duṣkṛtakarmā' sau labhate paramaṁgatim//

(A person who rememebers the river Gaṅgā even for a distance of a thousand *yojanas*, attains to *parama-gati* even if he has been a doer of misdeeds).

The Gaṅgā is resorted to by Ṛṣis and Munis (Rām., Bālakāṅḍa, 1.34.6-7). She is the eldest daughter of the Himālaya and his wife Menā (daughter of the mt. Meru) (Rām., Bālakāṇḍa 1.34.13). Umā is her younger sister (Rām., Bālakāṇḍa, 1.34.13). The gods requested Himālaya to give Gaṇgā to them to serve their cause (Rām., *ibid.* 15). They took her to Svargaloka (Rām., *Ibid.* 21).

Agni had dropped Śiva's semen in this river from which Skanda was born (Rām., Bālakāṇḍa 1.36; MBh, Śalyaparva, 9.43; Skandp. Vaiṣṇavakhaṇḍa, Vaiśākh-Māhātmya, 9.74).

Rām., Bālakāṇḍa, 1.38-43; Mbh, Āraṇyakaparva, 3.105-109; BrahmVP, Prakṛtikhaṇḍ,10; Devībhp. 9; and a large number of other Sanskrit texts narrate a legend about the descent of Gaṅgā on the earth (which is known as Sagaropākhyāna). Briefly the legend is as follows:

King Sagara of the Solar race performed successfully ninety-nine Aśvamedha (Horse) sacrifices. But when he commenced the hundredth one, his sacrificial horse was stolen by Indra fearing that he thereby would lose his throne of the king of gods, if the sacrifice was completed. Indra carried the horse down to the Pātāla-loka in the Āśrama of Ṛṣi Kapila. The king Sagra had sixty thousand sons from his wife Sumati. He ordered his sons to search for the horse. They went out in the search of the horse. They traced the horse in the Āśrama of Ṛṣi Kapila. They reproached the Ṛṣi for having stolen the horse. The innocent Kapila was enraged and reduced them to ashes by means of the power of his penance. Their death rites could not be performed because it was only Gaṅgā who could purify them. King Sagara's sons and grandsons up to three generations tried to bring Gaṅgā on the earth but without success. Finally Bhagīratha performed rigorous penance on the bank of the lake Bindusara (MBh, Sabhāparva, 2.3.9; Bhīṣmaparva, 6.7.40; Varāhp. 47.24). Brahmā thereupon agreed to his request that Gaṅgā be released on to the earth for the sake of his great-great-grandfathers. But he warned Bhagīratha that there was no one on the earth who could bear the mighty fall of Gaṅgā (Rām., Bālakāṇḍa, 1.41.23), no one except Śiva. Bhagīratha then propitiated Śiva. Śiva agreed to bear Gaṅgā. Gaṅgā accordingly fell down on the matted hair of Śiva and wandered there for a thousand years. When her pride was humbled, and for the sake of Bhagīratha, Śiva released her towards Bindusara. Gaṅgā then followed the chariot of Bhagīratha, and, flowing on the earth, she went to the Pātāla-loka and purified king Sagara's sons. Since king Bhagīratha had brought her down on the earth, she came to be called Bhāgīrathī (Rām., Bālakāṇḍa 1.43.5).

This entire legend of the descent of Gaṅgā from Brahmaloka on the earth is known as Gaṅgāvataraṇa. This has provided an excellent theme for the artists of the Gupta and the mediaeval periods who have portrayed it on the temple-walls and door jambs and made sculptures and drawings and paintings on paper and walls.

MBh, Ādiparva, 1.91;92 and Devībhp. 2.3;4 give another account of the descent of Gaṅgā.

A king named Mahābhiṣa of the Ikṣvāku dynasty performed one thousand Aśvamedha sacrifices and one hundred Vājapeya sacrifices. By virtue of these sacrifices he went to Svarga. Once Gaṅgā visited the grandsire Brahmā in the Brahmaloka.King Mahābhiṣa also happened to be there. The transparent white garment which Gaṅgā was wearing at that time was suddenly blown away by the wind. All the gods bent down their heads but the king boldly and longingly looked at her. Brahmā was annoyed by this act of the king, and cursed him to go back to the Mṛtyuloka. Gaṅgā also had, by that time, developed love for the king. She followed him to the earth. On the way, she saw the eight Vasus with their beauty dimmed because of the curse of Ṛṣi Vasiṣṭha. The Vasus had stolen the cow Nandinī of the sage. On being placated by them, Vasiṣṭha modified the curse in such a way that the curse was to become inoperative if and when they would be born from the womb of Gaṅgā (MBh, Ādiparva, 1.93). The Vasus, therefore, beseached Gaṅgā to be their mother so that they might be relieved of their curse. They also told her that king Pratīpa's son, Śantanu, would marry her and that they would be born of this union. They further told her that she should throw each one of them into her water so that they could regain their original forms.

Once king Pratīpa went to the bank of the river Gaṅgā for penance. Gaṅgā appeared before him and asked him to accept her as his wife. The king declined. He, however, assured her that he would accept her for his son provided he got one. In due course, the king got a son who came to be known as Śantanu. Indeed, it was the same king Mahābhiṣa who was born to king Pratīpa as his son Śantanu. When Śantanu grew up, Pratīpa told him of the promise he had made to Gaṅgā. Gaṅgā married Śantanu on the condition that she should not be prevented from whatever right or wrong she did. The couple begot eight sons. As Gaṅgā had told the Vasus, she threw seven of them into her water one by one. King Śantanu could not utter a word because of the promise he had made to her. But while she was about to throw the eighth one into the water, the king could not control his agony and pleaded with her to spare at least that child. The promise was broken. Gaṅgā forsook him and repaired to her abode. She brought up the eighth child and later returned him to Śantanu. The boy was named as Devavrata who later came to be known as the great Bhīṣma.

BrahmVP, Prakṛtikhaṇḍa, 6 and Devībhp. 9.6 relate yet another legened about the descent of Gaṅgā:

Lakṣmī, Gaṅgā and Sarasvatī are three wives of Viṣṇu. Once Gaṅgā passionately looked at the face of Viṣṇu. Sarasvatī could not tolerate this and complained to him that he was partial to Gaṅgā and Lakṣmī. Viṣṇu silently left the place. Then there ensued a heated argument among the three wives. Sarasvatī quarrelled with Gaṅgā while Lakṣmī kept quiet. Lakṣmī's silence irked Sarasvatī, and she cursed her that she would become a plant and a river. As the result of this, Lakṣmī did become a plant and a river, named Tulasī and Padmā respectively. Then she turned towards Gaṅgā and also cursed her that she would be turned into a river. This was too much for Gaṅgā. She, in turn, retaliated by cursing Sarasvatī that she too would become a river. They both became rivers.

Bhāgp. 5.17; Mārkp. 56; Viṣṇup. 2.2.31f and 2.8.99f mention that the river Gaṅgā issued from the foot of Viṣṇu when, in his Vāmana incarnation, he had stretched out his leg upward to measure the three worlds. The Brahmāṇḍakaṭāha of the nail of his left foot broke out and a stream issued forth which was named as Viṣṇupadī Gaṅgā. Flowing through the sky where she was known as Ākāśagaṅgā (MBh, Svargārohaṇaparva, 18.3.26), she fell on the periphery of the moon. After purifying the moon, she fell down on the summit of the mount Meru. There she divided herself into four streams.

1. The first stream flowed towards the east and is known as Sītā. Sītā flowed through the forest Caitraratha and, passing through the lake Varuṇodā, fell on the mountain

Śītānta. Descending on the earth she flowed through Bhadrāśva and joined the sea in the east.

2. The second stream, Alakanandā, flowed southward towards the Gandhamādana mountain and, coursing through the forest Nandana, entered the lake Mānasa. From there she flowed on the mount Himavat. Here lord Śiva stopped her. However, being propitiated by Bhagīratha, Śiva released her. She entered the southern ocean in seven streams and flowed towards the east in three streams.
3. The third stream is known as Sva-rakṣu which fell on the mountain Vipula on the west and, flowing through the forest Vaibhāga, entered into the lake Śītoda. Later, falling on the mt. Sva-rakṣu and Triśikha, she reached Ketumāla and finally entered into the Salt sea.
4. The fourth stream was known as Somā which flowed on the mountain Supārśva which is at the foot of the mt. Meru. Flowing through the forest Sāvitrī, she entered the lake Mahābhadra. From there, falling on the mountain Śaṅkhakūṭa and Vṛṣabha, she flowed through the northern Kurus and entered the great ocean.

The four streams mentioned in Bhāgp. 5.17 are slightly different. Their courses are also different. They are:

1. Sītā flows from the Brahmapurī, i.e., the Meru, and descends on the Gandhamādana. From there she flows through the country of Bhadrāśva and joins the sea in the east.
2. The second stream named Alakanandā falls from Meru to the south on the Hemakūṭa. From there, piercing the Himālayas, she comes to Bhāratavarṣa and flows into the south ocean.
3. The third stream named Cakṣu descends on the

Mālyavān mountain and, flowing through the Ketumāla-varṣa, joins the sea in the west.

4. The fourth stream Bhadrā falls from the Meru towards the north on the mountain Śṛṇgavān and falls into the ocean in the north.

MBh, Ādiparva, 1.158.17-20; and Bhīṣmaparva, 6.7.44-47 mention seven streams of the Gaṣgā as follows:

1. Vasvokasārā, 2. Nalinī, 3. Pāvanā, 4. Sarasvatī, 5. Jambunadī, 6. Sītā, and 7. Sindhu.

Matsyp. 121.40f mentions these seven streams slightly differently. The are: 1. Nalinī, 2. Hlādinī, 3. Pāvanī, (these three flow in the east), 4. Sītā, 5. Cakṣu, 6. Sindhu, (these flow in the west), and the seventh stream followed the course of Bhagīratha's chariot, and was, therefore, named as Bhāgīrathī. Vāyup. 47.38-40 agrees with the list of the Matsya-purāṇa.

BrahmVP, Prakṛtikhaṇḍa, 11;12 mentions that Gaṅgā was the beloved of Kṛṣṇa. She is regarded also as a portion *(aṁśa)* of Rādhā. Gaṅgā married Kṛṣṇa (BrahmVP, Prakṛti-khaṇḍa, 10.114).

Having been released by Śiva, Gaṅgā followed Bhagī-ratha. On the way, she inundated the sacrificial place of the sage Jahnu. Angered by her temerity, the sage drank the waters of Gaṅgā. However, on being pleaded by the gods and other Ṛṣis, he accepted Gaṅgā as his daughter and released her through his ear. Therefore, Gaṅgā is known as Jāhnavī (Vāyup. 91.54-58).

The river Jāhnavī came on the earth on the tenth of the bright half of the month of Jyeṣṭha (June-July) on Tuesday, and as she removes ten kinds of sins, this festive occasion is celebrated as a Daśa-harā festival particularly on the banks of the river Gaṅgā.

Gaṅgā meets the river Yamunā at Prayāga. The confluence of Gaṅgā and Yamunā is very sacred. A bath in the *saṅgama* in the month of Māgha (February-March) is regarded very fruitful and removes all sins. Every twelve years Kuṁbhaparva occurs. Devout Hindus take bath on this day in the confluence of the Gaṅgā and Yamunā. On this day, there is a large gathering of men, women, and sādhus in millions at Prayāga. Kuṁbha is celebrated in three parts: first is the Makarasaṅkrāntī, second is Pūrṇakuṁbha on the Amāvāsyā, and the third is on the Vasanta-pañcamī day.

Gaṅgā is a very sacred river. A bath in her waters on the full-moon days of the months of Āṣāḍha (July-August), Kārtika (November-December), Māgha (February-March), and Vaiśākha (May-June) brings great rewards. One obtains great merit after a bath in Gaṅgā on the seventh of the bright half of Māgha (February-March), on a Akṣaya *tithi*, on the Amāvāsyā days, on the days of Saṅkrānti, and on the days of solar and lunar eclipses.

Before taking bath in the Gaṅgā, there is a procedure to follow. Matsyp. 102.1-8 prescribes that first Gaṅgā should be invoked with the following mantras:

vinṣṇoḥ pādaprasūtā'si vaiṣṇavī viṣṇudevatā/
pāhi nastvenasātasmādājanmamraṇāntikāt//
tisraḥ koṭyo'rdhakoṭī ca tīrthānāṁ vāyurabravīta/
divibhuvy antarikṣe ca tāni te santi jāhnavī//
nandinītyeva te nāma deveṣu nalinīti ca/
dakṣā pṛthvī ca vihagā viśvakāyā'mṛtā śivā//
vidyādharī supraśāntā tathā viśvaprasādinī/
kṣemā ca jāhnavī caiva śāntā śāntipradāyinī//

Matsyp. 102.4-7

(You are born from the foot of Viṣṇu, you belong to Viṣṇu, your god is Viṣṇu. Therefore, free us from sins committed through birth to death. Vāyu has said that there are three and a half crores of holy places in the heaven, on the earth, and in the mid-air. All these, O Jāhnavī, belong to you. You are known as Nandinī among the gods, also Nalinī. There are other names of yours, such as, Dakṣā, Pṛthvī, Vihagā, Viśvakāyā, Amṛtā, Śivā, Vidyādharī, Supraśāntā, Viśvaprasādinī, Kṣemā, Jānhavī, Śāntā, and Śantipradāyinī).

The person then should invoke the clay (in the river) with the *mantras* (Matsyp. 102.10-12) and apply it to his body. He should sip water and perform *tarpaṇa* for Ṛṣis and Pitṛs.

Matsyp. 106.52; MBh, Āraṇyakaparva, 85.94; Kūrmp. I.37.32 prescribe that charred bones and ashes of the burnt body of a dead person should be cast in the river Gaṅgā. It brings benefits to the deceased. He stays in the heaven as long as his bones remain in the waters of the Gaṅgā.

The qualities of the water of the Gaṅgā are:

coolness (*śītatvam*), sweetness (*swādutvam*), pellicidity (*svacchatvam*), appetising (*rucyatvam*), wholesomeness (*pathyatvam*), purity (*pāvanatvam*), remover of sin (*pāpahāritvam*), quencher of thirst and greed (*tṛṣnāmohadhvaṁśanatvam*), digestiveness (*dīpanatvam*), and preserver of intelligence (*prajñādhāritvam*) (Śabdakalpadruma, s.v.).

Tīrthas (Places of pilgrimage)

The following tīrthas are situated on the bank of the river Gaṅgā:

1. Aśvatīrtha (Viṣṇup. 4.7.7-8).
2. Avimukta-tīrtha (Matsyp. 181.54;93;94; etc. and Chs. 181-186).
3. Bhūteśvara (Kūrmp. I.35.10; Padmp, Ādikhaṇḍa, 1.37.13.)
4. Brahma-tīrhta (Kūrmp. I.35.9; Padmp, Ādikhaṇḍa, 1.37.9-12).

5. Candra-tīrtha (Kūrmp. I.35.11).
6. Carmākhya-tīrtha (Kūrmp. I.35.4).
7. Citrāṅgadeśvara-tīrtha (Kūrmp I.35.11; Padmp, Ādikhaṇḍa 3.37.14; Vāmanp, SM, 25.35).
8. Daśāśvamedhika-tīrtha (Kūrmp. II.37.36; MBh, Araṇyakaparva, 3.81.11; 82.82; Matsyp. 185.68; Vāyup. 77.45).
9. Daurvāsika-tīrtha (Kūrmp. I.35.11).
10. Devī-tīrtha (Brahmp. 127.1).
11. Deveśa-tīrtha (Kūrmp. I.35.9; Padmp. Ādikhaṇḍa, 1.37.13).
12. Gandharva-tīrtha (Kūrmp. I.35.10; Padmp. Ādikhaṇḍa, 1.37.13).
13. Gaṅgādvāra (Haridvāra) (Kūrmp. I.15.4; 41.47;II.20.33; MBh, Anuśāsanaparva, 13.26.12 ViṣṇuSmṛ 85.28).

    Kūrmp. (ibid) mentions that Dakṣa performed his sacrifice in this place.
14. Gaṅgāsāgara-saṅgama is about 150 kms south of Kolkata. It is said that Āśrama of saga Kapila (of king Sagara legend) was at this place. On the occasion of Makara-Saṅkrānti people take bath here for three days.
15. Gaṅgeśvara-tīrtha (on the mouth of Gaṅgā) (Kūrmp. II.41.102-103).
16. Gaurī-tīrtha (Kūrmp. I.35.3; Matsyp. 22.31; Padmp, Ādikhaṇḍa, 1.37.3).
17. Haṁsaprapatana-tīrtha (Kūrmp. I.37.24-25; Matsyp. 106.32).
18. Jaṁbukeśvara-tīrtha (Kūrmp. I.35.4; Nāradp. II.50.67).
19. Jāpeśvara-tīrtha (Agnip. 112.4).
20. Jñāna-tīrtha (Kūrmp. I.35.6).

21. Kālakeśvara-tīrtha (Kūrmp. I.35.7; Padmp, Ādikhaṇḍa, 1.37.7).
22. Kālañjara-tīrtha (Kūrmp. I.35.12).
23. Kāla-tīrtha (Kūrmp. I.35.2).
24. Kanakhala (Kūrmp. II.37.10-11;MBh, Āraṇyakaparva, 3.82.26; Anuśāsanaparva, 13.26.12).
25. Kapālamocana (Kūrmp. I.35.15;MBh, Ārayakaparva, 3.81.118; Varāhp. 97.29-30; Vāmanp. 3.48-51; Padmp, Ādikhaṇḍa, 1.37.18).
26. Kapila-tīrtha (Kūrmp. I.35.9).
27. Kāśī (Matsyp. 180-185; Kūrmp. I.31-35; Padmp, Ādikhaṇḍa, I.33-37; Agnip. 112; Nāradp. II.48-51 Skandp, Kāśīkhaṇḍa, 6ff).
28. Kṛttivāśeśvara-tīrtha (Kūrmp. I.32.12-26).
29. Kubjāmra-tīrtha (near Haridvāra) (MBh, Vanaparva, 3.84.40; Matsyp. 22.66; Kūrmp. II.20.33; Garudp. I.81.10; Padmp, Ādikhaṇḍa, 1.32.5).
30. Kuśāvarta-tīrtha (MBh, Anuśāśanaparva, 13.26.12; Bhāgp. 3.20.4).
31. Maṇikarṇa-tīrtha (Kūrmp. I.35.8; Padmp, Ādikhaṇḍa, 1.37.8).
32. Nāga-tīrtha (Kūrmp. I.35.7; Padmp, Ādikhaṇḍa, 1.37.7).
33. Nakulīśvara-tīrtha (Kūrmp. II.44.12-14; Matsyp, 22.77).
34. Nārāyaṇa-tīrtha (Kūrmp. I.35.5; Padmp, Ādikhaṇḍa, 1.37.5).
35. Piśācamocana-tīrtha (Kūrmp. I.33.2;14; Padmp, Ādikhaṇḍa, 1.35.2).
36. Pitāmaha-tīrtha (Kūrmp. I.35.8; Padmp, Ādikhaṇḍa, 1.37.8).
37. Prājāpatya-tīrtha (Kūrmp. I.35.4; Padmp. Ādikhaṇḍa, 1.37.4).

38. Prayāga (Kūrmp. I.37.12; Matsyp. 104.5; 109.15; 111.14; Skandp, Kāśīkhaṇḍa 7.45; Padmp. Uttarakhaṇḍa, 6.23.27-35; Nāradp. II.63.127-28).
39. Saṅgameśvara-tīrtha (Liṅgp. I.92.88).
40. Śrī-tīrtha (Kūrmp. I.35.8; MBh, Āraṇyakaparva, 3.81.37; Padmp. Ādikhaṇḍa, 1.37.8).
41. Śakreśvara-tīrtha (Kūrmp. I.35.15; Lingp. I.92-93; Nāradp. II.50-65).
42. Svargadvāra-tīrtha (Kūrmp. I.35.4; Padmp., Ādikhaṇḍa, 1.37.4).
43. Uttara-tīrtha (Kūrmp. I.35.14; Padmp., Ādikhaṇḍa, 1.37.17).
44. Vāhneya-tīrtha (Kūrmp. I.35.10).
45. Vidyādhareśvara-tīrtha (Kūrmp. I.35.11; Padmp., Ādikhaṇḍa, 1.37.14).
46. Viśvarūpa-tīrtha (Kūrmp` I.35.2; Padmp., Ādikhaṇḍa, 1.37.2).
47. Vṛṣadhvaja-tīrtha (Kūrmp. I.35.13; Liṅgp. I.92.106; Nāradp. II.50.48).
48. Vyāghreśvara-tīrtha (Kūrmp. I.35.14; Liṅgp. I.92.107; Nāradp. II.50.56; Padmp., Ādikhaṇḍa, 1.37.17).
49. Yama-tīrtha (Kūrmp. I.35.6; Padmp., Ādikhaṇḍa, 1.37.6).

In literature and art, Gaṅgā is depicted as a charming young lady surrounded by white and red hue. She wears yellow garment. Sometimes she is shown wearing red garment also. She is shown either holding a pitcher or a lotus flower. Sometimes she is portryaed as smelling the lotus. Her vehicle is a crocodile. She is lustrous like hundred winter moons. Her lips are red like ripe *bimba* fruit and her teeth shine like pearls. Her breasts are hard like *Śrīphala*. Her face is always smiling. Her body is decked with numerous ornaments. She wears a garland made of Mālatī flowers. (These descriptions are based on Kṛyādhikāra, 5.180.181; Agnip. 50.16; Devībhp. 9.12; BrahmVP, Prakṛtikhaṇḍa, 10.97, and Viṣṇudhp. 3.52.6).

Gaṅgā is also known by the following names:

Adhvagā Alakanandā, Arghyatīrtha, Bhavamanā, Bhāgīrathī, Bhīṣmajananī, Bhīṣmasū, Dharmadravī, Gaṇḍinī, Haimavatī, Haraśekharā, Jyeṣṭhā, Khāpagā, Kumārasū, Kuṭilā, Mandākinī, Nandinī, Puṇyā, Ṛṣikulyā, Rudra-śekharā, Śailendrajā, Samudra-śubhagā, Saridvarā, Siddha-sindhu, Sīddhāpagā, Sitasindhu, Suradīrghīkā, Suranadī, Suranimnagā, Surāpagā, Śuddhā, Svarāpagā, Svaradhunī, Svargasaridvarā, Svargyāpagā, Svarvāpī, Tīrtharāja, Tridaśadīrghikā, Tripathagā, Trisrotrā, Ugraśekharā, and Viṣṇupadī,

For the *māhātmya* (eulogy) and *stuti* (prayer) of Gaṅgā see:

1. Agnip. 110.
2. BrahmVP, Prakṛtikhanda, 10.114; Śrīkṛṣṇakhaṇḍa, 34.
3. Devībhp. 9.12.18.
4. Gaṅgāṣṭakam, Sri Śaṅkaragranthāvalī, Śāradāpīṭham, Sringeri.
5. Gaṅgāstrotra by Sri Śaṅkarācarya.
6. MBh, Āraṇyakaparva, 3.85.88-97; Anuśāsanparva, 13.26; 27.
7. Skandp, Kāśīkhanda, 27-29. (This contains Gaṅgāsahasranāma).
8. Nāradp. II.38-45; 51.1-48.
9. Padmp, Ādikhaṇḍa, 33-37; Sṛṣṭikhaṇḍa, 5.60; 6.2.
10. Viṣṇup. II.8.120-121.

Geographical Details

Gaṅgā rises from the Himālayas. At her source, she is known as Bhāgīrathī. Her source is near Gaṅgotrī which is about 13,800 feet high. Though tradionally Gaṅgotrī is regarded as the source of the Gaṅgā, the actual source is little north of it. She emerges from Himachal Pradesh at Lachmanjhula and cuts across the Siwalik range at Haridvāra. At Haridvāra (also known as Gaṅgādvāra), she assumes the form of a big river. From Haridvāra she flows from north-west to south-east. After Allahabad, she flows in the easterly direction. In the last stage, she is divided into many branches and finally falls into the Bay of Bengal forming a delta known as Sundarbans.

About 400 kms before reaching the ocean, the Gaṅgā divides herself into several streams forming a triangle. She meets the river Brahmaputra. The main river is known as Padmā which, near the Bay of Bengal, is called Meghnā.

At Prayāga, Gaṅgā meets Yamunā and the concealed Sarasvatī. The Triveṇī-saṅgama is regarded very sacred.

Tributaries of the Gaṅgā

1. Kālī from the right bank near Kannauj.
2. Rāmagangā from the left near Kannauj.
3. Īśānā from the right.
4. Kalyāṇī from the left.
5. Pāṇḍu from the right.
6. Luni from the left.
7. Yamunā from the right.
8. Tons (Tamasā) from the right.
9. Varaṇā from the left near Vārāṇasī.
10. Gomatī from the left.

11. Gaṅgī from the left.
12. Besu from the left.
13. Mangoi from the left.
14. Karmanāsā from the right.
15. Ghāgharā from the left near Chapra.
16. Śoṇa from the right.
17. Gaṇḍaka from the left.
18. Kośī from the left.
19. Burhī Gaṇḍaka from the left.

Gaurī

She is mentioned in MBh, Bhīṣmaparva, 6.10.24; Kūrmp. I.46.35. She is identified with the modern river Panjkora which rises near a place named Punpat in the Gilgit area of Himachal Pradesh. She flows south-westward up to Chutiatur and then turns southwards and finally joins the Swat to the north-west of Kalangai. Then she is known as the Landoi, an affluent of the river Kabul (Vedic Kubhā).

Panjkora may be a corruption of Pañcagauḍa from the name of a town of that name situated on the bank of this river.

Gautamī

The river Gautamī rises from the Western Ghats. According to modern view, the northern branch of the Godāvarī is called Gautamī. According to the Śabdakalpadruma also, Gautamī is another name of Godāvarī. In fact, below Rajahmundry, Godāvarī divides herself into two main streams: The Gautamī Godāvarī on the east and the Vāsiṣṭhī Godāvarī on the west. (See under Godāvarī also).

The rivers Droṇa and Govardhinī are the two tributaries of the Godāvarī.

The cold water of Gautamī is believed to remove phlegm, and cure rheumatism, bile, and urinary diseases.

Godāvarī

The river Godāvarī rises from the Sahyādri in the Western Ghats (Kūrmp. I.46.36; Mārkp. 57.26; Matsyp. 114.29; Vāmanp. 13.30; Varāhp. 85; Vāyup. 45.104; Viṣṇup. 2.3.11). She is a sacred river which is resorted to by the Siddhas (MBh, Āraṇyakaparva, 3.83.30).

The source of the Godāvarī is at the village Tryaṁbaka where she is known also by the name Gautamī. One of the twelve Jyotirliṅgas, called Tryaṁbakeśvara, is found there. The famous temple of Tryaṁbakeśvara is also there.

The rivers Kaḍvā, Pravarā, and Muḷā meet Godāvarī in Aurangabad (Maharashtra) and together they are called Godāvarī in their onward journey. Godāvarī falls in three streams in the Bay of Bengal.

It is believed that all sacred places come to the river Godāvarī when Jupiter (Bṛhaspati) is in Leo (Siṁha). A bath in her water during this period brings merit.

BrahmVP 10.126ff narrates a story about the origin of the Godāvarī:

Once a Brāhmaṇa lady was going on a pilgrimage. The Aśvins saw her on the way, and, in spite of her protestations, violated her. She dropped the foetus in a garden and reported the incident to her husband. Her husband suspected her fidelity and forsook her. By her power of *Yoga*, the lady transformed herself into a river. That river is Godāvarī.

Rāma, Sītā, and Lakṣmaṇa lived on the bank of the Godāvarī in Pañcavaṭī near Nashik during their exile. Rāvaṇa had kidnapped Sītā from there (Rām., Araṇyakāṇḍa, 3.44.7f).

The word Godāvarī means the best giver of water

(*go*-'water' *dā*-'to give', *varī*-'best'), or the best of the rivers giving cows (*go*-'cow'), or the river (also known as Gautamī) which was brought down by the sage Gautama in order to expiate for his sin of having killed a cow. In this connection, Brahmp. chs. 69-175 and Gautamī Māhātmya 2-8 narrate the following legend:

Viṣṇu in his Vāmana incarnation measured heaven with his second step. Brahmā offered *arghya* by pouring water over that foot. The water flowed down from the foot of Viṣṇu on the mt. Meru. From there, it flowed in four directions. The southern streams was taken by Śiva on his head which is known as Gaṅgā. Pārvatī, Śiva's wife, felt jealous of another woman Gaṅgā, on her husband's head. Gaṇeśa, son of Pārvatī, contrived a plan to remove Gaṅgā from there. He asked Jayā, a maid servant of Pārvatī, to become a cow and go to Gautam's Āśrama at Brahmagiri. Disguised as a Brāhmaṇa, Gaṇeśa too reached there. At that time, although there was severe drought in other places, the Āśrama of Gautama had plenty of food and water. Therefore, a large number of Brāhmaṇas had gathered there. Jayā, as a cow, entered in Gautama's rice-field. Gautama took a blade of grass and tried to shoo the cow out. The moment the blade of grass touched the cow, she fell dead. All the Brāhmaṇas threatened to leave the Āśrama because of the sin Gautama had committed killing a cow. Gaṇeśa who was watchning all this, suggested to Gautama to bring water from the matted hair of Śiva. So, Gautama went to Kailāsa to get the water from Gaṅgā who was on Śiva's head. He prayed to Śiva to release Gaṇgā on to Brahmagiri. Siva gave Gautama a lock of his hair containing water of Gaṇgā. Gautama placed that lock of hair on Brahmagiri from which water began to flow. Gautama sprinkled this water on the dead cow. She became alive and pardoned the Ṛṣi. That water became the river

Gautamī. As the water of the river gave new life to the cow, the river is also called Godā or Godāvarī.

Gautama turned the course of the river with a blade of *darbha* grass (also called *kuśa* grass). The place where he did so is called Kuśāvarta which is a sacred tīrtha.

Godāvarī is as sacred as Gaṅgā. In fact, she is called Gaṅgā of the South (*Dakṣiṇa-gaṅgā*). All tīrthas on the Gaṅgā like Gaṅgādvāra, Kuśāvarta, Bilvaka, and Kanakhala, etc. are also said to situate on or around the Godāvarī.

According to tradition, Godāvarī is stated to divide herself into seven streams before she meets the sea. These streams are named after seven Ṛṣis, namely, Kaśyapa, Atri, Gautama, Bharadvāja, Viśvāmitra, Jamadagni, and Vasiṣṭha. Pilgrims take bath one after another in all the seven streams. This custom is known as Saptasāgara-Yātrā.

Tīrthas on the Godāvarī :

1. Ahalyā-tīrtha (Brahmp. 87.1).
2. Aśva-tīrtha (Brahmp. 89.43).
3. Bāṇa-tīrtha (Brahmp. 123.214).
4. Bhadrācalam (Rāma crossed the Godāvarī on his way to Laṅka at Bhadrācalam. There is an ancient temple of Rāma there).
5. Brahma-tīrtha (Brahmp. 113.23).
6. Daṇḍāraṇya (Brahmāṇḍp. II.13.56). Daṇḍārṇya is the valley of Godāvarī.
7. Daśāśvamedhika-tīrtha (Brahmp. 33.1).
8. Gaṅgādvāra. It is situated at a place where Godāvarī descends from Brahmagiri at Tryaṁbakeśvara.
9. Govardhana (Brahmp. 91).
10. Kapāleśvara-tīrtha. At Nashik there is a temple of Kapaleśvara Mahādeva.

11. Kapilā-tīrtha (Brahmp. 155.1-2).
12. Koṭi-tīrtha (Brahmp. 148.1-2).
13. Kuśāvarta-tīrtha (Brahmp. 80.1-3).
14. Mātṛ-tīrtha (Brahmp. I.45.6-14).
15. Nashik. Situated at a distance of 30 kms from the source of Godāvarī. Associated with Rāma, Sītā, and Laksmaṇa. Here Lakṣmaṇa had cut off the nose (*nāsa*) of Śūrpaṇakhā. Rāmakuṇḍa, Lakṣmaṇakuṇḍa, Sitākuṇḍa, Pañcavatī, and Tapovana are all located near Nasik. Every 12 years the Kumbhamelā takes place there.
16. Nāgatīrtha (Brahmāṇḍp. II.111.1).
17. Pravarā-saṅgama-tīrtha (Brahmp. 106).
18. Rajahmundry. Every thirteenth year the Pushkara festival is held at this place when a bath in the Godāvarī is held to bring great merit.
19. Soma-tīrtha (Brahmp. 105.1; 110.1).
20. Tryaṁbaka-tīrtha. There is an ancient Jyotirliṅga and temple of Tryaṁbakeśvara Mahādeva (Kūrmp. II.35.18; Matsyp. 22.47; Brahmp. 79.6).
21. Vañjārā-saṅgama (Brahmp. 159).
22. Vipra-tīrtha (Brahmp. 167.1).
23. Viṣṇu-tīrtha (or Maudgalya-tīrtha) (Brahmp. 125.1;3).

Godāvarī was brought on the earth before Gaṅgā; hence, Godāvarī is called Vṛddhā Gaṅgā. Godāvarī was brought by a Brāhmaṇa (Gautama) whereas Gaṅgā was brought by a Kṣatriya Bhagīratha. Therefore, Godāvarī is regarded more sacred.

Kubera became the lord of wealth after bathing in the Godāvarī (Godāvarī Māhātmya 27). Indra once lost his position of the king of gods. He regained it after he was sprinkled with the water of the Godāvarī (Godāvarī Māhātmya 52). The water with which Indra was sprinkled became a river Maṅgalā.

The water of Godāvarī is stated to be medicinal. It cures leprosy, consumption, blood pressure, and indigestion.

Eulogies and prayers of Godāvarī are found in the Godāvarī Māhātmya; Brahmp. 70-175; and Varāhp. 71.37-44.

Geographical Details

Godāvarī rises from a hill called Brahmagiri in the Western Ghats which is situated in the Nashik district of Maharashtra about thirty kms by the side of the village Tryaṁbaka which is situated about 80 kms from the shore of the Arabian sea. The hill Brahmagiri has five peaks which are named after the five faces of Śiva : Sadyojāta, Vāmadeva, Aghora, Tatpuruṣa, and Īśāna. The river Godāvarī flows from the Īśāna peak.

She flows first in the east and then in the south-east direction. She meets the river Prāṇahitā which is the united stream of the waters of Wardha, Paingaṅgā, and Waingaṅgā. Thereafter, the Godāvarī is joined by the river Indrāyaṇī and further on by the river Śabarī. Flowing through Maharashtra, she enters Andhra Pradesh.

At Dowlaiswaram, the river is divided into two main streams called by the names of Gautamī Godāvarī which is the eastern stream and Vāsiṣṭhī Godāvarī which is the western stream. The first stream passes by Yanan and enters the Bay of Bengal, while the second enters the same sea at Narsapur. They form a wide alluvial delta at their mouth.

Tributaries

1. The river Kaḍvā joins the Godāvarī from the left to the south of Niphad.

2. The combined flow of the rivers Pravarā and Muḷā joins from the right to the north-east of Gangapur.

   The confluence of the pravarā and Godāvarī is known as Pravarā-Saṅgama. It is a sacred place. The river Pravarā is regarded as the essence (*rasa*) of the best (*pravara*) part of the body of the demon Rāhu when he drank Soma in the legend Samudra-manthana. Viṣṇu had cut off his head in the legend (Godāvarī Māhātmya 36).
3. The river Shiv joins the Godāvarī from the left.
4. Sindhphaṇā from the right to the north of Manjlegaon.
5. Wān from the right near Sonepet.
6. The combined flow of Dudhnā and Pūrṇā from the left to the south of Lasina.
7. Asnā from the left near Nanded.
8. Manjrā from the right to the east of Kondalawadi.
9. Siddhā from the left to the south of Narsapur.
10. Peddavugu from the right.
11. Koddam from the left near Peddabellala.
12. Māner from the right to the east of Manthani.
13. Prāṇahitā from the right near Siroucha.
14. Indrāvatī from left to the east of Ankish.
15. Laknavaran from the right near Nagaram.
16. The combined flow of Talperu and Chirda from the left near Chirda.
17. The combined flow of Mureru and Kinarsani from the right near Borgampad.
18. Sabarī from the left near Kunavaram.
19. Pamuleru from the left.

20. The river Phenā meets the Godāvarī near Manjiratha. There is a story about the origin of the river Phenā:

Once Indra conquered all Asuras except Asura Namuci who resisted and even captured Indra. Indra requested Namuci to release him. Namuci agreed to let him go on the condition that he (Namuci) should not be killed by day or by night, with wet or dry. Indra promised this and he was released. But Indra out off Namuci's head at twilight and with foam (*phena*) of water. That foam became a river, Phenā, which flows into the Godāvarī. Phenā is also Called Sindhuphenā or Sindhuphaṇā (Godāvarī Māhātmya 59.4-8).

Gomatī

There are two rivers by the name Gomatī.

1. The first Gomatī is identified with the modern river Gomal. The Gomal rises from the Shinkai-Ohnak ranges of the Himālayas in Afghanistan. She flows in south-easterly direction up to Pakistan border and then eastward. After some distance, she takes a north-easterly course from Gul Kach Post. Wana Toi, a tributary, joins Gomal from the left bank at Kotkai. From Kotkai Gomal flows eastward and at Khajuri Kach she is joined by the Zhob from the right bank. From Kot Murtaza she takes a south-easterly direction and joins the Indus below Dara Ismail Khan.

2. The second Gomatī also rises from the Himālayan hills at Pilbhit and flowing southwards receives a left bank tributary named Kathnā. Thereafter she flows south-eastward and receives two tributaries, the Sarayū and the Kalyān, from the left and the Sāi from the right. Gomatī joins the river Gaṅgā to the west of Saidpur in Uttar Pradesh.

Haimavatī

She rises from the Himālayas. She is a sacred river and is resorted to by gods, Gandharvas, and ascetics (Matsyp.

116). Purūravas practised penance on the bank of this river to get rid of his ugliness (The ugliness of Purūravas, king of the Madras, is mentioned in Matsyap. 115. See also under Airāvatī above).

This river is identified with the modern river Ravi in Panjab. According to MBh, Ādiparva, 1.167.1-9, Haimavatī is another name of Śatadru (Sutlej).

Hairaṇvatī

The river Hairaṇvatī flows through the region named Hairaṇvat (MBh, Bhīṣmaparva, 6.95). She is identified with the river Choṭā (little) Gaṇḍaka which flows through the district of Gorakhpur, and falls into the Sarayū. (See also under Gaṇḍakī above).

Hiraṇvatī

She rises from the Himālayas (Vāmanp. 13.20). Viṣṇu lives in this river in the form of Rudra (Vāmanp. 63.22). She is the same river as Hairaṇvatī mentioned above.

Hrādinī

The river Hrādinī is one of the seven streams of the Gaṅgā that flows eastward (Matsyp. 121.4). Rām., Ayodhyākāṇḍa, 2.65.1 says that it was the first river that Bharata crossed while returning from Kekaya to Ayodhyā.

Ikṣu

The river Ikṣu rises from the Himālayas (Matsyp. 114.22; Vāyup. 45.96).

Sircar opines that the name Ikṣu may indicate the river Ikṣumatī (modern Kālīnadī, a tributary of the Gaṅgā); but the forms Cankṣu and Raṅkṣu (or Vaṅkṣu) in the Mārkaṇḍeya Purāṇa probably suggest that it is another name of the Vaṅkṣu or Oxus (Amu Daria). (See under Ikṣumatī and Raṅkṣu below).

Geographical Details

Kālīnadī (Purāṇic Ikṣu) has two headwaters: 1. the Kalapani, 2. the Kuthi Yankti. The Kalapani, the eastern headwater, is a collection of a few springs. The Kuthi Yankti, the western headwaters of the Kālīnadī, rises from the snow fields of the Himādri. After the confluence, the Kālīnadī flows in a south-westerly direction where the Gorī Gaṅgā meets her from the right at Jauljibi. The Sarayū, a greater feeder of the Kālīnadī, meets her at Panchameshwar from the right. Other important tributaries of the Kālīnadī joining down stream are the Lohamatī and the Laḍhiyā. The Kālīnadī enters the plains at Baramdeo, henceforth known as Sharada. Finally, Sharada joins the river Ghaghara.

Ikṣumatī

She is a river in Kurukṣetra (MBh, Ādiparva, 1.3.145). Kuśadhvaja, brother of king Janaka, lived in the city Saṅkāśya on the bank of this river. Prabably she is the same river as Ikṣu mentioned above.

Indrāyaṇī

The river Indrāyaṇī rises from the Sahyādri range near Kurvande. She flows past the village Dehu which is very famous for the great Sant Tukārāma. Dehu is a place of pilgrimage particularly for the Warkaris. After passing Dehu, the Indrāyaṇī flows past Alandi which is also very famous and holy because of its association with the celebrated poet and saint Sant Jñāneśvara. The temple of Sant Jñāneśvara is on the bank of the Indrāyaṇī.

Indrāyaṇī meets the river Bhīmā near Tulapur.

Irāvatī

The river Irāvatī rises from the Himālayas (Kūrmp. I.46.29; Mārkp. 57.17; Varāhp. 85; Vāyup. 45.95), at a place called Kapisthala. She falls into the river Asiknī (modern Chenab). She is the modern river Ravi. She was known as Paruṣṇī to the Vedic people (Nirukta 9.26). (See also under Airāvatī above and Paruṣṇī below).

Īśvarī

She is a river near the river Airāvatī in Kurukṣetra. Having heard that the demon Bali, son of Virocana, wanted to perform a sacrifice with the Bhārgavas as priests, Ṛṣis Atri, Gautama, Kauśika, and other Ṛṣis of the Aṅgiras clan are said to have left Kurujāṅgala (i.e. Kurukṣetra) and repaired to the bank of the river Īśvarī (Vāmanp. 62.1-6).

Jalā

The Jalā and the Upajalā are the two tributaries of the Yamunā (MBh, Āraṇyakaparva, 3.130.17). It was at the confluence of these two rivers that king Uśīnara had performed the sacrifice and had surpassed Indra in greatness. It was also here that the king's charity was tested by Indra. (For the story of Uśīnara, see MBh, Āraṇyakaparva, 3.130).

Jaṁbū

Jaṁbū is a mythical river. She is formed by the juice of *jaṁbū* fruits that fall from the tall *Jaṁbū* trees on the top of the mountain Gandhamādana (Kūrmp. I.45.18; MBh, Bhīṣmaparva, 6.7.15; 10.29; Vāyup. 35.26-32; Viṣṇup. II.2.19-20; Mārkp. 54.29-30). The fruits of this tree are said to be as large as elephants. From there the river falls on the mt. Meru and then enters Jambūdvīpa. The region was believed to be rich in gold.

The river Jaṁbū is also known as Jāṁbūnadam (masc.), a river of juice of *jaṁbū*. It flows from the top of the mt. Merumandara into Ilāvarta (Bhāgp. 5.16.19-20; Vāyup.

35.26-30). The Vāyup. refers to it as a river rising from a lake situated to the west of the Meru (Vāyup. 35.29;30; 47.65-66). It is also said to rise from Candraprabha lake on the slopes of Merumandara (Brahmāṇḍp. I.18.68-69; Bhāgp. 5.16.19).

Jaṁbū is also the name of one of the seven streams of Gaṅgā. (See also under Gaṅgā).

Jaṁbulā

She rises from the mount Ṛkṣa (Vāyup. 45.100). (See under Vañjulā below).

Jayantī

Once Bhīṣma observed Pitṛvrata on the bank of the river Bhāgīrathī. Ṛṣi Pulastya came there. Bhīṣma asked him what rewards a person obtains if he visits tīrthas on the earth. During the course of his narration of importance of tīrthas the Ṛṣi described the tīrtha in and around Kurukṣetra. Somatīrtha is situated on the bank of the river Jayantī in Kurukṣetra.

Jayantī is a sacred river and a dip in her water brings the fruits of the Rājasūya sacrifice (MBh, Āraṇyakaparva, 3.81.16).

Jyeṣṭhilā

This is the name of a branch of the river Śoṇa (MBh, Sabhāparva, 2.9.20 fn). (See Jyotirathā below).

Jyotirathā

The river Jyotirathā rises from the mt. Ṛkṣa (Varāhp. 85). In MBh, Āraṇyakaparva, 3.83.8, this river is called Jyotirathyā. She joins the river Śoṇa. A water ablution to gods and manes at the confluence of the Śoṇa and Jyotirathyā brings the fruits of the Agniṣṭoma sacrifice (MBh, Āraṇyaka-parva, 3.83.8). According to Pargiter (Mārkp. 57.21 footnote under Mahānadī), the Jyotirathā may be identified with the modern river Johilā, the southern of the two sources of the river Śoṇa. Surathā is probably another name of the Jyotirathā. (See below Surathā).

Jyotiṣmatī

There is a large lake named Sarpa behind the mountain Hemakūṭa from which the rivers Sarasvatī and Jyotiṣmatī rise. They later fall into the western and eastern seas respectively (Matsyp. 121.64; 65).

Kālikā

She is a sacred river. A person who bathes at the confluence of Kālikā and Sarayū and observes fast for three days is freed from all the sins (MBh, Āraṇyakaparva, 3.82.135). The modern name of Kālikā is Kālīnadī. The river Kālīnadī flows through Saharanpur and Muzzarffarpur districts of Uttar Pradesh.

There are two rivers bearing this name, 1. the eastern Kālīnadī, 2. the western Kālīnadī. The eastern Kālīnadī flows in Kumaun district and joins the Gaṅgā. The city of Saṅkāśya is situated on the eastern bank of this river, while Kanauj stands on the western bank. The western Kālīnadī is a tributary of the Hindan. From her source up to her junction with Dhavalā Gaṅgā, Gaurī, and Chandrabhāgā, she is called Kālī Gaṅgā (See Kṛṣṇā Gaṅgā below). After the junction, she is known by the name of Kālīnadī.

Geographical details

The Kālikā (or Kālī or Kālīnadī) has two headwaters: 1. Kalapani, 2. the Kuthi Yankti. The Kalapani, the eastern headwater, is a collection of springs. The Kuthi Yankti, the western headwater of the Kālī, rises from the snow fields of the Himādrī. After their confluence, they are known as Kālī.

The river Kālī flows in a south-westerly direction where she is met with the Gorī Gaṅgā at Jauljibi. Another tributary, Sarayū, meets Kālī at Pancheshvara. Other important tributaries of the Kālī joining down stream are the Lohavatī and the Laḍhiyā.

The Kālī enters the plains at Baramdeo, henceforth known as Shāradā. The river Shāradā (or Chanka) flows south-eastwards and finally joins the river Ghāghrā.

There are two more rivers known as Kālī West and Kālī East in Uttar Pradesh. Kālī West rises in the piedmont zone of Siwalik ranges to the north of Saharanpur and flows southward, and joins the river Hindan to the south-east of Budhana.

The Kālī East has her source in the plains of upper Gaṅgā-Yamunā doab to the north of Meerut. She flows south-eastward, receives a tributary Nim on the left bank, and finally joins the Gaṅgā from the right in between Fatehgarh and Kanauj.

Kālindī

The river Kālindī rises from the mountain Kalinda in the Bunderpunccha range of the Himālayas. Therefore she is known as Kālindī.

Kālindī is regarded also as another name of the Yamunā. After the death of Pārvatī, Śiva went amuck and fell into the river Kālindī which became black because of the heat of his body (Vāmanp. 6.26). Kālindī is the daughter of the sun (Vāmanp. 34.17).

Vāmanp. 3.8 mentions that Śiva approached the river Kālindī for the redemption of the sin that he had committed by cutting off one of the five faces of Brahmā (Vāmanp. 2.26). Seeing him approaching her the Kālindī became dry (Vāmanp. 3.8).

It was on the bank of this river that king Durjaya met and fell in love with Urvaśī (Kūrmp. I.23.6). (For the story of Durjaya, see Kūrmp. I.23.4-46).

Kālindī is married to Kṛṣṇa (Viṣṇup. 5.28.3; 32.4). (See further under Yamunā).

Kalmāṣī

King Drupada performed a sacrifice on the bank of the river Kalmāṣī with a view to obtaining a child. Draupadī was born as the result of that sacrifice (MBh, Ādiparva, 1.155.5).

Kaṁpanā

The river Kaṁpanā is variously known as Kulaṁpanā (MBh, Anuśāsanparva, 13.151.15 fn) and Kiṁpunā (MBh, Sabhāparva, 2.9.20 fn). She is resorted to by the Siddhas. A person who bathes in this river attains Sūryaloka (MBh, Āraṇyakaparva, 3.82-99).

Kāñcanākṣī

Kāñcanākṣī is the name of one of the seven streams of the Sarasvatī. Once some holy Munis took up their residence in the Naimiṣa forest. They were engaged in discources on the Vedas. There they thought of the Sarasvatī. The sacred river thereupon appeared before them and was named Kāñcanākṣī (MBh, Śalyaparva, 9.37.15-18; Vāmanp. 39.34; SM, 16.28).

Kapilā

This sacred river destroys all sins. The Kapilā is the southern portion of the river Narmadā. Running for about three kms, she falls down over a descent of seventy feet and is, therefore, known as Kapiladhārā (See below).

Kapiladhārā

This river is presumably the same as Kapilā mentioned above. During the course of his pilgrimage, Prahlāda bathed in this river and offered ablutions to gods and manes and visited the temple of Skanda there (Vāmanp. 57.47). This river joins the river Narmadā at Barwani in Central India. At the distance of about 38 kms to the south-west of Nashik occurs the first fall of the Narmadā from the mt. Amarakaṇṭaka. That is Kapiladhārā. The Āśrama of the sage Kapila was situated there. That is why the portion of the river is called Kapilā or Kapiladhārā.

Kapiñjalā

This river is enumerated with the Jyotirathā and the Viśvāmitrā (MBh, Bhīṣmaparva, 6.10.25). A tribe named Kapiñjala is mentioned in the Mārkp. 58.9.

Kapīvatī

Bharata crossed this river while coming back to Ayodhyā from Kekaya (Rām., Ayodhyākāṇḍa, 2.65.11). She is identified with the river Baigu, a branch of the Rāmagaṅgā.

Karamodā

The river Karamodā rises from the Ṛkṣa (Mārkp. 57.22; Vāmanp. 13.26). Pargiter opines that Karamodā is another name of the modern river Karmanāśā which joins the Gaṅgā on her right bank above the river Śoṇa (Mārkp. 57.22 fn).

There is a belief among the common folk that the river Karmanāśā has her source in the saliva of king Triśaṅku who is hanging between the earth and the heaven. Therefore, an orthodox Hindu would not wade through this river lest all his pious deeds might be washed away by the touch of her water.

The tīrtha Vaidyanātha (modern Baijnath) is near the river Karmanāśā south of Ghazipur (U.P.).

Karatoyā

The river Karatoyā rises from the mt. Ṛkṣa (Varāhp. 85; Vāyup. 45.100). The Śabdakalpadruma says that this river flowed out of the water that was poured on the hands of Śiva at the time of his wedding with Pārvatī. Therefore, she is known as Karatoyā. The Śabdakalpadruma further says that it is only this river which is full of pure water in the month of Śrāvaṇa while other rivers have streams of blood.

A person who observes fast for three nights and bathes in the river Karatoyā obtains the fruits of the Aśvamedha sacrifice (MBh, Āraṇyakaparva, 3.83.3). Sadānīrā or Sadānīramayā is regarded as another name of the Karatoyā.

Pargiter (Mārkp. 57.18 fn) identifies this river with the river Kuratee in the Bogra district in the north of West Bengal. According to Dey, she flows through the districts of Rangpur, Dingipur, and Bogra. The Karatoyā, the Pūrṇabhābhā, and the Atrai jointly form one channel known as old Tista, Sanskrit Trisrotā, and meet the river Gaṅgā near Goalundo.

Geographical details

Karatoyā rises in the northern part of West Bengal plains above Domar in the district of Rangpur. In her upper course, she has two tributaries, 1. Jambuneśvarī from the left, and 2. Ghirnī from the right. Flowing southwards parallel to the Brahmaputra, she is joined by the river Atrai (old course of the Tista) from the right and little down stream by the river Icchāmatī. The combined flow of these rivers finally joins the Brahmaputra from the right.

Kauśikī

The river Kauśikī rises from the mount Himālaya (Kūrmp. I.46.30; Mārkp. 57.18; Vāmanp. 13.22; Varāhp. 85; Vāyup. 45.96). She is identified with the modern river Kośī which rises in the southern part of the eastern Nepal. She represents a combined stream of four rivers, three of which rise in Tibet. The four rivers are 1. Kośī, 2. Sun Kośī,

3. Aruṇā, and 4. Tamour. In India, the Kauśikī flows through Bhagalpur and Purnea districts, and meets the Gaṇgā to the west of Manihari in Purnea district a little below Patna. Near her mouth she receives a small tributary named Saurā (See Kiraṇā below).

The Kauśikī is a very sacred river. She destroys even the greatest sins, and brings merits of the Rājasūya sacrifice to the person who resorts to her (MBh, Āraṇyakaparva, 3.82.113). A person who observes fast, consuming only air, on the bank of the Kauśikī ascends to the heaven in twenty-one days (MBh, Anuśāsanaparva, 13.26.30). It is very efficacious to give *dāna* and perform *śrāddha* on her bank (Brahmāṇḍp. I. 16.26).

The river Kauśikī is closely connected with sage Viśvāmitra. Vāyup. 91 narrates the following legend:

King Gādhi was the son of Kuśika. He had no son but a daughter by the name Satyavatī. She was very beautiful. The sage, Ṛcīka, became enamoured of her and asked Gādhi to give her to him in marriage. Gādhi thought that Ṛcīka was a very poor Brāhmaṇa, and in order to avoid giving his daughter in marriage to him, he asked Ṛcīka to produce and give him one thousand horses white in colour but with black ears by way of Śulka. Gādhi thought that it would be impossible for poor Ṛcīka to fulfill this condition. Sage Ṛcīka with his penance and austerities propitiated god Varuṇa and it is said that near the city of Kānyakubja, god Varuṇa produced 1000 horses, as requested by the sage, from the waters of the river Gaṅgā. That place is known as Aśvatīrtha.

Ṛcīka gave those 1000 horses to king Gādhi who was struck with wonder. He gave his daughter to him in marriage. As advised by her mother, Satyavatī requested the powerful sage to grant a boon to both, herself and her mother so that each of them might give birth to a virtuous son. Sage Ṛcīka gave two consecrated *carus* to his wife Satyavatī and told her that she should embrace the Udumbara tree and eat the *caru* meant for her. Her mother should embrace the Aśvattha tree and eat the other *caru* meant for her. The mother of Satyavatī thought that Ṛcīka must have given the best of the two *carus* to his wife Satyavatī. She prevailed upon her daughter to exchange the trees and the *carus*. They did so. In due course Satyavatī became pregnant. Ṛcīka came to know from the symptoms in her body that there was an exchange of trees and *carus* between the mother and the daughter. Ṛcīka told Satyavatī that as he was a Brāhmaṇa he wanted his son to have the best lustre and learning of a Brāhmaṇa and as Gādhi was a Kṣatriya, he wanted Gādhi's son to be a great warrior, and for that purpose he had concentrated the two *carus* accordingly but as the mother and daughter had made an exchange, Satyavatī would deliver a Kṣatriya like child of war—like nature, while King Gādhi would have a son of unequalled Brahmanical lustre. Satyavatī asked her husband Ṛcīka to intervene with his great powers and see that her son should have the temperament of a Brāhmaṇa. Ṛcīka agreed and said that instead of his son it would be the grandson of his who would have the Kṣatriya like temperament. Thereafter Satyavatī gave birth to sage Jamadagni and her mother gave birth to sage Viśvāmitra. Jamadagni married Reṇukā and one of her sons was Paraśurāma who was an unequalled warrior with a Kṣatriya like temperament and who had destroyed the Haihayas because they had killed his father Jamadagni. It is said that Paraśurama had destroyed clans of Kṣatriyas twenty-one times.

Satyavatī, the mother of sage Jamadagni and the elder sister of sage Viśvāmitra, followed her husband to the heaven and the legend says that she was then transformed into a river flowing from the Himālayas, and now known as Kauśikī. Sage Viśvāmitra who had great regard for his sister decided to stay and perform penance on the bank of this river. MBh, Ādiparva, 1.65.30 says that Viśvāmitra himself created this river for his daily ablutions. This river is known as Kauśikī as both Satyavatī and Viśvāmitra belonged to the family of Kuśika, the father of king Gādhi. (See also Rām., Bālakāṇḍa, 1.33).

The place where sage Viśvāmitra performed penance on the bank of the Kauśikī is known as Kauśikāśrama, and it is regarded so sacred that a bath in the river at that place yields merits equivalent to Rājasūya sacrifice (MBh, Āraṇyakaparva, 3.82.113). There is also the Kauśika lake connected with Viśvāmitra and a bath therein yields merit equivalent to the Aśvāmedha sacrifice.

The confluence of the river Kauśikī with the Tāmrā (modern Tambar) and the Aruṇā has been regarded to be a place of great pilgrimage.

The Āśrama of sage Ṛṣyaśṛṅga was situated on the bank of the Kauśikī.

Geographical Details

The river Kauśikī is the same river as the modern Kośī. She flows from the eastern Himālayan range in Nepal. The area is known as the land of seven Kośīs or Saptakauśikī. The Saptakauśikī is formed by seven streams: 1. Sun Kośī, 2. Bhotia Kośī, 3. Tamba Kośī, 4. Lakkhu, 5. Dūdha Kośī, 6. Aruṇā and 7. Tambar. The land of Saptakauśikī is also known as the land of Mahākauśika. The Triveṇī of Tambar, Aruṇā, and Sun Kośī is regarded very holy and a place of pilgrimage.

Out of the seven Kośīs, the most important is the Sun Kośī. The river Kośī is formed by the confluence of three major streams, the Sun Kośī, the Aruṇā, and the Tambar. The sacred tīrtha Varāha-kṣetra is situated there. It is also called Kokamukha. It is situated in the Purnea district on the Triveṇī above Nathpur. At this place, three Kośīs, namely, the Tambar, Aruṇā, and the Sun Kośī unite, and they come out into the plains. Kokamukha is described in the Varāhp. 140 and Nṛsiṁhp. 65. The place is sacred because of Varāha incarnation of Viṣṇu.

After the rise from Nepal, Kośī first moves in a south-western direction and then flows in the south and south-eastern direction. She is joined further on by the river Ghughrī. Kośī enters the plains of Bihar at Barakshetra.

Kośī brings water from the two sides of mount Everest and also from several other places of the Himālayas. The rains and the snow which melts on the Himālayas feed this river throughout the year.

The Kauśikī meets the Gaṅgā near Kargola. She has many other tributaries such as Saurā, Kamalā, Barhnadī, Dhusan, Tilbeh, Sugarvā, and Balan, etc.

Bharata-āśrama is situated on the Kauśikī (Padamp, Ādikhaṇḍa, 1.38.48).

Kāverī

Just as the Gaṅgā is highly venerated in north India, the Kāverī is regarded very sacred and worshipped in south India. Kāverī is called Dakṣiṇa Gaṅgā of the extreme south. The local legend has it that even the Gaṅgā comes down to the Kāverī once every year to purge herself of the accumulation of sins which the sinners have deposited in her by bathing in her waters.

The river Kāverī rises from the Sahya mountain in the Brahmagiri hills of the Western Ghats (Kūrmp. I.46.36;

Mārkp. 57.27; Matsyp. 114.29; Vāmanp. 13.30; Vāyup. 45.104).

She is a sacred river and a dip in her water brings the fruits of donating one thousand cows (MBh, Āraṇyakaparva, 3.83.20).

Several legends are current about the origin of the Kāverī. In ancient times there was a king by the name Kavera. He practised severe penance to propitiate Brahmā for liberation. Brahmā told the king that he had to wait for some time to get liberated, that the king should keep as his ward Viṣṇumāyā, the daughter of Brahmā. The king did so. Viṣṇumāyā grew up at the house of the king, and being a part incarnation of Viṣṇu, she went to the Himālayas to do penance. In the mean time, the king was liberated as promised by Brahmā. Viṣṇumāyā propitiated Viṣṇu who asked her to assume two forms for the benefit of the world. In one form she was to become a river. As she was the daughter (i.e. ward) of king Kavera, the river was called Kāverī.

In her other form this Viṣṇumāyā was to become Lopāmudrā who was married to sage Agastya. At this time sage Agastya was also performing penance on the Himālayas. He was asked by Brahmā to contact and get married to Lopāmudrā. Sage Agastya came to Viṣṇumāyā who had assumed the form of Lopāmudrā and married her. After some time Agastya came to know that there was scarcity of water in the south. So he asked Lopāmudrā to enter into his *kamaṇḍalu* which she did, and he carried her to the south on the Sahyādri. On this portion of the mountain even Brahmā used to perform penance. Therefore, the hill was known as Brahmagiri.

At this place, Viṣṇu had assumed the form of an Āmalaka tree. Brahmā had brought in his *śaṅkha* water from Kailāsa from the Vraja river to worship Viṣṇu in his form of Āmalaka tree. This pure water from Kailāsa was poured out by Brahmā. At this time, Agastya had placed his *Kamaṇḍalu* on a large slab of stone and had gone for his bath. As gods would have it, there were stormy winds, the *kamaṇḍalu* was overturned and Viṣṇunāyā Lopāmudrā or Kāverī came out of it.

According to another version, the Vindhya mountain was competing with the sun. The mountain grew taller and taller and blocked the path of the sun and so there was darkness. Sage Agastya was solicited to control Vindhya. Agastya agreed to do so, and propitiated god Śiva. As desired by Agastya, Śiva gave him the necessary power and also a continuous stream of water so that Agastya could perform his penance at any place. It is said that originally river Kāverī was flowing on the Kailāsa mountain but as ordered by Śiva, she entered the *kamaṇḍalu* of Agastya. Agastya came to the south from the Himālayas. On the way, in reverence to the sage, Vindhya lay prostrate before the sage. The sage told him that as he wanted to go to the south with ease, he should not get up till he returned. Vindhya obeyed and it is said that he is still lying low expecting the Ṛṣi to return. Agastya came to the Sahya mountain and started performing penance. At that time, one Asura named Surapadma had stopped all rains by his powers. Indra was worried. He requested Gaṇeśa to see that there was plenty of water in the south. Gaṇeśa assumed the form of a crow and overturned the *kamaṇḍalu* of Agastya on the Sahyādri, and thus Kāverī started flowing.

Kāverī is regarded as the daughter of Coorg. In the month of Śrāvaṇa (August-September) there is a festival every year. Just as when sending off a daughter to her husband's place her parents and relatives give ornaments to her, similarly devout people offer some gold ornaments or some money in the small lake situated at the source of the Kāverī.

Saint Jñānasambandhara was born on the bank of the Kāverī. The famous poet Kamban composed his Tamil Rāmāyaṇa on the bank of this holy river.

Geographical Details

The source of the Kāverī is at Talakāverī on the Brahmagiri range of hills which form part of the Western Ghats in the district of Coorg in Karnataka. Starting from Coorg, she flows in a south-easterly direction through Mysore and Thanjavur and falls in the Bay of Bengal. About nineteen kms north-west of Mysore city is built the celebrated Kṛṣṇasāgara dam across the Kāverī where is also the famous Brindāvana gardens.

Kāverī divides herself into two branches. The northern branch is called the Coleroon and the southern branch retains the name Kāverī. Both branches encircle the Śiva-sundaram island. On the right, there is the Bar Chukki Fall and on the left there is the Gagana Chukki Fall. They fall from the height of about 320 feet.

The river Kāverī has divided herself into two branches at three places forming three islands. All the three are regarded very sacred. The first is called Ādiraṅgam, the second Madhyaraṅgam, and the third Anantaraṅgam or Śrīraṅgam which is sixteen kms below Tiruchirapalli.

Śrīraṅgapattanam is at the Ādiraṅgam, Śivasamudram is at the Madhyaraṅgam, and the third, the Anantaraṅgam or Śrīraṅgam is regarded the most sacred. In all the three places, there are temples and images of Nārāyaṇa sleeping on the serpent Ādiśeṣa. Within a short distance of each of these temples, there are also temples of Śrīnivāsa. There are some Śaiva temples also on her banks. Chidambaram (where the temple of Naṭarāja is) is well known. The ancient temple of Jaṁbukeśvaram near Śrīraṅgam is also very famous. Thanjavur has the celebrated temple of Bṛhadīśvara Mahādeva. At Tiruchirapalli there is a temple of Mātṛbhūteśvara.

Tributaries

1. The river Hemavatī from the left joins the Kṛṣṇa-sāgara reservoir.
2. The river Lakṣmaṇatīrtha from the right joins the Kṛṣṇa-rājasāgara.
3. Kabbani from the right near Narsipur.
4. Shinsa from the left joins east of Malavalli.
5. Arkavatī joins from the left.
6. Chinnar joins from the left.
7. Palar from the right.
8. Bhavānī from the right near Bhavānī.
9. Tirumanimattar from the left near Puglar.
10. Amarāvatī from the right near Karur.
11. Aiyar from left to the east of Musiri.
12. A major branch of Kāverī, Coleroon, empties into the Bay of Bengal, near Chidambaram. Tiruchirapalli is situated at the head of the Kāverī delta below which the river has many distributaries, such as, Vennar, Vettara, Palvar, and Coleroon.

Kiraṇā

According to Vāmanp. 62.5, the river Kiraṇā rises out of the rays of the sun. She may be identified with the modern river Saurā, a small tributary of Kauśikī near her mouth. (See under Kauśikī).

Kośā

She is mentioned in MBh, Bhīṣmparva, 6.10.33 fn. Dey opines that this may be the river Kasai in district Midnapur in West Bengal.

Kṛpā

The river Kṛpā rises from the Śuktimat mountain (Mārkp. 57.30; Matsyp. 114.32); but according to Vāmanp. 13.25, she flows from the Ṛkṣa. She is identified with the modern river Kopā, a tributary of the river Babla in eastern India.

Kṛṣṇā

The river Kṛṣṇā rises from the Sahya mountain in the Western Ghats to the north of Mahabaleshwar (Kūrmp. I.46.36; Matysp. 57.26; Vāmanp. 13.30; Varāhp. 85; Vāyup. 45.104). Flowing through the states of Maharashtra, Andhra Pradesh, and Tamil Nadu, she falls into the Bay of Bengal.

She is the same as Kṛṣṇā-Veṇyā, i.e. the combined flow of Kṛṣṇā and Veṇā.

Kṛṣṇā is regarded as a form of Viṣṇu. There is a legend about this:

Once Brahmā wished to perform a yajña. Brahmā, Viṣṇu, and Śiva lived in Mahabaleshwar. Brahmā invited gods, Ṛṣis, and Gandharvas, etc. to attend the sacrifice. The fixed time for the sacrifice approached. But Sāvitrī, Brahmā's wife, forgot about the auspicious time and was delayed. In the meantime, Brahmā with the consent of Viṣṇu, took the Yajña-dīkṣā along with his other wife Gāyatrī. When Sāvitrī arrived and saw that the sacrifice had already commenced, she became angry. She cursed Brahmā, Viṣṇu, and Śiva as also Gāyatrī, other wife of Brahmā, to become rivers. Hearing the curse Viṣṇu also became angry and cursed Sāvitrī also to become a river. So all the five became rivers. Viṣṇu became Kṛṣṇā river, Śiva Veṇyā or Veṇā, and Brahmā Kakudmatī (modern koyna), and Sāvitrī and Gāyatrī by the same names. These five rivers rise from the top of the Sahya mountain.

Kṛṣṇā and Veṇyā flow together at Māhulī-kṣetra and

these two are joined by the Kakudmatī. All the three meet at Karhad-kṣetra.

Near the source of the Kṛṣṇā, stands an ancient temple of Mahādeva. In this temple there is a small reservoir into which the waters of the stream fall from the mouth of a cow. This is known as the traditional source of the Kṛṣṇā. It is regarded as a place of pilgrimage and as a holy spot. It is called Kṛṣṇābāi. At Mahuli, where the Yenna meets the Kṛṣṇā, a fair is held five times a year in Kārtika (November-December), Caitra (April-May), Āśāḍha (July-August), and twice in Śrāvaṇa (August-September).

The famous tīrtha Śrīśailam is on the river Kṛṣṇā in Andhra Pradesh. At Śrīśailam, the original image of god Mallikārjuna stands which resembles a termite mound.

Bathing in the confluence of the Veda and Kṛṣṇā rivers produces merit equal to donating ten thousand cows, or donating land (Kṛṣṇā Māhātmya 32.18). There is a tīrtha on the Kṛṣṇā where Śrī (goddess of wealth) practised penance to get Nārāyaṇa as her husband. The tīrtha is known as Śrītīrtha.

The town Wai is also situated on the Kṛṣṇā. Wai is identified with Virāṭanagarī where Pāṇḍavas had spent the thirteenth year of their exile incognito (*ajñātavāsa*).

A person who has the *darśana* of Kanaka-Durgā at Vijayawada on the Kṛṣṇā in Andhra Pradesh will not be widowed. Kṛṣṇā Māhātmya 54.35 mentions that a bath in the Kṛṣṇā on the days of Amāvāsyā, Paurṇamāsī, and Aṣṭakā days, or at the time of eclipses brings the reward of donating one thousand cows.

It is believed that the river Gaṅgā comes down to Kṛṣṇā every twelve years when Jupiter (Bṛhaspati) is in Vigro (Kanyā). This is known as *kanyāgata*. During the *kanyāgata*, the river Kṛṣṇā is decorated with *śaris* in Wai. It is a kind of honour paid to Kṛṣṇā when Gaṅgā comes to meet her.

Kṛṣṇā Māhatmya 56.56-57 mentions that feeding even one Brāhmaṇa at the tīrtha Devahrada on the bank of the river Kṛṣṇā is equal to feeding a crore of Brāhmaṇas in any other place.

Geographical Details

Kṛṣṇā rises about 64 kms from the Arabian sea in the Western Ghats to the north of Mahabaleshwar. On reaching the chain of the Eastern Ghats, the river turns sharply towards the south-east and flows for about 160 kms to the Bay of Bengal which she enters by two principal mouths. She has formed a wide alluvial delta. The city of Vijayawada is at the head of this delta.

Tributries

1. Koyna (Kakudmatī) joins the Kṛṣṇā from the right bank near Karad. Goddess Koyna is called *daityanivārinī* here.
2. Yerla from the left to the north-east of Sangli.
3. Varṇā from the right near Sangli.
4. Pañcagaṅgā from the right to the south of Shirol at Kurundwad.
5. Combined flow of Dūdhagaṅgā and Vedagaṅgā from the right to the east of Sadalgi.
6. Ghaṭaprabhā from the right to the east of Kolhar in the Bijapur district.
7. Malaprabhā from the right near Tangadi in Karṇāṭaka.
8. Don from the left to the south of Kodekal.
9. Bhīmā from the left to the north of Raichur.
10. Tuṅgabhadrā from the right to the north of Nandikothur in Kurnool district. Tuṅgā near Śriṅgerī meets the river Bhadrā. The joint stream is known as the river Tuṅga-bhadrā. Both of them rise from the Western Ghats.

11. Dindi from the left to the west of Veludurti.
12. Peddavagu from the left. The famous Nāgārjuna-sāgara is situated here.
13. Hallia from the left to the north-west of Rentachintala.
14. Kandaleru from the right to the north of Rentachintala.
15. Musi from the left to the north of Guruzala. Musi is the name given to the combined streams arising from the hilly area round about Hyderabad and the two streams of Musi and Aler meet river Kṛṣṇā.
16. Palleru from the left to the south of Jaggayyapeta.
17. Combined flow of the Muneru and Wira from left near Amaravati.
18. Veṇā joins Kṛṣṇā at Mahuli near Satara.

Kṛṣṇaveṇī

Kṛṣṇavenī is also known as Kṛṣṇaveṇā or Kṛṣṇaveṇyā. She rises from the mt. Sahya (Matsyp. 114.29; Viṣṇup. 2.3.11). Veṇṇā or Veṇā which meets Kṛṣṇā is the modern Yenna. Sometimes Kṛṣṇaveṇyā is held as the name of the river which flows after the confluence of the Kṛṣṇā and Veṇyā. The two rivers Kṛṣṇā and Veṇyā (Yenna) meet at Mahuli near Satara (Maharashtra).

According to Sircar the combined flow of Veṇvā (modern Varṇā that flows between Satara and Kolhapur districts) and Kṛṣṇā is known as Kṛṣṇaveṇī or Kṛṣṇaveṇvā.

Kṛtamālā

The river Kṛtamālā rises from the mt. Malaya in the Western Ghats. This mountain is famous for sandal trees (Kūrmp. I.46.37; Mārkp. 52.27; Matsyp. 114.30; Vāyup. 45.105; Viṣṇup. 23.12). The river Kṛtamālā is indentical with the river Vaigai which flows near Madurai in Tamil Nadu. The river is also known by the name of Ṛtumālā and Vegavatī.

Agnip. 2.4 says that Manu found in this river the fish which later became the basis of the Matsyāvatāra.

Geographical Details

The Kṛtamālā (modern Vaigai) rises from the Varushanad hills of the Southern Ghats (Cardamon hills) near Kottaimalai. She flows initially north-eastwards and then south-eastwards and empties herself into the Bay of Bengal to the east of Ramanathapuram.

The river Suruli joins her from the left near Allinagaram.

Krumu

Krumu is a Ṛgvedic river. She is mentioned in the Nadī-stuti-sūkta ṚV 10.75.6. In ṚV 5.53.9, she is mentioned along with Kubhā, Anitabhā, Sindhu, and Sarayu.

Max Müller identifies Krumu with the Kurram in Pakistan (*SBE*, Vol 32, *Vedic hymns*, Vol. I, 323) which is a tributary of the Sindhu below the river Kabul.

Geographical Details

Krumu rises from the Hindukush ranges in Afghanistan. She flows eastward and enters Pakistan at Kharlachi. She turns to south above Sadda and receives a major tributary Gambil (=Tochi) from the right bank to the north of Arsalakhan. After that, within a few kilometers, she joins the Indus near Kundal.

Kṣiprā

She rises from the Vindhyas (Matsyp. 114.27) or more accurately from a part of the Vindhya known as Śuktimat (Kūrmp. I.46.39). She is the same river as Śiprā mentioned below.

Kubhā

Kubhā is a Ṛgvedic river (ṚV 5.53.9; 10.75.6). She is identified with the modern river Kabul which rises from

Peukelaitis (Puṣkalāvatī) in Afghanistan and joins the Indus near Attock.

The Kubhā is known as Kuhū in the Purāṇas (See below).

Geographical Details

Kubhā is the modern Kabul which rises from Sanglakh range of the Hindukush and flows eastwards receiving the river Longar from the right to the east of the town Kabul. She joins the Indus near Attock.

Tributaries

1. Panjshir from the left to the west of Nagalu.
2. Alingar from the left near Chaharbagh.
3. Surkhab from the right to the west of Jalalabad.
4. Kunar (or Kameh or Khonar) from the left to the east of Jalalabad.
5. Swat from the left near Prang.

Kuhū

She is a Purāṇic river (Kūrmp. I.46.49;31.80; Markp. 57.17; Matsyap. 114.21; Vāmanp. 13.20; 31.80; Varāhp. 85; Vāyup. 45.95). She is identified with the Vedic Kubhā (modern Kabul). (See Kubhā above).

Kumārā

She rises from the mt. Śuktimat (Viṣṇup. 2.3.13). She may be the same river as Kumārī mentioned below.

Kumāradhārā

She rises from the Bislighat below Pushpagiri (i.e. Subrahmanya range of the Western Ghats).

By bathing in this river and worshipping god Skanda one becomes able to gain the presence of Skanda (Kūrmp. II.37.20-21).

She sprang from Pitāmaha's lake. One who keeps fast

there for six days is freed even from brahmahatyā (MBh, Āraṇyakaparva, 3.82.129-30).

The sacred Svāmī-tīrtha is situated near this river (Kūrmp. II.37.20; Vāmanp. 57.46).

Kumārī

The river Kumārī rises from the mt. Śuktimat (Mārkp. 57.29). She is identified with the modern river Kaorhari which rises from the Śuktimat range in south Bihar. In MBh, Bhīṣmaparva, 6.10.34, she is mentioned with Lohityā, Karatoyā, Ṛṣikulyā and Brahmakulyā. (See also Sukumārī below).

Kumudvatī

She rises from the mt. Vindhya (Kūrmp. I.46.34; Matsyp. 114.27; Vāmanp. 13.28; Varāhp. 85; Vāyup. 45.102), Pargiter opines that the name is perhaps Damudvatī and identifies this river with the river Damudā in West Bengal (Mārkp. 57.24).

However, there is a river named Kumudvatī which joins the river Tuṅgabhadrā from the left to the west of Harihar.

Kuntī

The river Kuntī rises from the Pāriyātra (Matsyp. 114.24). Sircar and Dey opine that she is a small tributary of the Chambal. Matsyp. (*ibid*) enumerates this river along with the river Avantī which is also a tributary of Chambal.

The river Kunti is known also by the name Aśvanadī or Aśvarathānadī.

Kūpā

This river rises from the Śuktimat mountain (Vāyup. 45.107). She is identified with the modern Kopā, a tributary of the river Bablā in eastern India.

Kuṭikā

The Kuṭikā was the first river which Bharata crossed

while returning to Ayodhyā from Kekaya (Rām., Ayodhyākāṇḍa, 2.65.11). She is identified with the modern river Kosila, an eastern tributary of the Rāmagaṅgā in Rohilkhand. (See also Kuṭilā below).

Kuṭilā

Vāmanp. 31;32 narrates the following legend regarding the river Kuṭilā and god Skanda:

Agni requested the Kuṭilā to bear the semen of Śiva. She accordingly bore the foetus for 5000 years, but no child was born. At last, on the advice of Brahmā, she dropped the embryo on the Udaya mountain. Skanda was born out of it. Therefore, he is known as Kauṭilya, son of Kuṭilā.

In the Vāmana incarnātion, Viṣṇu stretched his third leg as far as the river Kuṭilā. Therefore, the Kuṭilā is known as Viṣṇupadī. She is also known as Suranadī (Vāmanp. 65.34). In Vāmanp. 31.59, it is said that Śiva, Agni, Kuṭilā, and the Kṛttikās all felt very happy when Skanda was coronated as the chief of god's army.

On the basis of these stories, Kuṭilā is believed to be another name of the river Gaṅgā. In fact, the Śabdakalpadruma enumerates Kuṭilā among the names of Gaṅgā.

According to Dey, however, Kuṭilā is the same as Kuṭikā mentioned above, the modern Kosila.

Lāṅgulinī

The Lāṅgulinī rises from the Mahendra mountain in the Eastern Ghats (Mārkp. 57.29). Vāyup. 45.106 mentions the mount Śuktimat as her source. A river Lāṅghanī (or Lāṅgalī) is mentioned in MBh, Sabhāparva, 2.9.20. Prahlāda bathed in the river Lāṅgulinī during his pilgrimage (Vāmanp. 57.14).

This river is identified with the modern river Lāṅguliā

which flows in the district of Srikakulam in Andhra Pradesh. She rises from the Kalahandi hills and flows southwards through the districts of Ganjam and empties herself in the Bay of Bengal.

Lohitā

This river is variously known as Lohitā, Lauhityā, Lohityā, Lauhitā, Lohinī, Rohiṇī, and Brahmaputra (sometimes also as Brahmaputrā, Bhaviṣyottarp. 77.58-59).

This river is mentioned in Rām., Kiṣkindhākāṇḍa, 4.39.34; MBh, Sabhāparva, 2.27.24; 48.8; Bhīṣmaparva 6.10.34; Anuśāsanaparva 13.151.16; Kūrmp. 46.30; Matsyp. 114.22; Vāmanp. 13.22; Varāhp. 85; Vāyup. 45.96; 47.9; etc.).

The river Lohitā has her source in a large lake of red water which is situated at the foot of the mt. Hemaśṛṅga (Matsyp. 121.10-13; Vāyup. 47.9). A people named Lauhityās is mentioned in Mārkp. 58.13).

The Lauhityā is regarded also as the eastern portion of the Brahmaputra. The Brahmaputra rises from the eastern side of the Mānasa lake and flows towards the east. It meets the Gaṅgā a little above Goalundo.

Kane, HoD, Vol. V, pt. I quoting Bhaviṣyottarp. 77.58-59 mentions a Brahmaputrā-snāna on Caitra (April-May), Śukla, 8. It removes all sins as on that day all holy rivers and the sea are supposed to be present in that river. (See also Brahmaputra above).

Lūpī

The river Lūpī rises from the mt. Pāriyātra (Vāmanp. 13.24). It is suggested that this river may be the same as the modern river Lūnī which rises in the Aravalli hills and which is fed by six tributaries (S.K. Dave, "The rivers of the Vāmana

Purāṇa", *Purāṇa*, Vol. XII, No.1, 1970, p. 40). It is elsewhere suggested that she is known as Nūpī and Lopāmudrā also. (See also Sindhu-2 and Nūpī below).

The river Lūnī derives her name from *lavaṇa* (salt).

Geographical Details

The river Lūnī rises from the Bisal lake near Ajmer (Pushkar) in the hills situated in the south-west direction. She is called Lūnī at a later stage, but during her earlier course she is known as Sāgarmatī.

She flows through Marwar (Sk. Marusthalī). The Lūnī reaches the Ran of Kutch only during the rainy season.

It is stated that the half of the agricultural produce of Marwar is provided by this river. The river is full of water during rainy season. In the summer melons and *singhoda* are abundantly grown in the bed of the river.

Tributaries

1. The Lilri joins the Lūnī from the left bank.
2. Guhiyā (or Guhiyābālā) from the left at Dunara.
3. Bandi from the left above Bali.
4. Sukrī from the left above Bali.
5. Jawai from the left.
6. Mitri from the right.
7. Lik from the left.
8. The river Sarasvatī starts from the Pushkar lake and meets the river Lūnī where she is called Pushkar Sarasvatī. The legend says that a lotus (*puṣkara*) fell down from the hand of Brahmā and struck the earth at three places causing three hollows. These formed the three Pushkar lakes.

Mahāgaurī

The river Mahāgaurī rises from the Vindhyas (MBh, Bhīṣmaparva, 6.10.32; Matsyp. 114.28; Vāmanp. 13.29; Vāyup. 45.103). Pargiter (Mārkp. 57.25 fn) identifies her with the river Brāhmaṇī in Orissa. She has also been identified with the river Mahānadī.

Mahākośī

Viṣṇu is regarded as living in the Mahākośī in the form of a Haṁsa (Vāmanp. 63.27; 57.60). She may be identified with the river Koshī which rises from the Himālayas and meets the Gaṅgā near Kursela. The three streams Koshī, Aruṅā, and Tamur join to form Kośī. Mahākauśikī may be the same river as Kauśikī (Kośī) mentioned above.

Mahānadī

The river Mahānadī rises from the Ṛkṣa mountain (Kūrmp. I.46.32;34; Mārkp. 57.21; Vāmanp. 13.25; Vāyup. 45.99).

She is a sacred river. An ablution to the manes in this river secures Akṣayaloka for the performer (MBh, Āraṇyakaparva, 3.82.73; Garuḍp. 83.85). The river Mahānadī is resorted to by the Ṛṣis (MBh, Āraṇyakaparva, 3.93.10).

Geographical Details

The Mahānadī rises in the Bastar hills from the plateau of the Amarakaṇṭaka range of the Vindhyas. She rises from a small pool near Sihawa which is situated in the south-east of Raipur district in Madhya Pradesh. She turns to the north and passes through the district of Raipur. Thereafter, the river flows in the east and passes through the district of Bilaspur. She flows further through Sambalpur district and about twelve kms west of Cuttack the river pours down upon Orissa delta. She crosses Cuttack district from the west to the east. The river finally falls into the Bay of Bengal forming several channels. The place where she meets the sea is called False point.

After entering Cuttack district, Mahānadī puts forth a large stream called Katjuri which, in its turn, is divided into two streams. One of them is the southern stream called Koyakhai. She passes through the Puri district. Katjuri also divides into two branches known as the great Devī and the little Devī. Katjuri meets the Bay of Bengal where she is called Jotdar.

About sixteen kms from Cuttack starts the Paika branch of the Mahānadī. The other branch, Virupa, separates from the Mahānadī opposite the town of Cuttack. She moves in a north-eastern direction and then joins the river Brāhmaṇī.

The Mahānadī divides herself into two other streams called Chitratala and Nun. The two streams rejoin under the name Nun.

The most easterly branch of the Mahānadī is called the Koyakhai. She supplies water in Puri district. Further the Koyakhai divides herself into two streams called Dayā and Bhārgavī. Dayā flows into Chilka and the Bhārgavī divides herself into a number of small branches and channels. These channels form into huge lakes. One such is the Sur Lake and the other is the Chilka Lake.

Tributaries

1. Chhinar from the left above Kanker.
2. Silari from the right to the south of Acchota.
3. Combined flow of Pairi and Sondur from the right near Rajim.
4. Sūkhā from the right to the west of Mahasamund.
5. Seonath from the left to the north-west of Katgi at Seorinarayan.
6. Jonk from the right near Seorinarayan in the district of Bilaspur.

7. Hasdo from the left to the east of Seorinarayan.
8. Borai from the left to the south-west of Dadra.
9. Lath from the right near Chondalpur.
10. Mand from the left near Chondalpur.
11. Kelo from the left to the south-east of Raigarh.
12. Hirakund dam is built to the north-west of Sambalpur.
13. Ong from the right to the north-west of Sonepur.
14. Tel from the right near Sonepur.
15. Eb in Sambalpur.

Mahī

The river Mahī (also known as Mahatī) rises from the mt. Pāriyātra (Kūrmp. I.46.35; Mārkp. 57.19; Matsyp. 114.23; Vāyup. 45.97). Rām., Kiṣkindhākāṇḍa, 4.39.20 has Mahī and Kālamahī side by side.

The land between Mahī and Narmadā is called Mehwas (Sk Mahīvāsa).

There are several legends connected with the river Mahī. It is said that the river had her source in the perspiration coming from the body of king Indradymna of Ujjain, and that the river was the daughter of Mahī, the earth. The second legend is:

A young man was constantly looking at a young Gurjar girl who used to churn curds every day. She did not pay any attention to him. One day the man attentively gazed at her for a long time. The Gurjar lady suddenly became conscious of his attention, and out of fear she threw herself into the pot of curds. The pot overflowed and she came out in the form of a stream which became a river. As the river flowed from the pot of curds (*mahī*), the river is named so.

A third view is that the river has her source in the

Mehad lake. She was also called Mau, Mahu, or Mehda. It is said that the name of the river is connected with a lake of the similar name which is regarded as her source.

The river is very sacred to the tribals like Bhils and Kolis. They worship her as their mother. They take oath in the name of Mahī and never break it. They also believe that if a guilty person is made to drink the water of Mahī, he will not be able to gulp it down, and vomit.

It is believed that near the mouth of the river Mahī, god Śiva had killed the demon Andhaka in a cavern. The confluence of the river Mahī with the sea near Cambay is known as Mahīsāgara-saṅgama-kṣetra. The Stambha-tīrtha (modern Cambay, or Khambhat) is also situated on the confluence of Mahī with the sea. It is also believed that Skanda had killed demon Tāraka there. Skanda propitiated Śiva after killing Tāraka by establishing three Śiva liṅgas. Skanda, after killing Tāraka, also established a pillar of victory at Stambhatīrtha.

At the confluence of the river Mahī with the Śoṇa at Banesvar in Rajasthan, there is a temple of Śiva. Annual fairs are held here.

Mahī is called *paścima-vāhinī-gaṅgā,* and also as Rājanadī.

Geographical Details

Mahī rises in the Dhar district in Malwa in Madhya Pradesh and flows for about 160 kms through the State. The source of this river is in a lake known as Mehad near the town Amjhera. The lake is situated on the west side of the Vindhya ranges. From her source she flows towards the Aravalli hills. Flowing towards west and north-west, she reaches Dungarpur where she is deflected by the Marwar hill to the south-west, and the rest of the course in Malwa region forms the boundary between Dungarpur and Banswara districts. She empties into the Gulf of Cambay.

The river is well known for her high banks, floods, and deep ravines.

Tributaries

1. Eran from the right to the south of Bhangra.
2. Combined flow of the Son and the Jakam from the right near Sabala.
3. Anas from the left to the south of Galiakot.
4. Panan from the left bank near Lunavada.

Mahodakī

Mahodakī flows from the Pāriyātra (Vāmanp. 57.13; 63.30). Prahlāda is said to have bathed in this river in the course of his pilgrimage (Vāmanp. 57.13).

This river is also known by the name of Mahodā where Viṣṇu lives in the form of Kuśapriya (Vāmanp. 63.30).

The river Mahodakī may be identical with the river Mahī mentioned above.

Malavāsā

She is mentioned in MBh, Anuśāsanaparva, 13.151.20. (MBh, *ibid*, fn gives the variant Mālavā).

The river Malavāsā may be identified with the modern river Malaprabhā which is a tributary of the Kṛṣṇā,

Mālinī

The river Mālinī is linked with the story of Śakuntalā, Menakā, and Viśvāmitra. Ṛṣi Viśvāmitra met Menakā on the bank of the river Mālinī and the latter abandoned Śakuntalā there (MBh, Ādiparva, 1.66.8-9). Kaṇva's Āśrama was also situated on her bank (Abhijñāna-Śākuntalam, 6.19).

The Mālinī is another name of the river Campā which

formed the boundary between Aṅga in the east and Magadha in the west. She is probably the same river as the one flowing to the west of Bhgalpur in Bihar.

Mandagā

The river Mandagā rises from the mt. Śuktimat (Mārkp. 57.29). MBh, Bhīṣmaparva, 6.10.31; Mārkp. 57.30; Vāyup. 45.107 mention Mandagā and Mandavāhinī side by side, and both are said to have their sources in the Śuktimat. However, Varāhp. 85 mentions a river Mandagāminī also arising from the Śuktimat.

Mandākinī

There are two rivers by the name of Mandākinī.

1. The first Mandākinī rises from the north of the mt. Citrakūṭa (a branch of the Ṛkṣa) (Rām., Ayodhyākāṇḍa, 2.86.11). (Cf. also Matsyp. 114.25; Vāmanp. 13.25; Varāhp. 85; Vāyup. 45.99; Mārkp. 57.21 mentions only Vindhya).

   The present river Mandākinī rises from the Citrakūṭa and meets the river Paisuni, a tributary of the Yamunā between the rivers Ken and Tons. The Mandākinī is now called Mandākin.

2. The second Mandākinī is a tributary of the Alakanandā. She rises from the mt. Kedāranātha and flows towards the south. She has a few tributaries. Near Kālīmaṭha, she is joined by the river Kālīgaṅgā on her left bank. Above Okhīmaṭha, Mandākinī is joined by the Madhyamāheśvara-gaṅgā from the left side. At Rudraprayāga, the Mandākinī joins the river Alakanandā.

The Mandākinī is a sacred river and is believed to be a remover of sins (MBh, Āraṇyakaparva, 3.83.55). A person who worships manes and gods on the bank of the Mandākinī obtains the fruits of the Aśvamedha and also the final beatitude (MBh, Āraṇyakaparva, 3.83.56). Observing a fast on her banks brings wealth (MBh, Anuśāsanaparva, 13.26.27).

The tīrthas Dharmapṛṣṭha and Kedāranātha are situated on the second Mandākinī.

Mañjulā

She rises from the Ṛkṣa (Kūrmp. I.47.33). MBh, Bhīṣmaparva, 6.10.32 refers to a river Mañju which is full of crocodiles. Dey opines that she is the same river as Bañjulā mentioned in Brahmāṇḍp. I.16.31; and Matsyp. 114.29 which has Vañjulā.

The river Mañjulā (or Bañjulā) rises from the mt Sahya in the Western Ghats (Brahmāṇḍp. I.16.34; Matsyp. 114.29).

Manoharā

Manoharā is one of the seven streams of the Sarasvatī (Vāmanp. 36.54). She flows in Kośala. Once Ṛṣi Uddālaka meditated upon Sarasvatī. She appeared before him in Kośala where she came to be known Manoharā (Vāmanp, SM, 16.32-34). (See also Manoramā below).

Manoramā

The river Manoramā also is one of the seven streams of the Sarasvatī. She sprang from the sacrifice of Uddālaka in the north of Kośala (MBh, Śalyaparva, 9.37.4; Vāmanp. SM, 16.32).

Marudvṛdhā

She is a Ṛgvedic river (ṚV 10.75.5; Nirukta 9.26). She is mentioned along with the rivers Asiknī and Vitastā. Roth opines that Marudvṛdhā is the stream formed by the combined waters of these two rivers down to her junction with the Paruṣṇī (Ravi).

Dey identified her with the river Candrabhāgā. Other scholars identify her with the Maruvardhana, a small stream in Kashmir that flows from north to south and meets the river Chenab on her southern bank at Kishtwar (A. Cunningham, *The Ancient Geography of India*, Varanasi, 1963, p. XXXIX, note).

Mehatnu

She is also a Ṛgvedic river (ṚV 10.75.6). She is mentioned there along with rivers Tṛṣṭāmayā, Susartu, Rasā, Śvetyā, and Kubhā.

Mehatnu is a tributary of the Indus below the river Kubhā. Dey identifies Mehatnu with the river Argesan in Afghanistan which joins the river Gomal or Gomatī.

Mūlī

According to Matsyp. 114.31, the river Mūlī rises from the Mahendra mountain. She may be identified with the river Mūlā, a tributary of the Godāvarī.

Varāhp. 85 mentions a river Mūlinī which may be the same as the Mūlī.

Naḍvalā

The river Naḍvalā joins the river Irāvatī (present Ravi), and the confluence is believed to assume special sanctity on the Śrāvaṇa-dvādaśī of the Bhādrapada (September-October) (Vāmanp. 53.51). She flows near Sakalpur, the capital of the Madras (B.C. Law, *Journal of Indian History*, Vol. 38, Pt 3, December 1960, pp. 533-46).

Nalinī

Nalinī is one of the seven streams into which the Gaṅgā divides herself (MBh, Bhīṣmaparva, 6.7.45).

This river is identified with the river Padmā, an eastermost tributary of the Gaṅgā. Dey, however, identifies Nalinī with the river Brahmaputra.

Nandā

A river Nandā is mentioned in MBh, Ādiparva, 1.207.7; Āraṇyakaparva, 3.82.138; 85.21; Anuśāsanaparva, 13.151.23; etc. According to Dey, this is another name of the river Mandākinī which is a tributary of the Alakanandā. (See also Alakanandā mentioned above).

Narmadā

The word *narmadā* means 'giver of pleasure'.

There is a legend about this (Skandp, Revākhaṇḍa, 4):

The river Narmadā is born out of the perspiration of Śiva. Śiva had once assumed the form of a virgin, and deluded gods and demons alike by her beauty and charm. They began to go after her. Śiva told them that only the strongest among them and the most lustrous would be able to win her. The moment the gods and demons came near her, she would disappear. She was seen by them in different forms and no one from amongst them could catch her. Her movements gave delight to Śiva. Therefore, she is called Narmadā (*narma*- 'pleasure', *dā*-'to give'). She is also called Revā, for, she makes a lot of noise (*rava*).

Narmadā is a very sacred river. It is said about her that:

gaṅgā kanakhale puṇyā kurukṣetre sarasvatī/
grāme vā yadi vāraṇye puṇyā sarvatra narmadā//

(Gaṅgā is holy in Kanakhala, Sarasvatī is holy in Kurukṣetra, but the river Narmadā is holy in all places whether a village or a forest).

She is often referred to as Dakṣiṇa Gaṅgā (Skandap, Revākhaṇḍa, 4.24). A mere sight of her waters purifies a person. It is said about her (Matsyp. 186.11) :

tribhiḥ sārasvataṁ toyaṁ saptāhne tu yāmunam/
sadhyaḥ punāti gāṅgyaṁ darśanādeva nārmadam//

(The water of Sarasvatī purifies a person in three days, the water of Yamunā in a week, the water of Gaṅgā immediately, but the Narmadā, by her mere sight, purifies a person).

A person who bathes in the Narmadā and fasts for a night is said to liberate himself and his one hundred ancestors.

Narmadā is also called the mind-born daughter of the Pitṛs named Somapās who dwell in the Sumānasa lake above the Brahmaloka (Padmp, Sṛṣṭikhaṇḍa, 5.5.53), and *śrāddhas* are performed on her banks which brings to the performer great rewards. Matsyp. 186.19 says that an ablution to manes and gods in the river Narmadā renders seven generations eligible for perfect enjoyment. A person who bathes in her waters attains Rudraloka (Matsyp. 186.62). Even the trees on her banks attain redemption from the cycle of births and rebirths (Matsyp. 186.54-55). A person who offers water ablution to gods and manes obtains the fruits of the Agniṣṭoma (MBh, Āraṇyakaparva, 3.80.71).

Viṣṇup. 4.3 relates the following story about the Narmadā.

Once the Gandhravas defeated all the Nāga chiefs and usurped their kingdom. The latter approached Viṣṇu and apprised him of their misfortune. Viṣṇu assured them help. He told them that he would enter into the body of king Purukutsa, the son of Māndhātā and slay the Gandharvas. The Nāga chiefs returned to their abodes and sent Narmadā to secure the help of Purukutsa. She led the king to the nether-world. Viṣṇu filled the king with his energy. As the result of it, Purukutsa defeated the Gandharvas and restored the kingdom to the Nāgas. In recognition of the service thus done to them by Narmadā, the Nāga chiefs conferred a boon on her that whosoever thought of her, or mentioned her name, or prayed to her, would never have any fear of snakes (Viṣṇup. 4.3.10).

Skandp, Revākhaṇḍa, 4 narrates a legend about the birth of Narmadā.

Śiva practised penance with Umā on the mt. Ṛkṣa for the welfare of the universe. Perspiration flowed from his body which turned into a river. The river appeared before Śiva in a human form. She prayed to him that she should survive even the time of the Pralaya, and that Śiva with Umā should live on her bank. Śiva granted both the boons. Since she flowed from the sweat of Śiva, the river is known by the name Rudriyā (Skandp, Revākhaṇḍa, 4.10).

Narmadā Māhātmya 4.46 mentions that the Narmadā issued forth from the tears of joy that Śiva shed on killing the demon Andhaka.

Further Skandp, Revākhaṇḍa, 178 has another legend:

Gaṅgā once felt exhausted because of washing away sins of sinners. She propitiated Viṣṇu in order to find some way of relief for her. She performed penance at a place named Gaṅgāvāhaka on the bank of the Narmadā. Viṣṇu promised her that he would always be at the place of Gaṅgāvāhkatīrtha and she should visit the place in every rainy season when her banks would be full and overflowing. She should flow through a place named Śaṅkhoddhāra into the Narmadā and bathe there. Thereby her burden would be shared. Therefore, even now Gaṅgā comes down to Narmadā every year to purge herself.

According to the Amarakośa, Narmadā is also called Revā. However, according to another view, Narmadā and Revā are two different rivers. Narmadā starts from Mekala mountain which is a part of the mt. Ṛkṣa, while Revā starts from the mt. Amarakaṇṭaka in the Vindhya range. Both the streams merge into one and then they are described either as Revā or Narmadā.

Narmadā is also called Somodbhavā and Mekalakanyakā.

About ten kms from Mortakka, in the island of Māndhātā on the bank of the river Narmadā, is situated the famous temple of Oṁkāranātha which is worshipped as one of the twelve Jyotirliṅgas. It is believed that Emperor Māndhātā of the Solar race in the Satya-yuga worshipped Śiva at this place. The island Māndhātā is situated between the rivers Narmadā and Kāverī. This place is known as Śivapurī. On the full moonday of Kārtika every year, a religious festival is held there.

It is stated that Śukadeva, son of Vyāsa, renounced the world when he was just a child. Vyāsa, his father, ran after him to persuade him to come back. It is said that Vyāsa performed penance near Chandod while Śukadeva was on the other bank. There is a temple of Vyāsa about twelve kms from Chandod in an island in Narmadā. In the south of Vyāsa temple, there is a temple of Śukadeva Mahādeva and about seven kms away is the temple of Anasūyā (wife of Ṛṣi Atri).

There are many other temples on or near the Narmadā, such as, the temple of Kumbheśvara Mahādeva, the temple of Śani (Saturn), and the temple of Śūrpaṇeśvara on the north bank of the river Narmadā. In the west, Śuklatīrtha is an important place of pilgrimage. On the full moon of Kārtika (November-December), there is a religious festival there.

Little away from Śukla-tīrtha is the famous Kabīravaḍa in a small island. It is stated that saint Kabīra planted there a small wooden stick which he used as tooth-brush, and from that stick has grown the huge Kabīravaḍa.

Broach (ancient Bhṛgu-kaccha) is situated about sixteen kms from Śukla-tīrtha. It is stated to be the celebrated place where there was the Āśrama of sage Bhṛgu. Besides these, a large number of other tīrthas are situated on the banks of the Narmadā. Their names are given below:

1. Ahalyā-tirtha (Kūrmp. 41.43; Padmp. Ādikhaṇḍa, 1.18.84; Matsyp. 191.90-93).
2. Akolla (It is the present name of Agastyāśrama situated to the east of Nasik on the Godāvarī) (Kūrmp. II.41.63-65).
3. Anaraka (Kūrmp. II.41.91-92); Matsyp. 193.1-3).
4. Āṅgiras-tīrtha (Kūrmp. II.41.31-33; Padmp. Ādikhaṇḍa, 1.18.50).
5. Apasareśa-tīrtha (Kūrmp. II.42.24; Padmp. Ādikhaṇḍa, I.21.16; Matsyp. 194.16).
6. Aśva-tīrtha (Padmp. Ādikhaṇḍa, 1.21.3; Matsyp. 194.3).
7. Bāṇa-tīrtha (Kūrmp. II.4.9-10).
8. Bhadrakarṇa-tīrtha (Kūrmp. I.31-46; II.20.35).
9. Bhadreśvara-tīrtha (Kūrmp. II.41.4-5; Matsyp. 13.31; 22.25; 32).
10. Bhīmeśvara-tīrtha (Kūrmp. II.41-22; Padmp. Ādi-khaṇḍa, 1.18.5; Matsyp. 22.46; 75).
11. Brahmatīrtha (Kūrmp. II.41.56).
12. Brahmeśvara-liṅga (Kūrmp. II.41.18).
13. Candra-tīrtha (Brahmāṇḍp. II.13.28; Kūrmp. II.42.15-16; Matsyp. 193.75).
14. Daśāśvamedhika-tīrtha (Kūrmp. II.41.104-107; Padmp, Ādikhaṇḍa, 1.20.20).
15. Deva-tīrtha (Kūrmp. II.42.16-17; Padmp. Ādikhaṇḍa, 1.18-24; Matsyp. 191.24).

16. Dhautapāpā (=Dhūtapāpā) (Kūrmp. II.42.9-10; Matsyp. 22.39; 193.62).
17. Gaṇeśvara-tīrtha (Kūrmp. II.41.100-2).
18. Gaṅgeśvara-tīrtha (Nāradp. II.19.46; Matsyp. 193.14-20).
19. Gautameśvara-tīrtha (Kūrmp. II.42.6-8; Padmp. Ādikhaṇḍa, I.20.58; Matsyp. 22.68).
20. Go-tīrtha (Padmp. Ādikhaṇḍa, 1.20.3; Matsyp. 193.33; Vāyup. 45.104).
21. Haṁsa-tīrtha (Matsyp. 193.72).
22. Kallolakeśvara-tīrtha (Kūrmp. II.41.88-89).
23. Kāma-tīrtha (Garuḍp. I.81.9; Kūrmp. 41.54-56).
24. Kanakhala (Padmp. Ādikhaṇḍa, 1.20.67; Matsyp. 193.69).
25. Kanyātīrtha (Kūrmp. II.42.21; Matsyp. 193.76-77).
26. Kapila-tīrtha (Kūrmp. II.41.93.100; Padmp. Ādikhaṇḍa, 1.17.7; MBh, Āraṇyakaparva, 3.81.38).
27. Koṭi-tīrtha (Kūrmp. II.41.34; Padmp, Ādikhaṇḍa, I.13.33; 18.8; Matsyp. 191.7).
28. Kuśa-tīrtha (Kūrmp. II.41.33-34).
29. Liṅgi-Janārdana-tīrtha (Kūrmp. II.41.61-62).
30. Manohara-tīrtha (Kūrmp. II.42.20-21; Padmp. Ādikhaṇḍa, 1.21.7; Matsyp. 194.7).
31. Mātṛ-tīrtha (Kūrmp. II.41.40).
32. Nandī-tīrtha (Kūrmp. II.41.90; Matsyp. 191.6.37).
33. Nārada-tīrtha (Kūrmp. II.41.16;17; Padmp. Ādikhaṇḍa, 1.18.23; Matsyp. 191.5;23).
34. Pitāmaha-tīrtha (Kūrmp. II.42.18-19; Padmp. Ādikhaṇḍa, 1.21.4; Matsyp. 194.4).

35. Piṅgaleśvara-tīrtha (Kūrmp. II.41.21-24; Matsyp. 191.32-36).
36. Puṣkaraṇī-tīrtha (Kūrmp. II.41.10-11; Padmp. Ādikhaṇḍa, 1.17.12; Matsyp. 190.16).
37. Ṛṇa-tīrtha (Kūrmp. II.41.19; 29.31 Matsyp,191.27).
38. Śakra-tīrtha (Kūrmp. II.41.11-12; Padmp. Ādikhaṇḍa, 1.24.29; Matsyp. 22.23).
39. Saṅgameśvara-tīrtha (Kūrmp. II.41.36-37; Padmp. Ādikhaṇḍa, 1.18.53; Matsyp. 191.74).
40. Sargabindu-tīrtha (Kūrmp. II.42.23-24).
41. Sāvitrī-tīrtha (Padmp. Ādikhaṇḍa, 1.21.6; Matsyp. 194.6; Vāyup. 112.22).
42. Soma-tīrtha (Kūrmp. II.41.47; Padmp. Ādikhaṇḍa, 1.18.30; Matsyp. 191.30).
43. Stambha-tīrtha (=modern Khambhat on the Gulf of Cambay) (Kūrmp. II.41.51; Padmp. Ādikhaṇḍa, I.18.93).
44. Śukra-tīrtha (Kūrmp. II.41.69-83; Matsyap. 22.29; 191.20-21; 192.14).
45. Śūlabheda-tīrtha (Kūrmp. II.41.12-14; Padmp. Ādikhaṇḍa, 1.18.3; Matsyp. 191.3-4).
46. Tāpaseśvara-tīrtha (Kūrmp. II.41-66; Padmp. Ādikhaṇḍa, 1.18.96).
47. Tryaṁbaka-tīrtha (Padmp. Ādikhaṇḍa, 1.18.112).
48. Umāhaka-tīrtha (Kūrmp. II.41.47-59).
49. Vaṭeśvara-tīrtha (Agnip. 109.20; Kūrmp. II.41.19; Padmp. Ādikhaṇḍa, 1.18.27).
50. Viṣṇu-tīrtha (modern Yodhipur) (Kūrmp. II.41.52-54; Padmp. Ādikhaṇḍa, 1.18.94; Matsyp. 191.90).
51. Vṛṣotsarga-tīrtha (Kūrmp. II. 42.8-9).

52. Yama-tīrtha (Kūrmp. II.41.83-84).

Viṣṇu lives in the river Narmadā in the form of Vīra, Kuvalayārūḍha, Śaṅkhacakragadādhara, Śrīvatsāṅka, Udārāṅga, and Śrīpati (Vāmanp. 63.18).

The qualities of the water of Narmadā are: lightness (*laghutvam*), coolness (*śītalatvam*), pacifier of heat and bile (*dāhapittaśamanatvam*), and cause of gout (*vātadātṛtvam*).

Her water can be preserved for ten months. The Śabdakalpadruma says:

tribhiḥ sārasvataṁ toyaṁ saptabhistvatha yāmunam/
nārmadaṁ daśamāsair gāṅgaṁ varṣeṇa jīryati//

(Three days the water of Sarasvatī, seven days the water of Yamunā, ten months the water of Narmadā, and for a year the water of Gaṅgā can be preserved).

The following texts eulogize and pray to Narmadā:

1. Narmadā-Māhātmya
2. Agni Purāṇa 113
3. Kūrma Purāṇa II. 38-44
4. Matsya Purāṇa 186-194
5. Padma Purāṇa, Ādikhaṇḍa, 1.13-23
6. Skanda Purāṇa, Revākhaṇḍa (entire)
7. Narmadāṣṭakam of Śrī Śaṅkarācārya

Geographical Details

The source of the Narmadā is in the mt. Amarakaṇṭaka, one of the highest peaks of the Maikala ranges of the Vindhyas. Initially she flows north-eastward and then turns westward.

After issuing from her source at Amarakaṇṭaka, Narmadā first falls at Kapiladhārā in a descent of about seventy feet. Thereafter, she passes from the rugged hills of Mandla. She then moves through the rocks of marble and flows in the western direction between the Vindhya and the Satpura ranges forming the Narmadā valley.

Below Jabalpur, the Narmadā enters an open fertile plain. She enters the large gorge near Harinagpal and emerges in the Gujarat plains to the east of Rajpipla. Below the city of Broach, the river widens out and falls in the Bay of Cambay. The *saṅgama* of Narmadā with the sea is regarded as the holiest tīrtha.

At Mandhar and Dardi, there are two waterfalls of twelve meters each. About thirty-four kms before the Mandhar fall is the Punasa dam. Near Maheshwar the river again descends from another small fall of eight metres called the Sahasradhārā fall.

Tributaries

1. Kharmer joins Narmadā from the left to the west of Dindori.
2. Silgi from the right to the west of Mahadwani.
3. Banjar from the left near Mandla.
4. Temur from the left.
5. Soner from the left to the north-west of Chargawan.
6. Hiran from the right to the west of Chindwada in Jabalpur district.
7. Combined flow of Unner and Sher from the left bank to the north-west of Narsimhpur.
8. Sindhare from the right.
9. The combined flow of Chitarevā, Hard, and Shakkar from the left.
10. Dudhī from the left.

11. Tendoni from the right to the south of Bareli.
12. Barna from the right to the south of Bareli.
13. Tawa from the left to the east of Hoshangabad.
14. Kolar from the right to the south of Nasurallaganj.
15. Gunjal from the left to the south of Nasarullaganj in Hoshangabad district.
16. Jamner from the right near Nemawar.
17. Chankeshar from the right.
18. Machak from the left to the east of Pareda in Hoshangabad district.
19. Chota Tawa from the left near Pareda.
20. Kanar from the right to the east of Mandhata.
21. Beda from the left near Mandaleshvar.
22. Karam from the right to the west of Maheshwar.
23. Dev from the left to the west of Dharampuri.
24. Man from the right to the west of Dharampuri.
25. Goi from the left near Nisarpur.
26. Uri or Or from the right near Nisarpur in Gujarat. Erandi is another name of Uri or Or.
27. Hatani from the right.
28. The combined flow of Heran and Orsang from the right near Chandod.
29. Karjan from the left to the north of Rajpipla.
30. Kapilā (or Kapildhārā) from the right bank (Matsyp. 186.40).
31. Viśalyā (Matsyp. 186.46).

Nīlā

The river Nīlā rises from the Himālayas (MBh,

Bhīṣmaparva, 6.10.30 fn; Vāmanp. 13.20). In the opinion of Sircar and Dey, the name Nīlā may be equated with the name Nilab applied to a part of the river Sindhu (Indus).

Nirvindhyā

The river Nirvindhyā rises from the mt. Vindhya (Kūrmp. I.46.34; Matsyp. 114.27; Vāmanp. 13.28; Vāyup. 45.102). According to Mārkp. 57.24 and Viṣṇup. 2.3.11, she flows from the Ṛkṣa (which is a part of the Vindhyas).

The river Nirvindhyā flows between the rivers Daśārṇā (modern Dhasan) and Śiprā. Sircar and Dey identify Nirvindhyā with the river Newuj.

The river Newuj rises from the Vindhya mountain to the west of Ashta and flows between the Betwa and the Kālīsindha and joins the river Parwan east of Aklera. The Parwan flows north-eastwards and joins the Kālīsindha to the south of Palit.

The Nirvindhyā (Newuj) joins the Chambal between Betwa and Kālīsindha.

Kālidāsa describes Nirvindhyā in the Meghadūta I.28.

Niṣadhāvatī

The river Niṣadhāvatī rises from the mt. Vindhya (Vāmanp. 13.28; Vāyup. 45.102 has Niṣadhā). Mārkp. 57.24 is more accurate and says that she flows from the Ṛkṣa. The name Niṣadhāvatī suggests the connection of that river with Niṣadha, the kingdom of king Nala (Pargiter). According to him, she may be a small tributary of the Narmadā or Tāptī (Mārkp. 57.24 fn).

Nūpī

She rises from the mt. Pāriyātra (Mārkp. 27.20). (See under Lūpī mentioned above).

Oghavatī

The Oghavatī is one of the seven streams of the Sarasvatī (MBh, Śalyaparva, 9.37.3-4; Vāmanp, SM, 16.17-18; 36.54-55).

There is a legend about this river. Once Skanda was repenting, for, he had pierced the mt. Krauñca who was his own brother, and where Mahiṣāsura had been hiding after the death of Tārakāsura. Viṣṇu advised Skanda to go to the tīrtha Pṛrhūkaka and bathe in the river Oghavatī assuring him that that would make him as lustrous as before. Skanda did so and recovered his original form (Vāmanp. 32.109-115).

Uśanas, preceptor of Asuras, practised rigorous penance on the bank of the river Oghavatī with a view to securing the knowledge of Sañjīvanī. Śiva, being pleased, imparted to him the knowledge (Vāmanp. 36.40).

The river Oghavatī is identified with the present river Mārkāṇḍa, a tributary of the Sarasvatī. Pṛthūdaka (modern Pehoa) is situated on her bank.

Padmā

The Padmā is the easternmost left branch of the Gaṅgā (Vāmanp. 63.16). She is joined by the Brahmaputra at Goalundo in the Faridpur district of Bangladesh. The Padmā enters into the Bay of Bengal as the river Meghnā.

Palāśinī

There are two rivers by the name Palāśinī.

1. The first one rises from the mt. Śuktimat (Kūrmp. 46.39; Mārkp. 57.30; Varāhp. 85; Vāyup. I.45.107). According to Sircar, she is the modern river Paras, a tributary of the river Koel in Chotanagpur. The river Koel flows through the hilly terrain of Palamu. Dey identifies this Palāśinī with the river Paddair which falls into the sea near Kalingpatnam in Ganjam district.

2. The second Palāśinī (MBh, Bhīṣmaparva, 6.10.21) is identified by Dey with the river which rises from the foot of Girnar hills in Kathiawar, Gujarat. This river is known as the river Suvarṇarekhā.

Pārā

The river Pārā rises from the mt. Pāriyātra (MBh, Ādiparva, 1.65.32; Mārkp. 57.20; Matsyp. 114.24; Vāmanp. 13.24). In some other texts, she is mentioned as Parā (MBh, Bhīṣmaparva, 6.10.19; Vāyup. 45.98).

Pārā is a river near Indore which flows north-west to join the Chambal on the right. The Pārā is also known by the name Pārvatī.

Pārvatī (or Pārā) is the modern Parbati. She rises from the Vindhyas between Kannod and Asht. She flows north-eastwards initially and then northwards, and finally joins the Chambal from the right bank near Pali.

She receives tributaries Kui from the right, Bāngaṅgā from the left, and Aheli from the right.

Parṇāśā

The Parṇāśā rises from the mt. Pāriyātra (Kūrmp. I.46.31 has Varṇāśā; Matsyp. 114.23; Vāmanp. 13.23; 31.81; Vāyup. 45.97; Varāhp. 85 has Parṇā).

MBh, Droṇaparva, 7.67.44-53 gives the following legend about Parṇāśā:

Śrutāyudha was the son of Varuṇa and his mother was Parṇāśā. She asked Varuṇa to make their son invincible, not to be killd by anyone. Varuṇa gave the son a mace which was made powerful with the mantras. Varuṇa told him that the mace should never be released in fight, otherwise it will kill him. Kṛṣṇa caught hold of that mace from him and snatched it. Śrutāyudha was killed.

The Parṇāśā is identified with the present river Banasi or Banas, which, flowing through the north Gujarat, joins the Chambal towards the north of sheopur (Rajasthan).

Paruṣṇī

Paruṣṇī is a Vedic river (ṚV 4.22.2; 5.52.9; 7.18.8-9; 8.74.15; 10.75.5; and AV 6.12.3). Nirukta 9.26 also mentions this river.

The Vedic Paruṣṇī is the Purāṇic Irāvatī or Airāvatī and modern Ravi. She was the scene of the battle of the ten kings known as the Dāśarājña (ṚV 7.18.8-9). (For Dāśarājña, see R.N. Dandekar, "The Dāśarājña", *CASS Studies*, No.1, 1973, p. 129).

The name Paruṣṇī is variously derived. It is derived from *paruś* 'flocks' of wool; or 'bends of the river', or 'reeds on her banks' (Nirukta 9.26).

The name Irāvatī means 'full of water'.

Among the Purāṇas the Irāvatī is mentioned in Matsyp. 22.19 where Pitṛtīrtha is situated; Vāyup. 45.95; Vāmanp. 79.7; and in MBh, Sabhāparva 2.9.19; Bhīṣmaparva 6.10.15.

The river Irāvatī (=Paruṣṇī, present Ravi) flows between the rivers Chenab and Sutlej. The city of Lahore stands on her bank. The river rises from the southern slopes of the sub-Himalayan ranges in Kulu in Kangra district (Himachal Pradesh). Her source is located in the mountains of Bungall which is situated near the Rohtang Pass. In the starting stage the river is also called Raina. After Kangra district, she passes by the city of Champa. It is from this area that the river is given the name of Ravi.

Near the Town Jammu, she is met with the river Tawi. Ravi passes by the town Dera Nanak Saheb. Further passing through the Gurudaspur and Amṛtasara districts, she enters

Lahore. Here she is divided into three branches. The river Degh meets her in Montagomary district. She ultimately merges into the combined waters of Chenab and Jhelum near Ahmadpur. The water of Ravi is redder than that of the Chenab, (See also under Airāvatī and Irāvatī above).

Pāvanī

The river Pāvanī was one of the seven streams of the Gaṅgā which flowed towards the east (Matsyp. 121.40). Dey opines that this river is to be identified with the river Ghaggar, or the united streams of the Ghaggar and the Sarasvatī in Kurukṣetra.

Payasvinī

She is said to rise from the Western Ghats. Dey identifies this river with three rivers: 1. The river Pāpanāśinī in Travancore, 2. The river Paisuni or Pisani, a tributary of the Yamunā between the Ken and the Tons (Tamasā) near mt. Citrakūṭa, and 3. The river Candragiri in South Kanara district.

Payoṣṇī

The river Payoṣṇī rises from the Vindhyas (Kūrmp. I.46.34; Matsyp. 114.27; Vāmanp. 13.28; Vāyup. 45.102) or from the Ṛkṣa (a part of the Vindhyas) (Mārkp. 57.24; Viṣṇup. 2.3.11).

Payoṣṇī is the modern river Pūrṇā in Berar which rises from the Gavilgarh hills. She is a tributary of the Tāptī together with the lower part of the Tāptī. She meets the Tāptī north of Bhusawal in Khandesh (Maharashtra).

The description of Payoṣṇī in MBh, Āraṇyakaparva, 3.53.21 that she flows into the ocean would be true only when we accepted the lower part of the Tāptī as Pūrṇā because the Tāptī enters into the sea.

Payoṣṇī Māhātmya 1.49-6.90 narrates the following legend about the origin of this river.

There was a king named Gaya. He was very generous particularly for the Brāhmaṇas. Once there was famine. There was no grass for cattle. Cows stopped giving Milk. At that time seventy thousand ascetics came to Gaya and asked for milk. King Gaya searched all over the world for such a large quantity of milk. Even Kāmadhenu and the Kṣīra-sāgara were not able to provide so much milk. Finally, Gaya approached Śiva for help. Śiva gave the king a digit of the moon on his head who is the moon's daughter. She served each one of them a hundred cupfulls of milk at a time filling the cups again and again. There was such a huge quantity of milk that the Brāhmaṇa ascetics could not drink any more and the milk started overflowing. This became the river Payoṣṇī

The word *payoṣṇī* means 'warm milk' (*paya*—milk, *uṣṇa*—warm, *uṣṇī*, fem). The river is full of warm milk.

Payoṣṇī is a very sacred and foremost among the rivers. One who engages himself in the worship of gods and Pitṛs on her banks obtains the fruits of donating one thousand cows (MBh, Āraṇyakaparva, 3.83.37).

Viṣṇu lives in the river Payoṣṇī in the form of Akhaṇḍa (Vāmanp. 63.7). The tīrtha Akhaṇḍeśvara is on her bank (Vāmanp. 55.10;11). There is also the Koṭi-tīrtha on the Payoṣṇī. One who bathes in the Payoṣṇī at Koṭi-tīrtha and has *darśana* of Koṭeśvara gets the merit of giving away a hundred thousand Kapilā cows (Payoṣṇī Māhātmya 23.50). Many other tīrthas, such as, Umātīrtha, Avaidhavya-tītha, Aṣṭasaubhāgya-tīrtha, and Saubhāgya-tīrtha are also situated on the Payoṣṇī.

A bath in the confluence of the Payoṣṇī with the Mahā brings the reward of one hundred sacrifices (Payoṣṇī Māhātmya 18.9). A bath at Dhanyapur tīrtha gives the reward of ten thousand sacrifices (Payoṣṇī Māhātmya 20.23). At the confluence of the rivers Nala and Payoṣṇī, a bath brings the benefits of donating a hundred Kapilā cows (Payoṣṇī Māhātmya 38.44).

Phalgu

Phalgu (also Phālgunī) is a tīrtha as well as a river in Gayā (Bihar) (Kūrmp. II. 20.34; Viṣṇu Smṛti 85.22; Vāyup. 105.6; 36; 109.16). She is a sacred river where *śrāddha* is performed (Garuḍp. 83.18; Agnip. 115.25). Asura Gaya had performed a sacrifice there. The river flows through the town Gayā.

The Phalgu is a southern tributary of the Gaṅgā and joins her north-east of Lakhisarai in the district Monghyr. She is made up of the streams of two rivers rising from Hazaribag plateau: 1. Nairañjanā (present Nīlājana), and 2. Mahānad (modern Mohanā). They meet together near Mora hills below Bodhagaya.

The Tīrtha Phalgu (or Phālgunī) is situated on the river Phalgu in Gayā (Kūrmp. II.20.34; Garuḍp. I.52.27; 83.4; 22; 84.14; Vāyup. 105.6; 36; 109.16).

Pippalaśroṇī

She rises from the Ṛkṣa (Mārkp. 57.22). This river has been identified with the modern river Paisuni which meets the Yamunā between the Ken and Tons.

Pippalā (Varāhp. 85); Pippalāvatī (MBh, Bhīṣmaparva, 6.10.21) Pippalī (Matsyp. 114.25) are the variants of the name Pippalaśroṇī.

Piśācikā

She also rises from the Ṛkṣa (Kūrmp. I.46.32; Vāmanp. 13.26; Varāhp. 85; Vāyup. 45.100). According to Pargiter, she may be one of the two southern tributaries of the river Śoṇa, either Rer or Kanhar.

Pitṛsomā

The Pitṛsomā is one of the small rivers which flows from the Mahendra mountain (Eastern Ghats) (Mārkp. 57.28).

She is variously known as Trisomā, Triyāmā, Trisāmā, and Tribhāgā. (She under these different names).

Plakṣā

This is one of the names of the river Sarasvatī (MBh, Āraṇyakaparva, 3.82.5). This river rises from a fountain situated at the foot of a Plakṣa tree, hence the river is called Plakṣajā (Vāmanp. 23.13) or Plakṣā (Vāmanp. 3.8; 34.18) or Plakṣavatī (MBh, Anuśāsanparva, 13.151.20 fn).

Pravarā

She is a tributary of the Godāvarī (MBh, Bhīṣmaparva, 6.10.22). The place where she meets the Godāvari is called the Pravarā-saṅgama which is regarded as a very sacred place.

Praveṇī

Ṛṣi Kaṇva's Āśrama was situated on the northern bank of this river (MBh, Āraṇayakaparva, 3.86.8).

Puṣpajā

The river Puṣpajā rises from the mt. Malaya (Matsyp. 114.30). According to Dey, Puṣpagiri mentioned in Mārkp. 57.14 is a part of the Malayagiri from where the river Kṛtamālā rises. Therefore Puṣpajā may be the same river as the Kṛtamālā. Puṣpajātī (Vāyup. 45.105) is another name of the Puṣpajā.

Puṣpavatī

She rises from the mt. Malaya (Kūrmp. I.46.37; Varāhp. 85). Dey identifies this river with the river Pambai in Travancore.

Raṅkṣu

The river Raṅkṣu rises from the Himālayas (Mārkp. 7.18). Raṅkṣu seems to be another name of the river Ikṣu or the river Vaṅkṣu (See Ikṣu above and Vaṅkṣu below).

The Raṅkṣu has been identified with the modern river Oxus which rises from the Pamir lake.

Dey, however, identifies this river with the river Rangit which is a tributary of the Tista in Darjeeling district.

S.M. Ali identifies Raṇkṣu with the Rāmagaṅgā. To south of Mall Chandpur, there is a reserve forest (in U.P. Himālayas) which is regarded as the source region of Rāmagaṅgā. She flows to the south-west below Gairsain.

She receives a tributary Khoh from the right bank, Aosi from the left bank, Gaṅgan from the right bank, and Garra from the left bank. She finally joins the Gaṅgā from the left near Kannauj in Uttar Pradesh.

Rasā

The river Rasā is mentioned several times in the Vedic texts (ṚV 1.112.12; 5.41.15; 9.41.6; 10.108.1; 2; 5; AV 4.2.5; JB 2.240).

In ṚV 1.112.12, she is mentioned as a large river at times getting flooded. She is regarded as a great mother (ṚV 5.41.15).

The river Rasā rises from the Himavat (Vāmanp. 13.21). She was known to the Zorostrians as Ranhā (Max Müller, SBE 32, *Vedic Hymns*, I, p. 323). Ranhā is Avestan name for Jaxartes.

When the Aryans moved away from this river, the river got a mythical character and was believed to be surrounding the entire universe (ṚV 9.41.6). Stella Kramrisch regards

Rasā "the apparent annual path of the sun" ("Indian Great Goddess", *History of Religions*, Vol 14, No. 4, p. 241).

The river Rasā has been connected with the legend of Saramā and Paṇis. Saramā crossed this river and approached the Paṇis who had hidden the cows of the Aryans (ṚV 10.108).

Dey and Law identify the Rasā with the river Jaxartes. P.L. Bhargava identifies her with the river Panjsir which flows to the south of the Hindukush range.

Revā

Although the river Revā is regarded as another name of the Narmadā, Revā is actually a tributary of Narmadā. Revā flows north-west from the Vindhyas (Bhāgp. 5.19.18), but from the Sahya according to the Vāmanp. 13.31. She joins the river Narmadā. Thereafter the river is known either as Revā or as Narmadā. (For details see under Narmadā above).

Ṛṣikulyā

There are two rivers by the name Ṛṣikulyā.

1. The first Ṛṣikulayā rises from the Mahendra mountain in the Eastern Ghats (Mārkp. 57.28). She is the northernmost river in the district of Ganjam, Orissa, and flows into the Bay of Bengal near Behrampur. Although the river Trisāmā (Triyāmā, Tribhāgā, or Pitṛsomā) and Ṛṣikulyā are mentioned in the Purāṇas as two separate rivers, it seems that actually they are one and the same river. The Ṛṣikulyā is the descriptive name of the Trisāmā. The name Ṛṣikulyā was applied to the combined flow of the three upper streams. Between the river Ṛṣikulyā and the Vaṁśadharā, three other rivers also flow in the district of Ganjam.

Geographical Details

The first Ṛṣikulyā rises from the northern part of Eastern

Ghats to the north-west of Sorada. She flows south-eastwards and is joined by the Mahānadī from the left near Aska. (This Mahānadī is a small tributary, and should not be confused with the larger river of the same name). Further down stream, she receives from left rivers Bhājwa and Dhanāi to the north of Hinjilikatu, and also Ghodahada from the right near Hinjilikatu. Finally, she empties herself into the Bay of Bengal near Ganjam.

2. The second Ṛṣikulyā rises from the mt. Śuktimat, southern portion of the Eastern Ghats (Kūrmp. I.46.38; Mārkp. 57.29; Viṣṇup. 2.3.13). Sircar identifies the second Ṛṣikulyā with the river Kiul.

Sābhramatī

The river Sābhramatī is also known as the river Candanā (See Candanā above). The Sābhramatī is the modern river Sābarmatī.

The Sābarmatī rises from the hills of Mewar from Nandikund which is identified with Dhanbar lake near Mīrapur. At her source, the river is known by the name Sabar. She passes by the Arbuda (modern Abu) mountains and meets the Gulf of Cambay. The river Sabar becomes known as Sābarmatī after it meets the river Hathmatī.

According to Padmp, Uttarakhaṇḍa, 6.135-138 (which mentions a large number of tīrthas on the bank of Sābhramatī), there is a legend about her origin.

Once sage Vasiṣṭha was seated in contemplation and in that state, with his powerful and penetrating eyes, he saw sage Viśvāmitra. This powerful glance pierced two holes in the earth and from both of them two rivers came out. One was Sarasvatī and the other was Sābhramatī. The word *sābhramatī* means 'she is full of agitation.'

According to Padma-purāṇa, (ibid), seven rivers, namely,

Sābhramatī, Setikā, Valkinī, Hiraṇyagāminī, Hastimatī, Vetramatī, and Bhadramukhī, meet at the place called Vikīrṇa-tīrtha. At the village Vautha, a fair is held on the full moon-day of Kārtika (November-December).

There are many tīrthas and temples on the bank of the river Sābarmatī.

Khadgatīrtha is situated on the bank of the river Sābarmatī where there is a temple of Khaḍgadhareśvara. One who takes a bath in Sābarmatī and has *darśana* of the god there becomes entitled for a long stay in heaven. The temple of Nīlakaṇṭha Mahādeva is also situated nearby. There is also the temple of Dūdheśvara Mahādeva. It is said that the milk of the heavenly cow Kāmadhenu was poured at this place. Near this place, there was the Āśrama of the sage Dadhīchi who had given his bones to Indra for making the *vajra* with which the demon Vṛtra was killed.

On the bank of the Sābarmatī is the Sābarmatī Āśrama of Mahatma Gandhi.

Padma Purāṇa mentions some other tīrthas on the bank of the Sābhramatī:

1. Agni-tīrtha (Padmp. Uttarakhaṇḍa, 6.134.1).
2. Devī-tīrtha (Padmp. Uttarakhaṇḍa, 6.161.1).
3. Go-tīrtha (Padmp. Uttarakhaṇḍa, 6.156.1).
4. Saṅgameśvara-tīrtha (on the confluence of the Sābhramatī and Hastimatī) (Padmp. Uttarakhaṇḍa, 6.138.1).
5. Soma-tīrtha (Padmp. Uttarakhaṇḍa, 6.154.1).

Sadānīrā

Sadānīrā is another name of the river Karatoyā (modern Kurattee) (Eggelling on ŚB 1.4.1.14), or rather Gaṇḍakī which formed the boundary between Kośala and Videha.

According to Pargiter, however, she cannot be the Gaṇḍakī. He identifies her with the Rāptī, a tributary of the Sarayū (Mārkp. 57.19 fn). MBh, Sabhāparva, 2.19.27 mentions Sadānīrā with Gaṇḍakī and Śoṇa and says that they rise from one mountain (*ekaparvate*).

Sadānīramayā

MBh, Bhīṣmaparva 6.10.31 mentions this river. According to the Śabdakalpadruma, this is another name of the river Karatoyā. (See under Karatoyā and Sadānīrā above).

Śailodā

The Śailodā rises between the mt. Meru and the Mandāra (MBh, Sabhāparva, 2.48.2). In Matsyp. 121.23, Śailodā rises from the lake Śailoda which is situated at the foot of mount Śṛñgavān.

Sakṛnnandā

Sakṛnnandā is believed to be a sacred river which removes all sins, makes the soul pious, and sends the person who bathes in her waters to the Indraloka (MBh, Āraṇyakaparva, 3.82.138). This river may be the same as the Nandā mentioned above.

Śakulī

Although Mārkp. 57.23 mentions Śakulī only once, there seems to be two rivers by this name. She is the modern river Sakri.

1. The first Śakulī rises from the Vindhyas (Mārkp. 57.23). Pargiter identifies her with the river Sakri which flows into the Gaṅgā between Patna and Monghyr.
2. The second Śakulī, according to Sircar, also rises from the Vindhyas (from the Ṛkṣa mountain to be exact) and flows into the Seonath, a tributary of the Mahānadī.

Geographical Details

The first Sakri rises from the Kodarma plateau and flows north-westward for some distance and then northward to join the river Gaṅgā.

The second Sakri rises from the Maikal range and flows south-eastward. In her lower course, she is known as Hanp which joins the river Seonath, a tributary of Mahānadī to the west of Nandaghat.

Śālūkinī

A hill named Śālaveya was on the bank of this river (Vāmanp, SM, 38.3). A person who bathes in this river gets rid of all sins and obtains his desired *loka* (Vāmanp, SM, 13.22).

Samaṅgā

This river was formerly known as Madhuvilā, on the bank of which was situated the tīrtha Kardamila. Indra was guilty of having killed Vṛtra who was a Bṛahmaṇa. As a result of this, Śrī is said to have deserted him and he was put to great misery. He took bath in this river and got rid of the sin and regained his lost glory (MBh, Āraṇyakaparva, 3.135.1-2).

Sandhyā

She is a tributary of the Yamunā between Agra and Allahabad (MBh, Sabhāparva, 2.9.20 fn).

Sarasvatī

Among the Vedic rivers, Sarasvatī is the foremost (ṚV 2.41.16). She is a mighty river (*maho arṇah* ṚV 1.3.12). She has been celebrated in three entire hymns (ṚV 6.61; 7.95; 96), as also in many other scattered passages.

The river Sarasvatī rises from the Himavat (Mārkp. 57.16; Matsyp. 114.20; Varāhp. 85; Vāyup. 45.94). She enters into the ocean (ṚV 7.95.2; MBh, Āraṇyakaparva, 3.80.79; Anuśāsanaparva, 13.134.15) at a place called Prabhāsa (Mārkp. 57.52 fn). A person who bathes at the place where the Sarasvatī enters into the ocean obtains merits of the Aśvamedha sacrifice and fruits of donating one thousand cows (MBh, Āraṇyakaparva, 3.82.34).

A dip in the Sarasvatī gives fruits of the Agniṣṭoma sacrifice (MBh, Āraṇyakaparva, 3.81.42). She never fails a person who prays to her as Jamadagni and Vasiṣṭha did, and fulfills all his desires (ṚV 7.96.3). ṚV 6.61.1 says that Ṛṣi Vadhraśva worshipped Sarasvatī for obtaining a child and through her favours got a son, the fierce Divodāsa. MBh, Ādiparva, 1.9.24-28 narrates the story of king Matināra who performed a twelve-year long sacrifice on the bank of the Sarasvatī. After the sacrifice was completed, Sarasvatī married the king and begot a son named Taṁsu. Sarasvatī is also said to have helped the Nāhuṣas with her milk and fat in order that they should be enabled to complete the 1000-year long sacrifice. King Puru ruled on her banks (ṚV 7.96.2). A large number of Vedic hymns were composed on her banks. She is called the inspirer of songs and good thoughts (ṚV 1.3.11). People always desire to live along the banks of the Sarasvatī (ṚV 6.61.14).

The river Sarasvatī possesses celestial as well as terrestrial nature. In ṚV 5.43.11 her both forms are invoked. At one place she is addressed as lightning's child (ṚV 6.49.7).

The celestial Sarasvatī is said to have originated from the root of a Plakṣa tree; therefore she is called Plakṣajā (MBh, Āraṇyakaparva, 3.82.5-6).

The river Sarasvatī divides herself in seven streams which flow in seven different directions (MBh, Śalyaparva, 9.37.3-4; Śāntiparva, 13.255.39; Anuśāsanaparva, 13.75.12; Vāmanp, SM, 16.17.18; 36.54). They are:

1. Suprabhā, 2. Kāñcanākṣī, 3. Viśālā, 4. Mānasahradā (also as Manoramā or manoharā), 5. Oghavatī, 6. Suveṇu, and 7. Vimalodā. (About these rivers see under respective entries).

The river Aruṇā joins the Sarasvatī (MBh, Āraṇyakaparva, 3.181.131). (See also under Aruṇā above). If a person fasts for three nights and bathes at the confluence of the Aruṇā and the Sarasvatī, he is freed from the sin of Brahmahatyā and obtains the fruits of the Agniṣṭoma and the Atirātra sacrifices; his family up to the seventh generation is cleansed of all sins (MBh, Āraṇyakaparva, 3.81.131-32; Śalyaparva, 9.42.23-26; Kūrmp. 30.22).

MBh, Śalyaparva, 9.50 narrates a legend about Sarasvatī.

Once Ṛṣi Dadhīcī was practising penance on the bank of the Sarasvatī. Indra, apprehensive of the loss of his throne, sent the Apsaras Alambuṣā to seduce the Ṛṣi. The Apsaras succeeded in doing so. When Ṛṣi Dadhīcī looked at the beautiful Apsaras, his semen fell into the river Sarasvatī. She became pregnant, and after some time in due course presented the Ṛṣi with his child. The Ṛṣi was pleased and named the child as Sārasvata. In ṚV 7.96.4, a male Sārasvata has been alluded to. In MBh, Āraṇyakaparva, 3.82.59, it is said that a person who offers water ablution to gods and manes in the river Sarasvatī attains Sārasvataloka.

BrahmVP, Prakṛtikhaṇḍs, 6 and 7; and Devībhp. 9.6 narrate a legend about Sarasvatī, Gaṅgā, and Lakṣmī. (See the legend under Gaṅgā). The important point to note in that legend is that, by the time of the Purāṇas, the Sarasvatī seems to have lost much of her Vedic grandeur and importance. In the above mentioned legend, Viṣṇu is said to have sent Sarasvatī to Brahmā, while Gaṅgā and Lakṣmī remained with him.

In the opinion of Pargiter (Mārkp. 57.16 fn), the Sarasvatī is the modern river Sursooty which flows to the west of Thaneswar between the Yamunā and the Sutlej and is joined by a westerly stream Ghaggar. The Sarasvatī flows into the sea at Prabhāsa (present Somanāth). The famous tīrtha Pṛthūdaka (present Pehoa) is on the bank of the Sarasvatī. If a person leaves his body in this tīrtha, he attains godhood (Vāmanp, SM, 18.19-20). Brahmā meditated at this place at the time of the creation of the universe (Vāmanp, SM, 18.21).

By the time of the Mahābhārata, the river Sarasvatī had lost her perennial flow and was seen only at certain places (MBh, Bhīṣmaparva, 6.7.77). In Vāmanp, SM, 11.2, she is known as *dṛṣyādṛṣyā*. According to MBh, Āraṇyakaparva, 3.80.118, the Sarasvatī finally disappeared at a place named Vinaśana. (Cf. also PañcaviṁśaBr 25.104; Jaiminīya-Upaniṣad-Brāhmaṇa 4.26). MBh, Anuśāsanaparva, 13.139 tells the following legend about the disappearance of the Sarasvatī.

Once Varuṇa kidnapped the wife of Ṛṣi Utathya and violated her chastity. In revenge Utathya drank all the waters of the river Sarasvatī. There is another legend about the appearance and disappearance of the Sarasvatī:

Brahmā entrusted Sarasvatī with the task of throwing away the Vaḍavānala into the Western sea. The river hesitated to carry the fire of Vaḍavā on the ground that she would be touching sinners on the earth. Brahmā asked her to go underground and to re-appear whenever she felt exhausted.

The source of the river Sarasvatī is believed to be in Plakṣa Praśravaṇa in the Himālayas in the Sirmur hills of the Siwalik range. She comes out in the plain in Ambala district at Ad-Badri. The Plakṣa Praśravaṇa is considered as sacred as Gangotrī and Jamunotrī. Sarasvatī disappeared in the sands in a place known as Vinaśana.

Flowing southwards through Simla and Sirmur, the river flows past Patiala, and vanishes in the northern part of the desert of Rajputana at some distance from Sirsa. She disappears for a time in the sands near the village of Chalaur and reappears at Bhavanipur. At Balchapur, she again disappears but appears again at Bara Khera. This fully justifies her name Dṛṣyādṛṣyā (Vamanp, SM, 11.2). At Urnai near Pehoa, the Sarasvatī is joined by the river Mārakāṇḍa and the united stream bearing still the name Sarasvatī ultimately joins the Ghaggar which was the lower part of the Sarasvatī. In MBh, Āraṇyakaparva, 3.80.118;119 it is said that after disappearing at Vinaśana, the river Sarasvatī reappears again at three places, namely, 1. Camasodbheda, 2. Śivodbheda, and 3. Nāgodbheda. A bath in the Sarasvatī at Camasodbheda brings the fruits of the Agniṣṭoma, and a bath in the Sarasvatī at the Śivodbheda brings merit equal to donating one thousand cows, and a bath in the Sarasvatī at the Nāgodbheda entitles one to obtain the Nāgaloka (MBh, Āraṇyakaparva, 3.81.119).

In Vedic times, Sarasvatī flowed as an independent river into the Ran of Kutch. The Yamunā was then a tributary of the Sarasvatī, not of the Gaṅgā as she is today. But due to a subsidence in the Gaṅgā delta, a pre-Yamunā tributary of the Gaṅgā began moving headward to catch the stream of the Yamunā. Simultaneously, by a later uplift in the Aravalli-Delhi axis as well as the rise of the Eocene Sea floor of the Rajaputana desert, the Yamunā broke away from the Sarasvatī and joined that pre-Yamunā tributary of the Gaṅgā and became herself a tributary of the Gaṅgā and met her at Prayāga. It is assumed by the common folk that the Yamunā took away along with her the waters of the Sarasvatī; hence, her confluence with the Gaṅgā in Prayāga is called Triveṇī. (For other views regarding the identification of the Sarasvatī, see S.K. Lal, *Female Divinities in Hindu Mythology and Ritual*, University of Pune, Pune, 1980, s.v.).

Prabhāsa-khaṇḍa of the Skanda-Purāṇa and the Śalyaparva of the Mahābhārata mention a large number of tīrthas on the bank of the river Sarasvatī. A few of them are mentioned below:

1. Auśanasa-tīrtha (MBh, Śalyaparva, 9.38.16).
2. Camasodbheda (MBh, Śalyaparva, 9.36.1).
3. Dvaitavana, (MBh, Śalyaparva, 9.36.26).
4. Gandharva-tīrtha (MBh, Śalyaparva, 9.36.10-14).
5. Gargasrota-tīrtha (MBh, Śalyaparva, 9.36.14-18).
6. Kurukṣetra (Kūrmp. I.31.47; 37.37; II. 20.23; 40.7).
7. Nāgadhanvan-tīrtha (MBh, Śalyaparva, 9.36.29).
8. Plakṣapraśravaṇa-tīrtha (Brahmp. II.13.39; Vāyup. 77.67).
9. Prabhāsa-tīrtha (Bhāgp. 7.14.31; 11.30.6; Brahmāṇḍp. II.13.40 MBh, Śalyaparva, 9.34.36).
10. Puṣkara-tīrtha (Padmp. Sṛṣṭikhaṇḍa, 5.19.37; MBh, Āraṇyakaparva, 1.213.13).
11. Śaṅkha-tīrtha (MBh, Śalyaparva, 9.36.19).
12. Sapta-sārasvata-tīrtha (MBh, Śalyaparva, 9.36.63; 37.1).
13. Soma-tīrtha (MBh, Āraṇyakaparva, 3.81.96, Matsyp. 109.2).
14. Subhūmika-tīrtha (MBh, Śalyaparva, 9.36.8).
15. Vinaśana-tīrtha (MBh, Śalyaparva, 9.36.1).

As mentioned earlier, there are two more Sarasvatī rivers. One is the tributary of the Alakanandā at a place called Māna above Badarīnātha which joins from the left bank.

The other Sarasvatī rises from the Danta hills in Gujarat and flows south-westward to fall in the little Ran of Kutch. Pāṭan is located on her bank.

Śarāvatī

She is mentioned in MBh, Bhīṣmaparva, 6.10.19 fn. According to Dey, Śarāvatī is the name of the river Rāptī on whose bank the city Śrāvasti was situated.

Sarayu

The Sarayu (also as Sarayū in the post-Vedic literature) is a Ṛgvedic river. Indra killed kings Arṇa and Citraratha on the bank of the Sarayu (ṚV 4.10.18). The Sarayū flows from the mountain Himavat (Kūrmp. I.46.28; Matsyp. 114.21; Varāhp. 85; Vāyup. 45.94).

The river Sarayū rises from the Mānasarovara on the Kailāsa and joins the Gaṅgā (Rām., Bālakāṇḍa, 1.23.7-9), where wives of the Yakṣas bathe (Raghuvaṁśa 13.60-63).

King Daśaratha had performed the Putreṣṭi on the bank of the Sarayū and had obtained four sons (Rām., Bālakāṇḍa, 1.11.15; 13.1; 14.1-2). This river is connected also with the tragic death of Śravaṇakumāra resulting from the arrow unintentionally shot by Daśaratha and the consequent curse upon him of the pang of separation from his son (Rām. Ayodhyākāṇḍa, 2.58; Agnip. 6.38).

Kālikp. 23.126 mentions that at the time of the marriage of Arundhatī and Vasiṣṭha the water used in the nuptial and the Avabhṛtha baths flowed in seven streams and that the Sarayū is one of those streams.

Viṣṇu lives in the Sarayū in the form of Śaṁbhu (Vāmanp. 63.27).

The main stream of Sarayū is now known as the Ghāghrā which joins the Gaṇgā in the district of Chapra. At the north-west corner of the district of Bahraich, the Ghāghrā receives a tributary from the north-east which is now known as Sarayū. The ancient city of Ayodhyā (district Faizabad) is situated on the Sarayū.

According to Dey, the Sarayū rises in the Kumaon hills

and is called Sarayū, Ghāgrā (or Gogrā), or Devā after her confluence with the Kālīnadī.

Sarayū is a sacred river. Her water is called *sarvam-udakam*. Kālidāsa (Raghuvaṁśa 8.95) says that king Aja gave up his body at the confluence of the Sarayū with the Gaṅgā near Chapra in Bihar.

Geographical Details

At present, there are three rivers by the name Sarayū.

Sarayū-I

This Sarayū rises in the Terrain region of Uttar Pradesh and joins the Ghāgharā from the left bank to the east of Tambaur in Uttar Pradesh. After the confluence, the river is known as Ghāgharā or Ghogrā.

Sarayu-II

This also rises in the terrain region of U.P. to the east of the Sarayū-I. She has three head-streams which join together near Bahraich. Then the river flows southwards and joins Ghāgharā from the left bank.

Sarayū-III

The third Sarayū rises in the Kumaon range of the Himālayas in U.P. She is a greater feeder of the Kālīnadī. The Sarayū meets Kālīnadī at Pancheswar about 45 kms below Jaulajibi (Dey).

P.L. Bhargava identifies Ṛgvedic Sarayu with Siritoi, a tributary of the Gomal.

Śatadru

In the Ṛgveda, Śatadru (Purāṇic) is known as Śutudri (ṚV 3.33.1; 3; 10.75.5). Nirukta 9.26 explains the word as 'quick runner, rapid runner, or runs swiftly like one who is goaded.' In post-Vedic, particularly Purāṇic literature, this river is known as Śatadru.

Śatadru rises from the mount Himavat (Kūrmp. I. 46.28; Mārkp. 57.17; Vāmanp. 13.20; Varāhp. 85; Vāyup. 45.95; Viṣṇup. 2.3.14). She and the river Vipāś figure in the famous dialogue hymn (ṚV 3.33).

Why the river is called Śatadru is found in a story in the MBh, Ādiparva, 1.166;167. Once king Kalmāṣapāda (son of Sudāsa, MBh, Ādiparva, 1.168.8) went for hunting. In the forest, he came across Ṛṣi Śakti, son of Ṛṣi Vasiṣṭha who was coming along the same track from the opposite direction. The king ordered the Ṛṣi to make way for him. The Ṛṣi politely rejoined that it was the duty of kings to give way to the Ṛṣis. This infuriated Kalmāṣapāda and, out of anger, he whipped the Ṛṣi. The Ṛṣi cursed the king that he would become a Rākṣasa and eat human flesh. This incident was being secretly watched by Viśvāmitra, an arch rival of Vasiṣṭha. Viśvāmitra ordered a Rākṣasa named Kiṅkara to enter the body of the king.

Now turned into a demon, the king first killed Śakti. Viśvāmitra ordered the Rākṣasa to kill the other sons of Ṛṣi Vasiṣṭha. The king soon devoured all the sons of Vasiṣṭha. Beholding his Āśrama bereft of his children, Vasiṣṭha plunged into deep grief. If was impossible for him to live without his children. He tried to kill himself. But each time he was miraculously saved. Once he tied himself strongly with ropes and flung himself into a mighty river. But the river simply cut the ropes and brought the Ṛṣi safely on the bank. Because his cords were cut by the river, Vasiṣṭha named the river as Vipāś.

Still thinking of ending his life, Vasiṣṭha saw another mighty river named Haimavatī (flowing from the Himavat). The river was full of crocodiles and other aquatic monsters. The Ṛṣi thought that it was a proper place to end his life. He threw himself into the river. But the river saw him as a mass of burning fire and immediately flowed in a hundred directions. Therefore, the river is known as Śatadru (a river running in hundred courses).

The qualities of the water of Śatadru are: coolness (*suśītam*), lightness (*laghutvam*), tastefulness (*svādutvam*), destroyer of diseases (*sarvāmayaghnam*), purity (*nirmala-tvam*), digestive (*dīpanatvam*), appetising (*pācanam*), and giver of strength, intellience, and retaining power (*balabuddhi-medhāyuṣañca*). (Śabdakalpadruma, s.v.).

Geographical Details

Śatadru is the present river Sutlej. She has her origin in the highlands of Tibet. She rises at a height of 4630 metres in the western region of the Mānasarovara (also known as Rākṣasa-tāla. It is stated that Rāvaṇa had propitiated Śiva while standing there). From this region, the river has a westerly course until she turns a little towards south-west near Indo-Tibet border near Shippi La. The river Spiti joins her on the left from the north inside the Indian border.

Śatadru enters Panjab plains near Rupar. Later, she forms the boundary between India and Pakistan. She finally joins the river Chenab (Vedic Asiknī) at Panjnad near Khairpur-Jadid in Pakistan. The combined flow of the Sutlej and Chenab is known as Panjanad which joins the Indus near Chacharan in Pakistan.

Satīrā

The river Satīrā rises from the mount Pāriyātra (Vāyup. 45.97). She is the same river as Sadānīrā mentioned above.

Śilāmā

The river Śilāmā (Rām., Ayodhyākāṇḍa, 2.65.2) is a tributary of the Vitastā according to the Nīlamata-Purāna, 1394.

Sindhu

There are two rivers by the name of Sindhu.

1. The first Sindhu is a Ṛgvedic river which is regarded as surpassing all the streams that flow on the earth (ṚV 10.75.1). She has many big and small affluents, such as, Tṛṣṭāmā, Rasā, Susartu, Śvetyā, Kubhā, Krumu, and Gomatī (ṚV 10.75.6). She rises from the Himavat (Mārkp. 57.116; Matsyp. 114.20; Varāhp. 85; Vāyup. 45.94).

The Vedic Sindhu is the modern Indus which rises in Tibet and falls into the Arabean Sea near Karachi. It is from the river Sindhu that names Hindu, Hindusthāna, Sindha, Indus, and India are derived.

The tīrtha Pañcanada is on the confluence of the Sindhu with the sea (Brahmp. II.13.67; Vāyup. 77.56). Another tīrtha, Prayāga, is on the confluence of the Sindhu and the Vitastā. In this case, Sindhu is regarded as Gaṅgā and Vitastā as Yamunā (Nīlamata-Purāṇa 295-96).

The qualities of her waters are the same as that of the river Śatadru mentioned above.

Geographical Details

Sindhu rises in Tibet at an elevation of 5182 metres. At the source region, she is known as Singgekhabab and is a united flow of two streams, one flowing towards the north-west side of the Kailāsa and the other in north-westerly direction from a lake situated to the north-east of the Kailāsa. Beginning from this confluence, she flows north-west over a long distance to turn south below the Karakoram range. From this point she flows to south-west till she falls into the Arabian sea near Karachi forming two deltas at her mouth.

Tributaries

1. Hanle from the left.

2. Zaskar from the left near Nimu in Leh.
3. Shylok from the right near Kiris in Kashmir.
4. Shigar from the right at Skardu.
5. Gilgit from the right above Jaglot in Kashmir.
6. Kabul from the right near Attock (Pakistan).
7. Kurram from the right near Darrehtangi (Pakistan).
8. Combined water of five Panjab rivers, Jhelum, Chenab, Ravi, Beas, and Sutlej.
9. Astor from the left at Thalich.
10. Sohan at Makhad.

The second Sindhu rises from the Pāriyātra (Mārkp. 57.19; Matsyp. 114.23; Varāhp. 85; Vāyup. 45.97).

According to Pargiter, this Sindhu is the modern Kālīsindha, a tributary of the Chambal. In MBh, Āraṇyaka-parva, 3.130.6, it is said that Agastya had met Lopāmudrā at the bank of this river and had married her later. (See also under Lūpī and Nūpī above).

Sindhuparṇā

This river rises from the Pāriyātra (Varāhp. 85). She may be the same river as Sindhu-II above.

Sinīvālī

She rises from the Ṛkṣa (Mārkp. 57.24). According to Pargiter, she is probably the same as the Selye on whose bank the ancient city Tamraliptaka was situated. It was a famous port. Tamraliptaka is now known as Tamluk.

Śiprā

The river Śiprā rises from the Pāriyātra (Mārkp. 57.20; Matsyp. 114.24; Vāmanp. 13.24; 57.19; Vāyup. 45.98). The city Ujjayini stands on her bank. Kālidāsa gives a lively description of the river Śiprā in his Meghadūta I.31.

Kālikāp. 19.13 mentions that after the death of Pārvatī, Brahmā went to mt. Kailāsa to console Śiva. After some time, both of them came down the Himālayas to a lake named Śipra. Its water was clean and pure. Śiva gazed at the lake and a river flowed from the lake. The river was named Śiprā.

Śiprā is a river in Madhya Pradesh. She rises in Malwa on the Kokri Bardi hill. This place is situated about sixteen kms south-east of Indore. She flows into the Chambal a little below Sitamau. Śiprā is called Kṣiprā also.

Kālidāsa (in Raghuvaṁśa 6.34; 35; Meghadūta I.35) describes the city Avantī situated on the bank of the river Śiprā. This river is also known as Avantīnadī. She is described as Uttaravāhinī, i.e., flowing in the northern direction. The fight of Śiva with the demon Andhaka is said to have taken place in the Mahākānana near Avantī (Brahmp. 43.66).

The most important city Ujjayinī (modern Ujjain) is situated on the Śiprā. In Ujjain, there is the famous Jyotirliṅga of Mahākāla (Śiva). It is said that as there are two eyes on the face, similarly there are two sacred places on the earth, one Avimukta (Kāśī) situated on the bank of the Gaṅgā and the other Mahākāla in Ujjayinī situated on the bank of the Śiprā.

Śrī Kṛṣṇa, with Baladeva and Sudāmā, had taken his education in the Āśrama of sage Sandīpanī near Ujjain. This city is also famous as the capital of king Vikramāditya. Bhartṛhari is also associated with Ujjain. There is a cave near Ujjain where he is said to have practised penance.

Ashoka, when he was a young prince, was a Viceroy of Ujjain. Mahendra, his son, was born there. Ujjain was the capital of Pradyota kings. Caṇḍa Pradyota of Ujjain was a contemporary of the Buddha. King Udayana, the ruler of the Vatsa country, had married Vāsavadattā, the daughter of Caṇḍa Pradyota.

Every year on the full moon day of the month of Kārtika (November-December), a fair is held at Ujjain, and there is a Kumbhamelā every twelve years.

The river Kṣatā meets the Śiprā at Rudra-sarovara. This *saṅgama* is a tīrtha. The river Khan meets the Śiprā about ten kms south of Indore near the village Gotra. Another river Gambhīrā meets Śiprā at Murla Mar.

Sītā

The Sītā is one of the seven streams of the Gaṅgā which flowed to the west (MBh, Bhīṣmaparva, 6.7.45). Flowing through the forest Caitraratha and passing through the lake Varuṇodā, she falls on the mount Śītānta. Descending on the earth, she flows through Bhadrāśva and joins the sea (Mārkp. 56.5-7).

Sircar identifies the Sītā with the Tagdumbash branch of the Yarkand. Dey, However, identifies her with the Jaxartes (Sir-Daria) and regards Sir as a corruption of Sītā, *daria* means a river.

Vāmanp. 5.1 narrates a story about the origin of Sītā. Śiva went to the site of the sacrifice where Pārvatī had burnt herself. He became furious. Seeing his anger the Vasus melted out of fear, and a river flowed out of them which came to be known as Sītā.

S.M. Ali identifies Sītā with the river Kizil-Su-Kashgar-Tarim. The lake Aruṇodā is the modern Karkul which lies on the north-eastern corner of the Pamir (ancient mt. Meru) near the source of the river Kizil-Su. As the Kizil, she flows eastwards and reaches the town of Kashghar. She receives two tributaries from the north, and two from the south. As the river flows past the Kashghar town, she is also known as the Kashghar river. A few hundred kms down below, she receives another afluent of the Tarim, the Yarkand river. The combined waters of the rivers Tanshkand Daria and Kim-Arik flow across Akṣu and join the Tarim from the left. The Tarim finally ends in LopNor, the Salt-lake, which lies at the foot of the Altin Tag Range.

Somā

According to Mārkp. 56.16, the Gaṅgā is known as Somā on the mountain Supārśva which is at the foot of the mt. Meru. (See also under Suṣomā).

Śoṇa

Śoṇa is one of the seven rivers which is masculine. The seven rivers are: 1. Śoṇa, 2. Sindhu, 3. Hiraṇya, 4. Koka, 5. Brahmaputra, 6. Gharghara, and 7. Śatadru. However, MBh, Bhīṣmaparva 6.10.28 mentions a river Śoṇā (fem.) along with Kauśikī, Bāhudā, Candanā, etc.

The river Śoṇa rises from the mt. Ṛkṣa (Mārkp. 27.21; Varāhp. 85; Vāmanp. 13.25; MBh, Sabhāparva, 2.18.29; Āraṇyakaparva, 3.83.8). She is the modern river Son.

The Śoṇa forms the confluence with the river Jyotirathā. A person who offers ablutions to gods and manes at this confluence is said to obtain the merit of the Agniṣṭoma (MBh, Āraṇyakaparva, 3.83.8). Viṣṇu lives in the river Śoṇa in the form of Rukmakavaca (Vāmanp. 63.24).

The Śoṇa is also known by the name Hiraṇyavāha. Sands on the bank of this river look red-gold colour, hence she is called so. The Śoṇa is also identified with the river Māgadhī or Sumāgadhī. According to tradition, the fight between the Grāha (alligator) and the Elephant had taken place at Sonpur on the river Śoṇa. (For details, see Bhāgp. 8.2-3).

The modern river Son rises in the Maikal range in Gondwana near the source of the river Narmadā (i.e.

Amarakaṇṭaka) in the district of Bilaspur. Flowing north-east through Jabalpur, Baghelkhand, Mirzapur, and Shahabad districts, she joins the Gaṅgā at Patna. The ancient city of Pāṭaliputra stood at the confluence of the Śoṇa and the Gaṅgā. The rivers Śoṇa and Sarayū meet the Gaṇgā from opposite sides within a very short distance.

The river Johilla meets the Śoṇa on the left bank near Barawalu village. Rivers Banas and Gopat join Śoṇa on the right bank. In Mirzapur district, the river flows through a valley which is about fifteen kms broad. Here Śoṇa is met by two other tributaries, the Rihand and the Kanahar.

Sthāṇumatī

This may be the name given to the river Sarasvatī in Sthāṇeśvara (modern Thaneswar). She has been mentioned with the Gomatī in Rām., Ayodhyākāṇḍa, 2.65.11.

Śuktimatī

The river Śuktimatī rises from the mt. Ṛkṣa (Mārkp. 57.23; Vāmanp. 13.27; Vāyup. 45.101; Matsyp. 114.26 has Śuktimantī).

According to Sircar and Dey, she is to be identified with the modern river Ken, a tributary of the Yamunā which flows through Bundelkhand.

MBh, Ādiparva, 1.57.32 narrates the following story:

The river Śuktimatī flowed by the side of the capital of king Uparicara who was also known by the name Vasu. The mt. Kolāhala sought the river Śuktimatī who was in deep love with her. King Vasu did not like this, and so struck the mountain with his foot. The river came out of the embrace of Kolāhala. But by that time she had already conceived. In due course she gave birth to a twins. The river gave both children to Vasu. The king appointed the male child to the post of General of his army and married the female named Girikā.

Sukumārī

She rises from the Śuktimat mountain (MBh, Bhīṣmaparva, 6.12.30; Matsyp. 114.32; Vāyup. 45.107). (See also Kumārī above).

Dey identifies this river with the Kuārī-nadī which joins the river Sindha (or Kālīsindha), a tributary of Yamunā about twenty kms from Dholpur.

Suprabhā

The river Suprabhā is one of the seven streams of the Sarasvatī. MBh, Śalyaparva, 9.37.4; 12 and Vāmanp, SM, 16.21 relate the following legend about her:

Once Brahmā performed a great sacrifice. While the sacrifice was in progress at Puṣkara, many Ṛsis arrived there. They did not see Sarasvatī there. They complained that the sacrifice would not be perfect unless the Sarasvatī was summoned there. Brahmā thought of Sarasvatī and she appeared there under the name of Suprabhā.

Suprayogā

This river rises from the Sahya (MBh, Āraṇyakaparva, 3.212.24; Bhīṣmaparva, 6.10.20; Kūrmp. I. 46.35; Mārkp. 57.26; Matsyp. 114.29).

Pargiter opines that she is one of the western tributaries of the Kṛṣṇā (Mārkp. 57.26 fn). But according to Sircar, she is a small river in the Nellore-Guntur division and has been identified with the modern river Manneru.

Surasā

She rises from the mt. Ṛkṣa (Bhāgp. 5.19.18; Kūrmp. I.46.32; Vāmanp. 13.25; Viṣṇup. 2.3.10).

Surathā

The river Surathā rises from the mt. Vindhya. According to Pargiter (Mārkp. 57.21), Surathā is another name of the

Jyotirathā which is a tributary of the Son. (See Jyotirathā above).

Susartu

She is a Ṛgvedic river (ṚV 10.75.6), and was a tributary of the Sindhu. P.L. Bhargava opines that she is probably identical with the river Ghorband.

Suṣomā

Suṣomā is another name of the river Sindhu in her course through Panjab. In ṚV 8.64.11, she is mentioned with Ārjikīyā and in ṚV 10.75.5 she is mentioned with Śutudri, Sarasvatī, Paruṣṇī, etc. She is also mentioned in Bhāgp. 5.19.18.

P.L. Bhargava identifies her with the river Sohan, an eastern tributary of the Sindhu flowing south of Hāro. Sohan is the same as Suwan in the Rawalpindi district.

Sūtpalāvatī

She rises from the mt. Malaya (Mārkp. 57.28). (See Utpalāvatī above).

Suvāmā

She is mentioned in MBh, Bhīṣmaparva, 6.10.27. According to Dey, it is another name of the Rāmagaṅgā.

Suveṇū

She is one of the seven streams of the Sarasvatī. Dakṣa once performed a sacrifice at the source of the Gaṅgā. The Sarasvatī appeared there under the name of Suveṇu (MBh, Śalyaparva, 9.37.24; Vāmanp. SM, 16.37). According to Vāmanp. SM, 16.34, the Sarasvatī is known as the Suveṇu at Kedāra tīrtha.

Śvetyā

Śvetyā (ṚV 10.75.6) and Śvetayāvarī (ṚV 8.26.18) are

the same rivers. A portion of the Himālayas to the east of Tibet is called Śvetagiri.

The river Śvetyā is identified with the modern Swat which rises above Dadarila in the Gilgit area of Hindukush mountains, and flows south-wards up to Manglaur (Pakistan), then flows westwards up to Kalangai where a tributary, Panjkora, joins her from the left bank. Then she flows in the south-westerly direction up to Bazargai. She again takes a south-easterly course, and finally joins the river Kabul at Prang.

Syandikā

This river is mentioned in Rām., Ayodhyākāṇḍa, 2.43.10 with Vedaśruti and Gomatī. According to Dey, Syandikā is to be identified with the modern river Sai which flows about ten .kms south of Jaunpur and about thirty kms north of Varanasi.

Śyenī

She rises from the mt. Ṛkṣa (Matsyp. 114.25). Dey identifies her with the river Ken in Bundelkhand.

Śiphā

Śiphā is mentioned in ṚV 1.104.3 as a river. No detail is available.

Tamasā

The river Tamasā rises from the mt. Ṛkṣa (Mārkp. 57.22; Matsyp. 114.25; Vāmanp. 13.26; Vāyup. 45.100) in the Vindhyas. She is also known as Tāmasī (Kūrmp. I.46.32).

The river Tamasā is linked with the Ṛṣi-poet Vālmīki. It was on her bank that the Ṛṣi witnessed the *Krauñca-vadha* and the first verse emerged from his mouth (Rām., Bālakāṇḍa, 1.2.3 ff). The Raghuvaṁśa 9.20 mentions that king Daśaratha had raised golden yūpas on the banks of the river Tamasā and Sarayū.

The river Tamasā is the modern river Tons. The Tons rises from the Bhandar Plateau of the Kaimur hills area and flows north-eastwards to Maihar, and then flows northwards. She receives a tributary named Satna from the left. After the confluence, she again flows north-eastwards and receives another tributary, Bikar, from the right. Tons joins the Gaṅgā on the right bank below Allahabad.

Tāmraparṇī

The river Tāmraparṇī rises from the mount Malaya. Kūrmp. I.46.37; Mārkp. 57.27; Matsyp. 114.30; Varāhp. 85; Viṣṇup. 2.3.12; MBh, Āraṇyakaparva, 3.186; 95; Bhīṣmaparva, 6.10.27; Anuśāsanaparva, 13.151.16 all have short form Tāmrā; Vāyup. 45.105 has Tāmravarṇā. MBh, Āraṇyakaparva, 3.212.22 has Tāmravatī which too may be another name of the Tāmraparṇī.

There is a legend about this river. Gods and goddesses had gathered on mount Kailāsa for the marriage of Śiva and Pārvatī. From the Kailāsa sage Agastya came down to the south. He carried with him a garland of lotus flowers. The garland turned itself into a beautiful damsel. The sage asked the damsel to transform herself into a river which she did. Sage Agastya moved after her course and established tīrthas on her banks. He established 32 tīrthas above Pāpanāśana tīrtha for gods and 86 tīrthas below Pāpanāśana tīrtha for men.

Tāmraparṇī is a sacred river. A bath in her waters gives liberation like a bath in the river Gaṅgā. She is also called Dakṣiṇa Jāhnavī.

At the mouth of the river Tāmraparṇī in the Gulf of Mannar is situated Korkai. It was the capital of the Pandya kings and a very flourishing port. Near the port, at Kayal, Marco Polo had landed.

The city of Tirunelveli is on the bank of the Tāmraparṇī. In the city there are famous temples of Varadarāja, Śaṅkara, and Subrahmanya. The main temple is that of Salivatisvara which is regarded as the Svayaṁbhū-liṅga. There are many other images, one of them of Rāvaṇa.

Another city Tenkashi on the bank of Tāmraparṇī is called as Dakṣiṇa-Kāshī. There is also a temple of Kāshī-Vishvanātha. The Fall of Kuṭṭalam is about six kms from Tenkashi. There is also the temple of god Kuṭṭaleśvara.

Another important tīrtha on the Tāmraparṇī is Śrī-vaikuṇṭham (Viṣṇu). It also has the images of Śrī Devī and Bhūdevī and different Alvars.

In Vāyup. 77.24-27, it is stated that when the river meets the southern ocean, there are found conches and pearls. Since ancient times Tāmraparṇī is well known for pearl fishery. (Cf. also Raghuvaṁśa 4.49-50; Bhāgp. 10.79).

Geographical Details

The Tāmraparṇī rises from the southern part of the Western Ghats from a hill known as Agastya Malai. She descends on the plains in five beautiful falls near Pāpanāśana. Pāpanāśana is a famous tīrtha. It is also called Kalyāṇatīrtha. She flows through the Tirunelveli district. That portion of the Western Ghats which begins from Nilgiris and goes up to Kanyākumarī is also called the Malaya mountain.

The sand in the bed of the river is reddish; hence she is sometimes called Tāmravarṇī. The river falls in the Gulf of Mannar in the east near Pannaikayal.

After her rise from the mt. Agastya Malai, she receives several tributaries which also rise in the Western Ghats. The chief among them is the Chittar which joins the Tāmraparṇī near Sivalapperi.

Tāpī

Tāpī is also known as Tāptī and Tapatī. She rises from the Ṛkṣa (Bhāgp. 5.19.18; Kūrmp. I.46.34; Mārkp. 57.24; Matsyp. 114.27; Vāmanp. 13.28; etc.).

The Tāpi is the modern river Tāptī which flows from the east to the west. She rises near Multai (Mūlatāpī) in Betul district, Madhya Pradesh. Her source region is called Vindhyapada or the Satpura range. She flows westwards and falls into the Arabian sea in the Gulf of Cambay near Surat.

After flowing for about 200 kms, she flows through the Satpura Plateau. Then she passes through Khandesh flowing further west into Gujarat and passing through Surat district.

It is stated that Tapatī is the daughter of the sun-god Vivasvān through his wife Chāyā. She married the king Saṁvaraṇa and begot a son named Kuru.

According to another legend Rāma established the Rāmeśvara liṅga at Rāmanātha Ghela near Surat. The ocean came to Rāma as a Brāhmaṇa asking for *dāna*. Rāma agreeing, the ocean said that Rāma should not bathe in the Tāpī-sāgara-saṅgama, for, that would yield such a great merit that he would never be separated from his wife and the very purpose of his incarnation to annihilate demons would remain unfulfilled. Rāma agreed not to bathe there.

River Tāpī is said to be born on Āṣāḍha (July-August), Śukla, seven, at midday. This day is celebrated as a great festival. In fact, the whole month of Āṣāḍha is regarded holy for *snāna, dāna, yajña*, and *tapa* on the banks of the river Tāpī. During this month by burning lamps on Tāpī, one gets the reward of donating one's weight in gold in Kurukṣetra (Tāpī Māhātmya 4.40).

The Tāpī meets the river Pūrṇā near Bhusawal. At the confluence, there is the old and famous temple of Changadeva.

Prakash is another holy place about forty kms north-west of Dhulia (in Maharashtra) situated on the *saṅgama* of Tāpī and Pūrṇā.

The Tāpī-sāgara-saṅgama is a very holy spot near Hazira. On the Amāvāsyā of the month of Mārga-śīrṣa (December-January), a bath in this *saṅgama* and the *darśana* of god Nāgeśvara and Jaratkāreśvara brings great merit. Bathing on the Paurṇamāsī (full-moon day) of the month of Māgha (January-February) at Galiteśvara on the Tapi brings reward equal to donating ten million gold coins at Puṣkara.

There are several tīrthas on the banks of the Tāpī:

1. Ambarīśvara in the town of Abrama.
2. Aśvītīrtha at Aśvinīkumāra near Surat.
3. Darbheśvara in the village of Narsana.
4. Dhāreśvara in the village Dharoli.
5. Gautameśvara in the town of Bahudhan (also called Bodhan) near Dhulia.
6. Gupteśvara in the village of Phulpada near Surat.
7. Jaratkāreśvara in the village of Mora near Hazira.
8. Kāntāreśvara in Katagram near Surat.
9. Kaṭeśvara in the village of Kamalej.
10. Mukteśvara in the village of Mota.
11. Rāmeśvara at Rāmanāthaghela near Surat.

Tributaries

1. River Pūrṇā flowing from the hills of Berar meets Tāpī from the left to the north of Bhusawal in Khandesh and north-west of Edalabad.
2. Vaghur from the left to the west of Bhusawal.
3. Girnā from the left to the north of Dharangaon.

4. Bori from the left above Amalner.
5. Aner from the right above Amalner.
6. Panjhra from the left to the north-east of Betvad.
7. Aruṇāvatī from the right to the west of Shirpur.
8. Buray from the left to the north-east of Sindhkheda.
9. Gomai from the right to the south-west of Shahada.
10. Vākī from the right to the south of Taloda.
11. Nesu from the left to the south of Vajpur.

Tribhāgā

She rises from the mt. Mahendra (Matsyp. 114.31). (See Ṛṣi-kulyā above).

Tridivā

The river Tridivā rises from the Ṛkṣa (Kūrmp. I.46.30; Mārkp. 57.23; Vāyup. 45.101).

There is another river Tridivā which flows from the mount Mahendra (Mārkp. 57.28; Matsyp. 114.31; Vāyup. 45.106).

Trisāmā

According to Kūrmp. I.46.38, the Trisāmā rises from the Śuktimat mountain which is the southern portion of the Eastern Ghats. But according to Vāyup. 45.106 and Viṣṇup. 2.3.13, she flows from the Mahendra mountain which is also a portion of the Eastern Ghats.

The river Trisāmā is the same as the Ṛṣikulyā. The name Ṛṣikulyā was applied to the united flow of the three upper streams.

Trisrotasī

She is mentioned in MBh, Sabhāparva, 2.9.20 fn. The Trisrotasī represents the combined flow of three rivers, namely, Pūrṇabhābā, Atrai, and Karatoyā. Today she is known as the modern river Teesta (Sk Trisrotā) which flows in North Bengal.

Tṛṣṭāmā

She is mentioned in the Nadi-stuti-sūkta (ṚV 10.75.6) along with Rasā, Susartū, Śvetyā, etc.

Tṛtīyā

The river Tṛtīyā rises from the Himavat (MBh, Sabhāparva, 2.9.20 fn; Matsyp. 114.22; Vāyup. 45.96). In Vāyup. (*ibid*), she is mentioned with the rivers Kauśikī, Gaṇḍakī, Ikṣu, and Lohitā. Similar is the case with the Matsyp. occurrence.

According to Sircar, the name Tṛtīyā is a mistake for the name Karatoyā which flows in North Bengal. But according to Dey, she is a river in Gaya, presumably the river Tiliyā.

Triyāmā

She flows from the mount Mahendra (Varāhp. 85). (See Ṛṣikulyā above).

Tuṅgabhadrā

The river Tuṅgabhadrā rises from the mt. Sahya. She is made up of two streams, namely, Tuṅgā and Bhadrā (Mārkp. 57.26; Kūrmp. I.46.36; Matsyp. 114.29; Vāyup. 45.104). There is a legend about it:

The demon Hiraṇyākṣa, son of Kaśyapa and Diti, seized the earth and plunged it into water. Viṣṇu, was requested by gods to lift the earth from the water. Viṣṇu, assuming the form of a Varāha, killed the demon with his tusks and lifted the earth which was submerged in water. In fighting with the demon, Varāha (Viṣṇu) had perspiration and the stream that trickled down from his high (*tuṅga*) left tusk became the Tuṅgā river, and the stream coming from his right tusk which was firm and steady (*bhadra*) became the river Bhadrā. A third stream flowing from his eye became the river Netravatī.

There is another legend connected with this river:

There was a demon named Guha. He performed penance to propitiate Brahmā. He obtained a boon from him that neither Viṣṇu nor Śiva should be able to kill him. After obtaining the boon, Guha started persecuting gods and men. Because of the boon, it was necessary for Viṣṇu and Śiva to have a combined form. They became Harihara. It is stated that the Harihara *avatāra* took place at Kudlur where the river Tuṅgabhadrā meets the river Haridrā. Demon Guha while being killed prayed that the place might be known after him. Therefore, the place is known as Guhāraṇya kṣetra.

The famous Śriṅgerī-maṭha is situated on the left bank of the river Tuṅgā. It is said that Śrī Śaṅkarācārya brought the image of Śāradāmbā (Sarasvatī) from Kashmir and founded here one of his four chief *maṭhas*.

The waters of river Tuṅgabhadrā are known as particularly very sweet. A saying goes that one should bathe in Gaṅgā but drink the water of Tuṅgabhadrā.

In the Rāmāyaṇa, the Tuṅgabhadrā is known as Pampā. Paṁpā is the same as Hampi. Hampi is famous as Paṁpā-kṣetra.

Geographical Details

The Tuṅgabhadrā is the chief tributary of the Kṛṣṇā. Tuṅgabhadrā is formed by the united waters of two rivers, Tuṅgā and Bhadrā. These two rivers meet at Kudli about 15 kms from Shimoga. Tuṅgā and Bhadrā rise from the Western Ghats at a place called Gaṅgāmūla. The Tuṅgā rises at Gangāmūla on the Varāha-parvata in the Kadul district. The source of this river is very close to that of Bhadrā.

The Tuṅgā flows in the north-east past Śriṅgerī and then by the side of Tirthahalli. Flowing past Shimoga, she comes to Kudli and meets the Bhadrā. For some distance near Mandagadde, the Tuṅgā is divided in seven streams.

The river Bhadrā also has her source in the Western Ghats at Gaṅgāmūla in the Varāha-parvata in Kadur district. Bhadrā flows in the north-east and meets Tuṅgā at Kudli.

The combined stream moves north-wards and reaches Honnali which is situated on the left bank of the Tuṅgabhadrā. Honnali is the Bhāskarakṣetra. Leaving the town of Honnali, the river flows further north and receives rivers Choradi and Kumudvatī as her tributaries. The Tuṅgabhadrā then passes the town of Harihara which is situated on her right bank. After Harihara, the Tuṅgabhadrā meets the river Varadā.

After meeting the Varadā, the Tuṅgabhadrā flows past Hamphi which is also called Vijayanagar or Vidyanagar. Thereafter, she receives the Vedavatī (or Huggari). Then she passes by the town of Kurnool and joins the river Kṛṣṇā a few kilometres beyond the town Kurnool in Andhra Pradesh.

Tributaries

1. Two streams, Tuṅgā and Bhadrā, join to the north-east of Shimoga to form the river Tuṅgabhadrā.
2. Choradi joins Tuṅgabhadrā near Harihara.
3. Kumudvatī from the left to the west of Harihara.
4. The Haridrā near Kudlur. It is believed that the incaranation Harihara took place at this junction to kill the demon Guha.
5. Varadā meets the Tuṅgabhadrā from the left a little away from Harihara at Gulnath. There is a legend about the river Varadā. Śiva had cut off one of the five heads of Brahmā. In order to atone for the sin, Śiva started a severe penance on the Varadamūla hill. The penance was so severe that it would have consumed the world by its heat. Viṣṇu therefore poured the water of the Bhāgīrathī on the head of Śiva. A river flowed as the result which was named Varadā.

6. The river Vedavatī (or Huggari) from the right to the north of Sirguppa.

Tuṅgaveṇā

She is mentioned in MBh, Āraṇyakaparva, 3.212.24 fn. This river may be the same as the Tuṅgabhadrā mentioned above.

Uśīrā

The Uśīrā rises from the Himavat (Vāmanp. 13.21). According to Dey, Uśīragiri is the name of the Siwalik hills, or the hills at Haridwar through which the Gaṅgā flows down on the plains. Therefore, Uśīrā may be the name of the Gaṅgā in that region.

Utpalāvatī

The river Utpalāvatī rises from the mt. Malaya (Kūrmp. I.46.37; Matsyp. 114.30; Varāhp. 85; Vāyup. 45.105). In the Matsyp and Vāyup, she is mentioned with the rivers Kṛtamālā and Tāmraparṇī.

Dey opines that she is the modern river Vypar in Tinnevelly.

Vadhūsarā

The river Vadhūsarā rises from the Himavat (Vāmanp. 13.22). MBh, Ādiparva, 1.5;6 narrates a legend about the origin of the river Vadhūsarā:

Pulomā was the wife of Ṛṣi Bhṛgu. Once Bhṛgu went for bath. Seeing his wife Pulomā alone in the hermitage, a demon named Puloma came in the guise of a Varāha and kidnapped her. (Puloma had earlier wanted to marry her but her father had refused, and she was married to Bhṛgu). At the time of kidnapping, Pulomā was pregnant. Her foetus fell on the ground and thereby Cyavana (from *cyu* 'to slip, drop down') was born. The lustre of the fallen *garbha* killed the demon. Pulomā wept for her misfortune, and a great river flowed from her tears. Brahmā named it as Vadhūsarā.

Vadhūsarā is a sacred river. When the lustre of Paraśurāma had been dimmed by the arrow of Rāma (See the legend in MBh, Āraṇyakaparva, 3.97.27, Appendix 1.14.77), he regained it only after bathing in the river Vadhūsarā.

Vaihāyasī

She is mentioned in Bhāgp. 5.19.18. Dey opines that the river Vaihāyasī is the same as the river Vegavatī which he identifies with the Vaigā or Vygī in Tamil Nadu. The town Madurai is situated on the bank of this river. (See Vegavāhinī mentioned below).

There are two rivers bearing the name Vegavatī in south India. One of them flows near Kāñcipuram in Chingalput district of Tamil Nadu. The other rises in the Palni hills and flows past Madurai into the Bay of Bengal.

This river, popularly known as Vaigai, is called Kṛtamālā in later Sanskrit literature. (See also under Kṛtamālā).

Vaitaraṇī

The river Vaitaraṇī rises from the Ṛkṣa (Kūrmp. I.46.34; Matsyp. 114.27; Vāmanp. 13.28; Varāhp. 85; Vāyup. 45.102; Mārkp. 57.24).

She is a sacred river (MBh, Āraṇyakaparva, 3.81.70; 83.6). She removes sins. Gaṅgā is known as Vaitaraṇī in the Pitṛloka (MBh, Ādi-parva, 1.158.19). Even Dharma is said to have performed sacrifices on the bank of the river Vaitaraṇī (MBh, Āraṇyakaparva, 3.114.4).

The Vaitaraṇī is a mythical as well as a terrestrial river. She is identified with the present river Bytarani which rises in the southern part of the district Singhbhum and flows to the north of Orissa. She empties herself into the Bay of Bengal at Dharma.

As a mythical river, Vaitaraṇī flows in the realm of Yama (MBh, Bhīṣmaparva, 6.55.125; 99.38; Droṇaparva, 7.146.47). It is said that she is very difficult for sinners to cross (MBh, Ādiparva, 1.158.19; Udyogaparva, 5.107.14; Śāntiparva, 12.290.31; Mausalaparva, 16.6.10; Svargārohaṇa-parva, 18.3.4). The river is full of pus, fat, blood, and senews (Mārkp. 8.217). She flows at the door of Yama's palace and is 100 *yojanas* long (Garuḍp. II.35.1). Sinners are filled with terror just by a mere sight of this horrible river (Skandp, Revākhaṇḍa, 159.56). About the origin of this river, Kālikp. 18.93 relates the following story.

Śiva was too much agrieved by the death of Pārvatī in Dakṣa's sacrifice. He was sighing heavily, so much so that a mass of vapour issued forth from his body and flowed down. It was named as Vaitaraṇī.

The Adbhuta-Rāmayāṇa 10.5; 6 mentions that the river Vaitaraṇī rose from the tears of Rāma when he was crying and searching for Sītā.

Dharma-sindhu, p. 648 prescribes a rite in which a cow is donated which enables the performer to cross the river.

Kane (HoD, Vol. V, Pt. I, p. 418) provides details of Vaitaraṇī-vrata. The *vrata* commences on Mārgaśīrṣa (Dec.-Jan), Kṛṣṇapaksa, Ekādaśī (which is called Vaitaraṇī Ekādaśī), and continues for a year. The performer should worship a dark cow from its front foot to its tail, apply sandal-wood paste to its body, wash its feet and horns with water scented with sandal-wood paste and worship its limbs. This *vrata* is for one year in three parts of four months each in which *Naivedya* of boiled rice, cooked barley and *Pāyasam* is offered respectively in four months from Mārgaśīrṣa, in four months from Caitra, and in four months from Śrāvaṇa. One third of each *Naivedya* is given to the cow, to the priest, and to the performer. At the end of one year, gifts of bed-stead and a golden cow to the priest and one droṇa of iron are given to the priest.

The modern river Baitarani rises from the Keonjhar Plateau. She flows north-eastward and turns to south-east. She empties herself into the Bay of Bengal to the east of Chandbali. She has three tributaries, Khirani, Deo, and Salandi.

Vāluvāhinī

She rises from the mt. Ṛkṣa (Kūrmp. I.47.33; Vāyup. 45.100). she is identified with the river Bāgin in Bundelkhand which is a tributary of the Yamunā (Dey).

Vaṁśadharā

This river rises from the mt. Mahendra (Vāyup. 45.106). According to Dey, this is a river in Ganjam district in Orissa. Kalingapatanam is situated on her bank.

She is also known as Vaṁśadhāriṇī (Kūrmp. I.47.39). In Mārkp. 57.29, she is mentioned as Vaṁśakarā.

Vaṁśakarā, Vaṁśavarā, and Vaṁśadhāriṇī seem to be the variants of the same river.

Vañjulā

The Purāṇas do not agree on the origin of this river. According to Mārkp. 57.23, she rises from the Vindhya; according to Vāmanp. 13.22; 31.76 from the Śuktimat; according to Matsyp. 114.29; Varāhp. 85; and Vāyup. 45.104, she rises from the mt. Sahya. Vāyup. 45.100 has another river Jaṁbulā which rises from the Ṛkṣa. However, all these mountains are parts of the Vindhyas.

Sircar and Dey identify Vañjulā with the modern river Mañjīrā which is a southern tributary of the Godāvarī. She rises from the Balaghat range of the Western Ghats and, flowing south-east, meets the river Godāvarī to the east of Kandalwadi.

Vaṅkṣu

The river Vaṅkṣu (MBh, Anuśāsanaparva, 13.151.17) is also known by the name of Cakṣu. She is the modern river Oxus (Amu Daria). (See also Raṅkṣu above).

Oxus rises from the Victoria lake in the southern Pamirs (ancient Meru) on the Russian-Afghanistan border. It is known there as Pamir river which meets the river Wakhan Darya to the west of Qala Panj. After her junction with the Wakhan, she is known as Pyandzh. She flows through the Wakham range and near Ishkamish takes a sharp turn towards north. She turns again first south and then west. Then she turns in north-westerly direction from Khamiab and finally falls into the Aral Sea.

She receives tributaries like Shakh Darya, Gunt, Bartang, Yazzulam and Vanch on her right bank and a minor stream Shivā on her left bank. Further down she meets Yakṣu before her junction with her most important right bank tributary Vakhsh. The combined waters of the Vakhsh and the Panj are called the Amu Daria or the Oxus. Thereafter, the major tributaries like the Nigam, Surkhan, and Shirabad meet her on the right bank while Kokcha and Kunduz from the left.

Varā

She is mentioned in MBh, Bhīṣmaparva, 6.12.25 fn. Dey identifies the river Varā with the Varaṇā in Varanasi. (See Varaṇā below).

Varadā

The Varadā is a sacred river. A bath in her waters gives

benefits of donating one thousand cows (MBh, Āraṇyaka-parva, 3.83.31). She is the same as the modern river Wardha which rises in the Mahādeva hills and joins the Vaingaṇgā.

There is a legned about the origin of this river:

Śiva had cut off one of the five heads of Brahmā. In order to perform *prāyaścitta*, Śiva started performing a severe penance on the Varadamūla hill. The penance was so severe that it would have consumed in its flame the entire universe. Viṣṇu therefore poured the waters of Bhāgīrathī from his conch over the head of Śiva on the Varadamūla hill and it is said that this gave rise to the river Varadā.

At present there are two rivers by the name Varadā.

1. The first Varadā (modern Wardha) rises from the Betual plateau at 810 metres altitude to the east of the source of the river Tāpī. She flows southwards initially and then south-eastward to join Waingaṇgā from the right near Seoni. The combined flow of Varadā and Waingaṅgā below Seoni is known as Prāṇahitā.

Tributaries

1. Jam from the left to the south of Mowar.
2. Bembla from the right to the south of Pulgaon.
3. Asoda from the left to the north of Wadki.
4. Wunna from the left to the east of Wadki.
5. Erai from the left to the south of Chandrapur.
6. Pengaṅgā from the right to the south of Ghugus.

2. The second Varadā rises from the Western Ghats north of Anantpur, and meets the Tuṅgabhadrā east of Karajgi. She receives a tributary Dharmā from the left to the south of Bankpur.

Varaṇā

Vāmanp. 3.27;28 mentions that the river Varaṇā flowed

from the right foot of Yogaśāyī, a form of Viṣṇu, who lives in Prayāga. From his left foot flowed the river Asi. Vārāṇasī lies between these two rivers (Liṅgp. I.92; Padmp. Ādikhaṇḍa, 1.33-37; Matsyp. 180-185). Vāmanp. 16 narrates the following legend:

Once the sun destroyed the city of Sukeśī who was a pious devotee of Śiva. Śiva, by way of helping Sukeśī, looked at the sun who, as the result of that gaze, came down rolling. On the way, the Ṛṣis advised him to fall on the land of Hara, i.e., Vārāṇasī between the rivers Varaṇā and Asi. The sun fell there and rolled between these two rivers until Brahmā propitiated Śiva who came there and raised the sun up in the sky. Therefore, the sun received the name Lola. See also Vāmanp. 57.30; 31.

Varṇāśā

She is also known by the name of Parṇāśā or Parṇā.

The Parṇāśā rises from the mt. Pāriyātra (Kūrmp. I.17.31; Brahmāṇḍap. I.16-28; Vāyup. 45.97). She is identified with the river Banas in Rajasthan.

There is another river of the same name rising near Abu and falling into the Gulf of Kutch.

Varuṇā

She is mentioned in MBh, Bhīṣmaparva, 6.10.30 fn. She is presumably the same as river Varaṇā mentioned above.

Vasaukasārā

The Vasaukasārā is one of the seven streams of the Gaṅgā (Rām., Ayodhyākāṇḍa, 2.88.26; MBh, Āraṇyakaparva 3.186.94; Bhīṣmaparva, 6.7.45). Some Purāṇas (Matsyp. 121.40; Vāyup. 47.38) read Nalinī in place of Vasaukasārā which is one of the eastern streams of the Gaṅgā. (See also under Nalinī).

Vāsiṣṭhī

In MBh, Āraṇyakaparva, 3.82.43; she is mentioned with Ṛṣikulyā. It is said about her that anyone who goes to the river Vāsiṣṭhī becomes a Brāhmaṇa irrespective of his original caste.

The Vāsiṣṭhī is a branch of the river Godāvarī. Below Rajahmundry, the Godāvarī divides herself into two main streams, namely, the Gautamī Godāvarī in the east, and Vāsiṣṭhī Godavarī in the west.

Vedasmṛti

The Vedasmṛti rises from the Pāriyātra (Mārkp. 57.19; Bhāgp. 5.19.18; Matsyp. 114.24; Vāyup. 45.97; etc.).

Sircar identifies her with the river Besula in Malwa, a tributary of the river Sindh. Dey, however, identifies her with the river Baita which flows between the rivers Tons and Gomatī in Uttar Pradesh.

Vedaśruti

Rāma had crossed this river during his exile (Rām., Ayodhyākāṇḍa, 2.43.8). This river may be the same as Vedasmṛti mentioned above, for, the Rāmāyaṇa (Ayodhyā-kaṇḍa, 2.43.9) says that, after crossing Vedaśruti, Rāma crossed the river Gomatī.

Vedatrayī

This river rises from the mt. Pāriyātra (Varāhp. 85). (See under Vetravatī below).

Vedavatī

The Vedavatī rises from the Pāriyātra (Mārkp. 57.19). Dey identifies this river with the river Hagari, a tributary of the Tuṅgabhadrā in Bellary district.

Vedavatī rises in the form of two streams from the

Chandra Drona or Baba Budan mountain. The two streams are Veda and Avatī. Vedavatī joins the Tuṅgabhadrā from the right to the north of Sirgupta.

Vegavāhinī

This river rises from the Vindhyas (Mārkp. 57.23). She may be identified with the Vegavatī (modern Vaiga or Vygi) in Tamil Nadu. The town Madurai is situated on the bank of this river. Kāñcīpuram stands on the northern bank of this river. (See also Vaihāyasī above).

Veṇṇā

There are two rivers by the name Veṇṇā (also Veṇā or Suveṇā). Bhāgp. 5.19.18 has Veṇī; Mārkp. 57.19 has Veṇā.

1. The first Veṇṇā rises from the mountain Vindhya in the Seoni district of Madhya Pradesh (Matsyp. 114.27; Vāmanp. 13.28; Varāhp. 85). She joins the Wardha which later joins the river Prāṇahitā, a tributary of the Godāvarī. Sircar identifies the river Veṇṇā with the Waingaṅgā.

   The Veṇṇā is a sacred river. She grants the fruits of the Vājapeya sacrifice to the person who bathes in her water (MBh, Āraṇyakaparva, 3.83.31). A person who offers ablutions to gods and manes obtains a chariot drawn by peacocks and haṁsas (MBh, Āraṇyakaparva, 3.83.29).

2. The second Veṇṇā rises from the Mahabaleshvar hills in the mt. Sahya (Matsyp. 114.29; Kūrmp. I.46.36; Vāmanp. 13.20). Sircar identifies this Veṇṇā with the modern Varṇā which flows between the districts of Satara and Kolhapur (in the state of Maharashtra) and which is a tributary of the river Kṛṣṇā. The combined flow of the two rivers (Varṇā and Kṛṣṇā) is called Kṛṣṇaveṇā or Kṛṣṇaveṇī.

Veṇumatī

She rises from the mt. Pāriyātra (Matsyp. 114.24) where she is mentioned with the rivers Śiprā, Avantī, and Kuntī.

Veṇyā

Mārkp. 57.24 and 26 mentions this river twice. If they are two different rivers, they may be identical with the two Veṇṇās (I and II) mentioned above. Pargiter suggests the identification of Veṇyā which rises from the Sahya with the modern Pennar which flows between the Kṛṣṇā and the Kāverī. According to Vāyup. 45.102 (which has Veṇvā), she flows from the mt. Vindhya.

Vetravatī

She is mentioned in MBh, Āraṇyakaparva, 3.186.93; Kūrmp. I.46.31; Mārkp. 27.20; Matsyp. 114.23; Vāyup. 45.98).

She is the modern river Betwa which rises from the mt. Pāriyātra in the Vindhyas near Ubaidullaganj in Raisen district. She flows in north-eastern direction and joins the Yamunā from the right bank to the east of Hamirpur.

Tributaries

1. Halali from the left joins Betwa near Vidisha.
2. Nion from the right.
3. Bah from the left.
4. Sagar from the left to the west of Baroda.
5. Jamni from the right.
6. Dharan from the right.
7. Birma from the right.

Vipāśā

In the Ṛgveda she is known as Vipāś and in the post-Vedic Purāṇic texts as Vipāśā.

At present there are two rivers by the name of Vipāśā.

1. The first Vipāś is a Ṛgvedic river and, with Śutudri, forms part of the dialogue with Ṛṣi Viśvāmitra in the famous Nadī-saṁvāda hymn (ṚV 3.33). Vipāś occurs also in ṚV 4.30.11.

She is a very sacred river (MBh, Āraṇyakaparva, 3.130.8). The Vipāśā rises from the Himavat (Kūrmp. I. 46.29; Mārkp. 57.18; Varāhp. 85; Vāyup. 45.95).

Besides her terrestrial form, she is alluded to as a celestial river also. Indra crushed the chariot of Uṣas (ṚV 2.15.6; 10.138.5) which thereupon fell into the river Vipāś broken into pieces. (The destruction of the chariot of Uṣas by Indra is regarded as the extinction of her light after the sun-rise).

The meaning of the word *vipāś* is 'fetterless' (Nirukta 9.26). The Nirukta further says that the earlier name of Vipāś was Uruñjirā.

There is a legend as to why the river is called Vipāś:

Being agrieved by the murder of his sons, Vasiṣṭha tried to commit suicide. He tied himself with a rope and jumped into a river. The river cut the rope and saved his life. Hence she is known as Vipāś. (For the full story, see under Śutudri).

The qualities of her waters are the same as that of the Śatadru (=Śutudri above).

The famous temple of Amoghākṣī Devī stands on the bank of the river Vipāśā (Devībhp. 7.30.65).

The river Vipāśā is the same as the modern river Beas in Panjab which is a tributary of the Sutlej (Vedic Śutudri).

The river Beas rises from the Pir Panjal range near the Rohtang Pass in Lahoul at an elevation of about 4000 metres in the Kulu Valley. She flows south-eastward and crosses

Dhauldhar range at Larji. Then she flows westward and turns south to east of Gurdaspur. Finally, she joins the Sutlej at Harike in Panjab.

She has a large number of tributaries such as, Parbati, Harda, Sainz, Tirthan, Uhl, Baner, Gaj, Suketi, Luni, Awa, Banganga, Manuni, Chaki, etc.

2. The second Vipāśā rises from the Vindhyas (Mārkp. 57.22; Vāmanp. 13.26; Vāyup. 45.100).

According to Pargiter, she may be the modern river Bias which flows past Saugar in Madhya Pradesh and joins the river Ken, a tributary of the Yamunā at her right bank. He suggests another river. This Vipāśā may be the Sarasvatī Viśālā (modern Lilājana) at Bodhgaya (Mārkp. 57.22 fn).

Viṣṇu lives in the river Vipāśā in the form of Dvijapriya (Vāmanp. 63.4).

Virajā

Virajā rises from the mt. Ṛkṣa (Varāhp. 85). She is a sacred river and by bathing in this river one goes to the Brahmaloka (Kūrmp. II.35.26).

Kane opines that she is a river in Orissa.

Vīriṇī

She is mentioned in MBh, Āraṇyakaparva, 3.185.6. Manu was practising penance on this river when the fish of the famous legend of deluge approached him (MBh, Āraṇyakaparva, 3.185 describes the Matsyopākhyāna).

Viśālā

The Viśālā is one of the seven streams of the Sarasvatī (MBh, Śalyaparva, 9.37.4).

Once king Gaya, while performing a sacrifice at Gayā, thought of sarasvatī. The river appeared before him and was known as Viśālā (MBh, Śalyaparva, 9.37.19).

According to Kūrmp. I.47.33; Brahmāṇḍp. I.16.31, she rises from the mt. Ṛkṣa. Pargiter identifies her with the modern river Līlājana (Mārkp. 57.22 fn under Vipāśā). However, Dey identifies her with a tributary of Gaṇḍaka in Vaisali.

Viśalyā

The river Viśalyā rises from the mt. Amarkaṇṭaka in Kalingdesh (Brahmāṇḍap. II.13.12; Vāyup. 77.12). She is a branch of the Narmadā. The confluence of the Viśalyā and Narmadā is regarded full of sanctity. A person who observes fast for a day and bathes there liberates a hundred generations (Matsyp. 186.46). Rudraloka is obtained by a person who stays on her bank (Kūrmp. 40.27-30; MBh, Anuśāsanaparva, 13.151.15.

The river Viśalyā is famous for her sacredness in three worlds. A person who offers worship to manes and gods on her bank obtains the fruit of the Agniṣṭoma sacrifice (Garuḍp. 83.50).

Viśvāmitrā

This river is mentioned in MBh, Bhīṣmaparva, 6.10.25. She is the modern river of the same name which flows in Gujarat. The city of Vadodara (Baroda) is situated on her bank.

Vitastā

Vitastā is a Ṛgvedic river (ṚV 10.75.5) She rises from the Himavat (Kūrmp. I.46.29; Mārkp. 57.17; Matsyp. 114.21; Vāmanp. 13.20) at the spot where Śiva had placed his feet at the time of killing the demon Jalodbhava who had fled to the Himālayas (Vāmanp. 55.30). Śiva had taken *cakra* and Viṣṇu *triśūla* for killing the demon.

Viṣṇu lives in the Vitastā in the form of Kumārila (Vāmanp. 63.7).

The Nirukta 9.26 explains Vitastā as 'not burnt', 'mighty', 'having high banks'. Durga, commenting on this, says that the fire called Vaidehaka consumed all rivers except Vitastā.

Kane prescribes Vitastā-pūjā. From Bhādrapada, Śukla 10, for seven days one should see, bathe in, drink the water of, worship, and contemplate on the river Vitastā who is deemed to be an incarnation of Pārvatī (or Umā, Kūrmp. II.44.4). Special worship at the confluence of the Vitastā and the Sindhu is prescribed (HoD, Vol V, pt. 1, 407).

The water of Vitastā is so clear that if a poppy seed is thrown in it, it will be visible till it reaches the bottom.

A legend says that the land of Kashmir was originally a lake called Satīsara, and the place around was called Satīdeśa. The river Vitastā is like the *sīmanta* line of the holy country flowing in the centre and dividing the country into two parts.

Another legend says that the serpent Vāsuki propitiated Viṣṇu and sought protection from Garuḍa. Vāsuki was provided a safe place in the Satīdeśa along with other *nāgas*. The Nīlanāga was made the king. He resided in the famous Verang fountain. A demon, Jalodbhava, also resided in Satīsara. He used to kill men and *nāgas*. The Nāga king propitiated Viṣṇu. Viṣṇu asked Ananta Nāga to pierce the hills round about so that the water in the Satīsara might flow away, the lake might become dry, and the demon might be killed. Umā herself became river Vitastā.

It is also held that the Matsyāvatāra and the Varāhāvatāra of Viṣṇu had taken place in this land. Viṣṇu became Matsya in Kashmir. The ship (*nau*) in which the creatures were carried in order that they may be saved from the deluge was in fact goddess Durgā and the ship was carried to the west of the Banhal Pass in the Pir Pantsal range to the highest snowy peak called Nau-bandhana-tīrtha. It is further believed that Viṣṇu took the incarnation of Varāha (boar) at Baramula which is the same as Varāhamūla on the Śūkarakṣetra and which is situated at a distance of about fifty kms from Śrīnagar on the right bank of Vitastā.

The Greek invader Alexander is said to have crossed the river Vitastā at a place identified with Jalapur in the Jhelum district, and there he had met king Puru.

Geographical Details

The Vitastā is known today as Jhelum. In Kashmir, she is known as Vetha. She has her source in Verinag in the upper end of Kashmir valley. She enters the Wular lake and leaves it near Sopar. After Muzzafarabad, she takes a sharp turn and flows in southerly direction. She enters the plains near the town of Jhelum in Pakistan, and joins the Chenab at Trimmu in Pakistan.

Tributaries

1. Liddar from right near Anantnag.
2. Sind from the right bank near Shadipur.
3. Kishangaṅgā from the right near Muzzafarabad.
4. Punch from the left at Dhangrol.
5. Kahan from the right below the town Jhelum.
6. Bunha from the right above Darapur.
7. Adpat, Bring, and Sandran near Khanabad.
8. Pohru after the Wular lake.
9. Vishav, Rembiva, Ramshi, Dudhaganga, and Suknag from the left bank.

Vrataghnī

She rises from the mt. Pāriyātra (Kūrmp. I.46.30). (See Vṛtraghnī mentioned below).

Vṛṣabhā

She is mentioned in MBh, Bhīṣmaparva, 6.10.31. This river may be the same as the river Somā, the fourth stream of the Gaṅgā which falls on the mountain Vṛṣabha. (See also under Somā and Gaṅgā).

In MBh, Bhīṣmaparva, 6.10.34, the river Vṛṣabhaṅginī may be the same as Vṛṣabhā.

Vṛtraghnī

The river Vṛtraghnī rises from the mt. Pāriyātra (Kūrmp. I.47.30; Matsyp. 114.23; Vāyup. 45.97). According to Sircar, she is the modern river Vatrak, a tributary of the Sabarmati in Gujarat. However, Dey identifies her with the river Vetravatī. (See Vetravatī mentioned above).

Yamunā

The river Yamunā is mentioned even in the Ṛgveda (ṚV 5.52.17; 7.18.19; 10.75.5). She flows from the Himālayas. She is a very sacred river (MBh, Āśramavāsikaparva, 15.30.16) and removes the fear of sin from the minds of people (MBh, Āraṇyakaparva, 3.125.22).

Yamunā is the daughter of the sun (Vāmanp. 37.69) and his wife Sanjñā. The Mārkp. 77.1 narrates the following story in this connection:

Saṅjñā was the wife of the sun. She however was not able to bear the lustre of her husband and used to close her eyes in his presence. The sun cursed her that, since she closed her eyes, her son would be the imprisoner of people. And thus Yama was born. Upon this Saṅjñā opened her eyes wide and looked at him boldly. The sun then said that, since she had looked at him with bold and agitated eyes, she would give birth to a daughter who would be known as Vilolā. The Yamunā is known also by the name Vilolā.

The Yamunā is linked with Kṛṣṇa who subdued the serpent Kāliya living in her waters (Bhāgp. 10.6; Harivaṁśap. 2.12; Viṣṇup. 5.7; Agnip. 12.18). The young days of Kṛṣṇa were passed on her banks. Kālindī is also the name of a wife of Kṛṣṇa.

Near the glacier from which river Yamunā rises, there are a number of hot springs.

The waters of the river Gaṅgā are white while that of the Yamunā are black or blue. At Prayāga where the two rivers meet, one can distinguish the white and blue waters of the Gaṅgā and Yamunā.

A person, desirous of a son should bathe in the Yamunā on each Śrāvaṇa- nakṣatra for a year. He will get a son like Parāśara, son of Śakti and grandson of Vasiṣṭha.

Kane (HoD, Vol V, Pt. 1, p. 372) mentions that Mārga-śīrṣa, Śukla 12, is called Malladvādaśī. On the banks of Yamunā, Kṛṣṇa sported at the foot of Bhāṇḍīra-vaṭa on Govardhana hill amidst cowherds who were wrestlers, and Gopīs. Even today wrestlers worship Kṛṣṇa with flowers, milk, curds, and edibles for one year on each 12th. The reward is health, strength, prosperity, and Viṣṇuloka.

Yamunā called her brother Yama for dinner on the second day of the bright half of the month of Kārtika and Yama being highly satisfied with the sumptuous dinner blessed Yamunā that whoever being a brother takes a dinner at his sister's place on the second day of the bright half of the month of Kārtika would enjoy eternal happiness.

One who worships god Janārdana on the bank of the river Yamunā at Mathurā on the 12th of the bright half of Jyeṣṭha (June-July) and offers *piṇḍas* to ancestors acquires great merits.

Viṣṇu lives in the Yamunā in the form of Śrīkaṇṭha

(Vāmanp. 63.26). In Prayāga, Yamunā is looked after by the sun (Kūrmp. I.36.23).

The following tīrthas are situated on the banks of the river Yamunā:

1. Agni-tīrtha (Kūrmp. I.39.4; Padmp. Ādikhaṇḍa, 1.45.27; Matsyp. 108.27).
2. Anaraka-tīrtha (Kūrmp. I.39.5-6; Padmp. Ādikhaṇḍa, 1.27.56).
3. Madhuvana (Kūrmp. II.36.9; Viṣṇup. I.12.2-4).
4. Ṛṇapramocana-tīrtha (Kūrmp. I.38.14-16).

(For other tīrhtas see under Gaṅgā also).

The qualities of the waters of Yamuna are; 1. tastefulness, 2. generator of wind, 3. digestiveness, 4. generator of heat, 5. aggreeableness, 6. giver of strength.

The following are the texts which eulogize and pray to Yamunā:

1. Yamunāṣṭaka by Śaṇkarācārya.

2. Prayāga-māhātmya, Kūrmp. I. 36-39; II.35.

Geographical Details

The river Yamunā rises from the Himālayas about twelve kms to the west of Bandarpunch. About six kms from the glaciers from which the river Yamunā rises is the temple of Jamunotrī having an image of goddess Yamunā. About the name Bundarpunch, the legend says:

The monkey chief Hanumān had gone to Laṅkā in search of Sītā. He had set fire to Laṅkā with his burning tail and, after putting Laṅkā on fire, Hanumān leaped on to the peak of Bundarpunch and there he extinguished the fire in his tail.

The Yamunā after flowing in south-westerly direction up to Banog in Himachal Pradesh turns westward. While passing through the Siwalik hills, she meets the river Tons at right bank near Kalsi and emerges from the Siwalik range at Khera which is about 150 kms from the source of the river Yamunā.

The rivers Giri and Betwa join the Yamunā upstream and downstream of Poonta. Then Yamunā flows south-eastwards and joins the Gaṅgā at Prayāga.

The place from which Yamunā rises is also known as Kalinda mountain. Therefore, Yamunā is also called Kalinda-Kanyā or Kālindī.

Tributaries

1. Tons from the right at Kalsi.
2. Giri from the right above Poonta.
3. Ason from the left near Poonta.
4. Katha from the left to the west of Kairana.
5. Hindana from the left near Dankaur.
6. Uttangan (Bāngaṅgā) from the right.
7. Chambal from the right.
8. Kunwari from the right.
9. Sind from the right.
10. Betwa from the right near Hamirpur.
11. Non from the left.
12. Rind from the left.
13. Ken from the right.
14. Baghain from the right.
15. Paisuni from the right.

ABBREVIATIONS AND BIBLIOGRAPHY

A. Primary Sources

ĀśŚS — *Āśvalāyana-Śrauta-Sūtra,* Anandashram Sanskrit Series, Pune, 1917.

AV — *Atharva-Veda-Saṁhita,* VVRI, Hoshiarpur, 1960-64.

Bhāgp — *Bhāgavata-Purāṇa,* Gita Press, Gorakhpur.

Brahmp — *Brahma-Purāṇa,* Anandasharam Sanskrit Series, Pune, 1885.

BrahmVP — *Brahmavaivarta-Purāṇa,* Anandasharama Sanskrit Series, Pune, 1935.

Devībhp — *Devībhāgavata-Purāṇa,* (Ed.) Ramtej Pandey, Varanasi, 1963.

Dharma-Sindhu (With Marathi Com.), Kashinath Sastri Upadhyaya, Shri Gajanan Book Depot, Pune, 1979.

Garuḍp — *Garuḍa-Purāṇa,* (Ed.) Ramashankar Bhattacharya, Varanasi, 1964.

GB — *Gopatha-Brāhmaṇa,* (Ed.) Rajendrlal Mitra. Rep. Varanasi, 1972.

Godāvarī-Māhātmya — 1. Nasik, 1875.
2. Jñanadīpaka Press, Bombay (Mumbai), 1872.

JB — *Jaiminīya-Brāhmaṇa,* (Ed.) Raghuvira and Lokesh Chandra, Nagpur, 1954.

Kālikp — *Kālikā-Purāṇa,* Varanasi, 1972.

Kauśika-Sūtra M. Bloomfield, (Ed.) Rep. Delhi, 1972.

Kṛṣṇā-Māhātmya	Gangadharsastri Abhyankar, Virāj Vaibhava Press, Wai, 1885.
Kūrmp	*Kūrma-Purāṇa,* (Ed.) Ramashankar Bhattacharya, Varanasi, 1967.
Liṅgp	*Liṅga-Purāṇa*, Venkateshvar Press, Bombay, 1924.
ManuS	*Manusmṛti* with nine com. (Ed.) J.H. Dave, Bharatiya Vidya Bhavan, Bombay, 1972.
Matsyp	*Matsya-Purāṇa*, Anandashram Sanskrit Series, Pune 1981.
MBh	*Mahābhārata,* Cr. Edn., Bhandarkar Institute, Pune.
Narmadā-Māhātmya	Joglekar Sadashiva Atmaram, Prasad Prakashan, Pune, 1952.
Padmp	*Padma-Purāṇa*, Anandasharam Sanskrit Series, Pune, 1894.
PañcaviṁśaB	*Pañcawiṁśa-Brāhmaṇa* (Ed.) W. Caland, The Asiatic Society, Calcutta (Kolkata), 1982.
Payoṣṇī-Māhātmya	Ballal Tryambak, Sankar Printing press, Bombay, 1913.
Rām.	*Rāmāyaṇa*, Cr. edn., Baroda (Vadodara).
ṚV	*Ṛgveda-Saṁhitā,* Vaidika Samshodhan Mandlal Pune.
ŚB	*Śatapatha-Brāhmaṇa,* Laxmi Venkateshvar Press, Bombay, 1940.
Skandp	*Skanda-Purāṇa*, (Ed.) Mansukh Roy Mor, Calcutta.
Tāpī—Māhātmya	Arya Vijay Press, Poona, 1905.
Vāmanp	*Vāmana-Purāṇa,* All-India Kashiraj Trust, Varanasi, 1968. (SM = *Saromāhātmya* of Vāmanp.)
Varāhp	*Varāha-Purāṇa,* (Ed.) Hrishikesha Sastri, Bibliotheca Indica, Calcutta, 1888.
Viṣṇup	*Viṣṇu-Purāṇa*, Purāṇaprakashaka Mandali, Wai.

Viṣṇudhp — *Viṣṇudharmottara-Purāṇa*, 3rd Khanda, (Ed.) Priyabala Shah, Vadodara, 1958.

ViṣṇuSm — *Viṣṇu-Smṛti*, Chowkhamba Sanskrit Series, Varanasi, 1962.

B. Secondary Sources

Ali S.M. — *The Geography of the Purāṇas,* People's Publishing House, New Delhi, 1960.

Anne Feldhaus *Water & Womanhood*, Religious Meanings of Rivers in Maharashtra, Oxford University Press, 1995.

Bhargava P.L. *India in the Vedic Age*, D.K. Printworld (P) Ltd., New Delhi, 3rd Rev. Edn., 2001.

Cunningham *Ancient Geography of India*, Indological Book A. House, Rep. Varanasi, 1963.

Dave J.H. *Immortal India,* Bharatiya Vidya Bhavan, Bombay, 1991.

Dey N.L. *Geographical Dictionary of Ancient and Medieval India*, 3rd Edn., New Delhi, 1971.

Kane P.V. *History of Dharma-Śaśtra*, (HoD), Vols. IV & V, BORI, Pune.

Law B.C. (Ed.) 1. *Mountains and Rivers of India*, 21 International Geographical Congress, India, 1968, National Commitee for Geography, Calcutta, 1968.

2. *Historical Geography of Ancient India,* Oriental Book Reprint Corporation, Rep., New Delhi, 1984.

Pargiter F. *The Markaṇḍeya-Purāṇa*, (Eng. tr.), Rep., Eden.Varanasi, 1969.

Sircar D.C. 1. *Studies in the Geography of Ancient and Medieval India, Delhi*, 1960.

2. *Cosmography and Geography in Early Indian Literature, Calcutta*, 1967.

Sivaramamurti *Gaṇgā*, Orient Longman, New Delhi, 1976.

LIST OF MOUNTAINS

Agastya-hill	-	Southern part of the Western Ghats. Also known as Agasti-Kūṭa.
Amarakaṇṭaka	-	Name of that part of the Vindhya range which is near the source of the rivers Narmadā and Śoṇa. A part of the Mekala hills in the Gondawana region of Nagpur.
Arbuda	-	Mountain in the west of India. Modern mt. Ābu.
Brhamagiri	-	Part of the Sahyādri where Brahmā used to practise penance.
Citrakūṭa	-	A range of mt. Ṛkṣa near Prayāga.
Gandhamādana	-	Name of a mountain to the east of the Meru; renowned for its fragrant forests. Part of the Rudra Himāalyas.
Govardhana	-	A hill near Mathura and Vṛndāvana. Identified with the Nasik hills.
Hemakūṭa	-	Situated to the south of the mt. Meru. Identified with Bandarapuncha range of the Himālayas.
Hemaśṛṅga	-	Name of the mt. Sumeru.
Himālaya (= Himavat)	-	Situated to the south of the mt. Meru, east of the lake Aruṇoda, and south of the Mānasarovara. The mountain ranges from Sulaiman along the west Panjab and the whole of northern boundary of India up to Assam.
Kaliāsa	-	A peak of the Himālayas, residence of Śiva and Kubera. Pārijāta-vana is

	situated on the Kailāsa where Indra dwells.
Kesarācala -	Situated to the north of Mānasarovara, east of the lake Aruṇoda, west of the lake Asitoda, and south of the lake Mahābhadra.
Krauñca -	Part of Kailāsa on which Mānasarovara is situated.
Mahābaleshvara hills -	Part of the mount Sahya.
Mahendra -	Range of hills extending from the mouth of the Gaṅgā to the district of Madurai. There is also a peak called Mahendra-giri in the Ganjam distirct. It is believed that Hanūmān had jumped off to Laṅkā from this peak.
Malaya -	Name of a mountain range in south India. Identified with the southern part of the Western Ghats extending from Nilagiris to Kanyā-Kumārī. Abounds in sandal trees.
Mālyavān -	A mountain range to the west of the Meru. Identified with the Hindukush which starts from the north-western parts of the Himālayas and covers India, Pakistan, and north-eastern Afghanistan.
Mandara -	A portion of the Himālayas to the east of the Sumeru. Gods and demons used it as the churning rod when they churned the Kṣīrasāgara for Amṛta.
Mekala (Maikala) -	Part of the mt. Ṛkṣa in Gondawana.
Meru -	Also called Brahmapurī. Identified with the modern Pamirs. Said to consist of gold and gems.
Pāriyātra -	Western part of the Vindhya extending

(Pāripātra)		from the sources of the Chambala to the Gulf of Cambay. Modern Aravalli hills.
Puṣpagiri	-	Subramanya range of the Western Ghats. Part of the Malayagiri.
Ṛkṣa	-	Eastern part of the Vindhyas extending from West Bengal to the sources of the Narmadā and Śoṇa.
Sahya (Sahyādri)	-	Part of the Western Ghats to the north of the Travancore hills.
Śītāmta	-	A mountain in Jambūdvīpa inhabited by Yakṣas, Kinnaras, and Gandharvas. Pārijātavana of Indra is situated there.
Śṛṅgavān	-	Situated to the north of mt. Meru. It has three peaks (Śṛṅgāṇi). Eastern peak is brilliant like *sphaṭika* (crystal), southern peak shines like silver (rajata), and the central one glitters like gold.
Śuktimat	-	Southern portion of the Eastern Ghats including Garo Khasi and Tripura Hills (Pargiter) Portion of the Vindhya range which joins the Pāriyātra and the Ṛkṣa including the Hills of Gondawana, Chota Nagpur and the Mahendra range.
Supārśva	-	A mountain at the foot of mt. Meru.
Śvetagiri	-	A portion of the Himāalayas to the east of Tibet. Eastern part of mt. Meru.
Uśīragiri	-	Name of the Siwalik Hills. Hills at Haridvāra through which Gaṅgā flows.
Varāha-Parvata	-	Situated on the west of the lake Asitoda. Identified with a hill near Baramul in Kashmir.
Vindhya	-	The whole chain of hills from Gujarat to the Gaya distinct in Bihar lying both sides of the Narmadā.

INDEX OF RIVERS

A

Acchodā 1;2
Acchodakā 1;2
Acchodikā 1
Adapat 152
Adrijā 2;3
Adṛryā 3
Aheli 100
Airāvatī 3; 53; 55; 101
Aiyar 69
Ākāśagaṅgā 35
Alakanandā 4; 5; 7; 36; 85; 88; 116
Aler 73
Alinger 6; 75
Amarāvatī 69
Amarju 18
Aṁbumatī 5
Aṁbuvaśyā 5
Ami 14
Aṁśumatī 5; 6; 23
Amu Daria 53; 142
Anas 84
Aner 134
Anitabhā 6; 74
Ans 11
Antaḥśilā 6
Antaḥsirā 6; 7
Antaśilā 6
Antaśirā 6
Antyāgirā 6
Aosi 106
Āpagā 7
Aparā 30
Aparanandā 7
Āpayā 7
Argesan 87
Ārjikīyā 8; 128
Arkavatī 69
Aruṇā 8; 9; 10; 62; 64; 65; 80; 113
Aruṇāvatī 134
Asi 10; 144
Asiknī 10; 2; 23; 55; 86; 120
Aśmanvatī 11
Asnā 51
Asodā 143
Ason 156
Astor 122
Aśvanadī 11; 76
Aśvarathā 12
Aśvarathānadī 76
Atrai 12; 61; 134
Ātreyī 12
Avantī 12; 147
Avantīnadī-(Uttaravāhinī) 123
Avarṇī 12
Avatī 145
Awa 8; 149
Ayuk 7

B

Bahlā 70; 76

Baḍavā 12
Baghain 156
Bāgin 14; 141
Bāh 147
Bāhudā 13; 22; 125
Baigu 60
Baitā 145
Baitaraṇī 141
Balan 65
Balavāhinī 14
Bāluvāhinī 14
Bamani 24
Banas 24; 101; 126; 144
Banasi 101
Bandi 79
Baner 149
Bāngaṅgā 8; 100; 149
Banjar 96
Bañjulā 86
Barakar 26
Barhnadī 65
Barnā 97
Bartang 142
Barudi 21
Beas 122; 148
Beda 97
Bembla 143
Besu 45
Besula 145
Betwa 26; 98; 147; 156
Bias 149
Bhadrā 14; 37; 72; 135; 136; 137
Bhadramukhī 109
Bhāgā 10; 11; 23
Bhāgīrathī 4; 5; 29; 33; 37; 44; 56; 137; 143
Bhājwā 108
Bhakla 14
Bhāradvājī 14; 15; 22
Bhareli 21
Bhārgavī 81
Bhavānī 69
Bhīmā 15; 16; 17; 18; 23; 54; 72
Bhīmarathā 15
Bhīmarathī 15
Bhiundar Gaṅgā 4; 5
Bhogavatī 18
Bhotiā Kośī 64
Bhutnā 11
Bichlari 11
Bikar 130
Birahī Gaṅgā 5
Birma 147
Borai 82
Bori 18; 134
Brahmakulyā 76
Brāhmaṇī 7; 18; 19; 29; 80; 81
Brahmaṇī 18
Brahmaputra 19; 20; 21; 44; 61; 78; 88; 99; 125
Brahmaputrā 19; 78
Brahmaputrā-snāna 78
Bring 152
Bunha 152
Buray 134
Burhi Dihing 21
Burhi Gaṇḍaka 31; 45
Burhi Rāptī 14
Buriā Gaṇḍaka 30
Bytaraṇī 139

C

Cakṣu 36; 37; 142
Cakṣusī 22
Cakṣuṣmatī 21
Campā 84
Candanā 15; 22; 108; 125
Candrā 10; 11; 23
Candrabhāgā 10; 11; 16; 22; 23; 57; 87

Candrabhāgī 22
Candragiri 102
Candrikā 22; 23
Cankṣu 53
Carmaṇvatī 11; 12; 23; 24
Chaki 8; 149
Chambala 12; 23; 76; 98; 100; 101; 122; 123; 156
Chambla 24
Chanka 5 8
Chankeshar 97
Chautang 28
Chenab 3; 4; 10; 11; 22; 23; 87; 101; 102; 120; 122; 152
Chinnar 69; 81
Chirdā 51
Chitarevā 96
Chitratala 81
Chittar 131
Chordi 137
Choṭā Gaṇḍaka 53
Choṭa Tāwā 97
Chotī Kālīsindha 24
Citrā 25
Citrakūṭā 25
Citrarathā 25
Citraśilā 25
Citrotpalā 25
Cittutola 25
Coleroon 68; 69

D

Dakṣiṇa Gaṅgā 48; 65; 88
Dakṣiṇa Jāhnavī 130
Dāmodara 25; 26
Damudā 76
Damudvatī 76
Daśārṇā 26; 98
Dayā 81
Deeg 26
Degh 102
Deo 141
Deog 26
Dev 97
Devā 118
Devikā 26; 27; 30
Dhabalā 14
Dhanai 108
Dhanasiri 21
Dharan 147
Dharmā 143
Dhasan 26; 98
Dhaulī Gaṅgā 4
Dhavalā Gaṅgā 57
Dhavalī Gaṅgā 4; 5
Dhopāpā 28
Dhumalā 14
Dhusan 65
Dhūtapāpā 27
Dibang 19; 21
Digaru 21
Dihang 21
Dikhow 21
Dindi 73
Disang 21
Don 72
Droṇa 45
Dṛṣadvatī 8; 9; 28
Dṛśyādṛśyā 114; 115
Dūdhagaṅgā 29; 72; 152
Dūdha Kośī 64
Dudhī 96
Dudhnā 51
Dudhnai 21
Dugdhodā 29
Durgā 2; 29
Durgamā 29
Durgandhā 29

E

Eb 82
Erai 143

Eran 84
Erandi 97

G

Gaj 8; 149
Gambhīrà 29; 124
Gambil 74
Gaṇḍaka 30; 31; 45; 149
Gaṇḍakī 26; 29; 30; 31; 53; 109; 110; 135
Gandhakālī 31
Gandhavatī 31
Gaṅgā 2; 4; 5; 7; 12; 13; 14; 19; 21; 22; 25; 26; 27; 29; 31; 33; 34; 35; 37; 38; 39; 42; 44; 47; 49; 52; 53; 56; 57; 58; 60; 61; 62; 65; 71; 72; 77; 78; 80; 87; 88; 89; 90; 95; 99; 102; 104; 106; 110; 111; 113; 115; 117; 118; 121; 123; 124; 125; 128; 130; 138; ;139; 144; 153; 154; 156; (names of) 39; 43
Gaṅgan 106
Gaṅgī 45
Garra 106
Gaurī 45; 57
Gautamī 45-48
Gautamī Godāvarī 45; 50; 145
Gāyatrī 70
Ghaggar 102; 114; 115
Ghāgharā 45; 54; 118
Ghāghrā 14; 58; 117
Gharghara 125
Ghaṭaprabhā 72
Ghiranī 61
Ghod 17
Ghodahada 108
Ghogra 118
Ghonghī 14
Ghorband 128
Ghughrī 65
Gligit 122
Giri 156
Girnā 133
Godā 48
Godāvarī 18; 45; 46; 48-52; 87; 105; 142; 145; 146
Gogrā 118
Goi 97
Golan Lar 11
Gomai 134
Gomal 52; 87; 118
Gomatī 13; 27; 28; 44; 52; 87; 121; 126; 129; 145
Gopat 126
Gorī Gaṅgā 54; 58
Govardhinī 45
Great Devī 81
Guhiā 79
Guhiābālā 79
Gujatī 24
Gunjal 97
Gunt 142

H

Hagarī 145
Haimavatī 52; 119
Haimvatī 3
Hairanvatī 53
Halalī 147
Hallia 73
Hanle 121
Hanp 111
Hard 96
Hardā 149
Haridrā 136; 137
Hasdo 82
Hastimatī 109
Hatanī 97
Hathmatī 108
Hemavatī 69

Heran 97
Hindan 57; 58; 156
Hiran 96
Hiraṇvatī 53
Hiraṇya 125
Hiraṇyagāminī 109
Hiraṇyavāha 125
Hlādinī 37
Hooghly 26
Hrādinī 53
Huggarī 137
Hurla 8

I

Icchāmatī 61
Ikṣu 28; 53; 54; 106; 135
Ikṣumatī 22; 53; 54
Indramatī 8
Indrāvatī 51
Indrāyaṇī 16; 50; 54
Indus (Sindhu) 19; 52; 74; 75; 87;120
Irāvatī 3; 54; 87; 101
Iśānā 44
Iśvarī 55

J

Jāhnavī 37; 39
Jakam 84
Jalā 55
Jam 143
Jambū 55
Jambulā 56; 141
Jambūnadam 55
Jambunadī 37
Jambuneśvarī 61
Jamner 97
Jamni 147
Jawai 79
Jaxartes 106; 107; 124
Jayantī 56
Jhanji 21
Jhelam 11; 102; 122; 152
Jiriram 21
Johilā 57
Johillā 126
Jonk 81
Jotdar 81
Jumbū 56
Jyeṣṭhilā 56
Jyotirathā 56; 57; 60; 125; 128
Jyotirathyā 56
Jyotiṣmatī 57

K

Kabbanī 69
Kabul 6; 45; 74; 75; 122; 129
Kaḍvā 46; 50
Kagnā 18
Kahan 152
Kakudmatī 70; 71; 72
Kalapani 54; 57
Kālī 30; 44; 57; 58
Kālī Gaṅgā 57; 85
Kālikā 57
Kalinda-Kanyā 156
Kālindī 58;154
Kālīnadī 22; 53; 54; 57; 118
Kālīsind 24
Kālīsindha 98; 122
Kalmāśī 59
Kalyāṇa 52
Kalyāṇī 44
Kamalā 65
Kameh 75
Kaṁpanā 59
Kana 26
Kanahar 126
Kanar 97
Kāñcanākṣī 59; 113
Kandaleru 73
Kanhar 104
Kaorhari 76

Kapilā 59; 97
Kapiladhārā 59; 95
Kapilī 21
KapiñJalā 60
Kapivatī 60
Karam 97
Karamodā 60
Karjan 97
Karmanāśā 45; 60
Karatoyā 60; 61; 76; 109; 110; 134; 135
Kasai 69
Kashghar 124
Katha 156
Kathnā 52
Katjurī 81
Kauśikī 7; 10; 15; 22; 28; 61; 62; 64; 65; 69; 80; 125; 135
Kāverī 65; 66; 67; 69; 91; 147
Kelo 82
Ken 25; 85; 102; 104; 126; 129; 149; 156
Khān 124
Kharmer 96
Khīrā Gaṅgā 4;5
Khiranī 141
Khoh 106
Khonar 75
Kim-Arik 125
Kiṁpunā 59
Kinarsanī 51
Kiranā 62; 69
Kishangaṅgā 152
Kiul 108
Kizil-Su-Kashgar-Tarim 124
Koddam 51
Koel 99
Koka 125
Kokcha 142
Kolar 97
Konar 26
Kopā 70; 76
Kośā 69
Kosi 80
Kośī 45; 61; 64; 65; 80
Kosila 77
Koyākhāi 81
Koynā 70;72
Kṛpā 70
Krishṇai 21
Kṛṣṇā 15; 23; 29; 70; 71; 72; 73; 84; 127; 136; 137; 146
Kṛṣṇā Gaṅgā 57
Kṛṣṇa-Veṇā 73; 146
Kṛṣṇa-Veṇī 73; 146
Kṛṣṇa-Veṇyā 70; 73
Kṛtamālā 73; 105; 138; 139
Krumu 74; 121
Kṣatā 124
Kṣiprā 74; 123
Kuarī-nadī 127
Kubhā 6; 74; 75; 87; 121
Kuhū 75
Kui 100
Kulaṁpanā 59
Kulsi 21
Kumārā 75
Kumāradhārā 75
Kumārī 75; 76
Kumudvatī 76; 137
Kunar 75
Kunduz 142
Kuni 25
Kuntī 76; 147
Kunwari 156
Kūpā 76
Kuratī 61
Kurattee 109
Kurram 74; 122
Kuthi Yankti 54; 57

Kuṭikā 76; 77
Kuṭilā 77

L

Ladhiyā 54; 58
Lakku 64
Laknavaran 51
Lakṣmaṇatīrtha 69
Landoi 45
Lāṅgalī 77
Langhanī 77
Lāṅguliā 77
Lāṅgulinī 77
Lath 82
Lauhityā 78
Lidar kol 11
Liddar 152
Lik 79
Lilājana 149; 150
Lilri 79
Little Devī 81
Lohamatī 54
Lohavatī 58
Lohitā 21; 78; 135
Lohityā 76
Longar 75
Luhit 19
Luni 8; 44; 78; 79; 149
Lūpī 78;98

M

Machak 97
Madhuvilā 111
Madhyamāheśvara-Gaṅgā 85
Madi 30
Māgadhī 125
Mahā 103
Mahāgaurī 80
Mahākauśikī 64; 80
Mahākośī 80
Mahānada 104
Mahānadī 6; 25; 80; 81; 108; 110
111
Mahatī 82
Mahī 82; 83; 84
Mahodā 84
Mahodakī 84
Mahu 83
Malaprabhā 72; 84
Malavāsā 84
Maleni 24
Mālinī 84
Man 97
Māna 17
Mānagaṅgā 17
Manas 21
Mānasahradā 113
Mand 82
Mandagā 85
Mandākin 25; 85
Mandākinī 1;2;4;5;85; 86; 88
Mandagāminī 85
Mandavāhinī 85
Maner 51
Maṅgalā 50
Mangoi 45
Mañjīrā 142
Manjrā 51
Manju 86
Manjulā 86
Manneru 127
Manoharā 86; 113
Manorama 86; 113
Manuni 8; 149
Markand 28
Mārkaṇḍa 99
Mārkāṇḍa 115
Marudvṛdhā 86
Maruvardhanā 87
Maruvardwan 11
Mau 83
Meghnā 19; 44; 99

Mehatnu 87
Mehda 83
Mej 24
Mitri 79
Mohanā 104
Mūḷā 46; 51; 87
Mūḷā-Mūṭhā 16; 17
Mūlī 87
Mūlinī 87
Muneru 73
Mureru 51
Musi 73

N

Naḍvalā 87
Nairanjana 104
Nala 103
Nalinī 37; 87; 144
Nandā 7; 88; 110
Nandākinī 4;5
Nandinī 34
Narmadā 59; 60; 82; 88-92; 95; 96; 98;107; 125; 150
Nesu 134
Netravatī 135
Newuj 98
Nigam 142
Nīlā 97
Nilab 98
Nīlājana 104
Nim 58
Nion 147
Nīrā 17
Nirbindhyā 98
Niṣadhāvatī 98
Noa-Dihing 21
Non 156
Nun 81
Nūpī 79; 98

O

Oghavatī 99; 113
Ong 82
Or 97
Orsang 97
Oxus 11; 53; 106; 142

P

Paddair 99
Padmā 12; 19; 21; 35; 44; 87; 99
Pagladia 21
Paika 81
Paingaṅgā 50
Pairi 25; 81
Paisunī 85; 102; 104; 156
Palar 69
Palāśinī 99;100
Palleru 73
Palvar 69
Pambai 105
Pamir 142
Paṁpā 136
Pamuleru 51
Panan 84
Pañcagañgā 72
Pāṇḍu 44
Panj 142
Panjnad 11; 120
Panjhra 134
Panjkora 45; 129
Panjshir 75; 107
Pāpanāśinī 102
Pārā 100
Paras 99
Parbati 24; 100; 149
Parṇā 144; 100
Parṇāśā 100; 144
Pārvatī 8; 100
Paruṣṇī 3; 55; 86; 101; 128
Parwan 98
Paścima-Vāhinī-Gaṅgā (Mahī) 83
Pāvanā 37
Pāvanī 37; 102

Payasvinī 25; 102
Payoṣṇī 102; 103
Peddavugu 51; 73
Pengaṇgā 143
Pennar 147
Phalgu 104
Phalgunī 104
Phenā 52
Picchilā 22
Pindar 4; 5
Pindar Gaṅgā 4
Pippalī 104
Pippalaśroṇī 104
Pippalavatī 104
Piśācikā 104
Pitṛsomā 105; 107
Plakṣā 105
Plakṣajā 112
Plakṣavatī 105
Pohru 152
Prāṇahitā 50; 51; 143; 146
Pravarā 46; 51; 105
Praveṇī 105
Punch 152
Pūrnā 51; 102; 132; 133
Pūrṇabhābhā 61; 134
Puṣkara Sarasvatī 79
Puṣpajā 105
Puṣpajāti 105
Puṣpavatī 105
Pyandzh 142
Pyri 25

R

Raina 101
Rājanadī 83
Rakṣī 28
Rāmagaṅgā 14; 44; 60; 77; 106; 128
Ramshi 152
Rangit 106
Ramhā 106
Raṅkṣu 53; 106
Rāptī 14; 30; 110; 117
Rasā 6; 87; 106; 107; 121; 135
Ravi 3; 7; 11; 26; 53; 55; 86; 87; 101; 102; 122
Rembiva 152
Revā 88; 90; 91; 107
Rer 104
Rihand 126
Rind 156
Rohin 14
Rohiṇī 22
Ṛṣikulyā 76; 107; 134; 145
Ṛtumālā 73
Rudriyā 90

S

Sabar 108
Sabarī 50; 51
Sābarmatī 22; 29; 108; 109; 153
Sābhramatī 108; 109
Sadānīrā 61; 109; 110; 120
Sadānīramayā 61; 110
Sagar 147
Sāgaramatī 79
Sai 52; 129
Śailodā 22; 110
Śailodakā 22
Sainjā 8
Sainz 149
Sakri 110; 111
Sakṛnnandā 110
Śakulī 110
Salandi 141
Śālūkinī 111
Samaṅgā 111
Sandhyā 111
Sandran 152
Śaṅkha 18
Śaṅkhoddhāra 90

Sankosh 21
Saptakauśikī 64
Saraisindhu 4
Sarasvatī 4; 8; 9; 10; 13; 18; 28; 35; 37; 44; 57; 59; 79; 86; 88; 89; 95; 99; 102; 105; 108; 111; 112; 113; 114; 115; 116; 126; 127; 128; 149
Śarāvatī 117
Sarayū 26; 52; 53; 54; 57; 58; 74; 110; 117; 118; 126; 129
Śatadru 53; 118-121; 125
Satīrā 120
Satna 130
Saurā 62; 65; 69
Sāvitrī 70
Selye 122
Seonath 81; 110; 111
Seti 30
Setikā 109
Shakh Daria 142
Shakkar 96
Sharada 28; 54; 58
Sher 96
Shigar 122
Shinsa 69
Shirabad 142
Shiv 51
Shivā 142
Shudi 11
Shylok 122
Siddhā 51
Sighnā 22
Śilāmā 120
Silari 81
Silgi 96
Sina 18
Sind 152; 156
Sindh 145
Sindha 127
Sindhare 96
Sindhu 6; 11; 37; 74; 98; 121; 125; 128; 151
Sindphaṇā 51
Sindhuparṇā 122
Sindhuphenā 52
Singgekhabab 121
Singra 21
Sinīvālī 122
Śiprā 24; 31; 74; 98; 122; 123; 124; 147
Śiphā 129
Sir-daria 124
Siritoi 118
Sītā 2; 22; 35; 36; 37; 124; 155
Śītānta 124
Sohan 122; 128
Somā 36; 125; 153
Somodbhavā 91
Son 84; 125; 128
Śoṇa 15; 22; 45; 56; 57; 60; 83; 104; 110; 125; 126
Sondur 81
Soner 96
South Koel 18
Spiti 120
Sthāṇumatī 126
Subansiri 21
Sugarva 65
Suketi 8; 149
Sūkhā 81
Suknag 152
Sukrī 79
Śuktimatī 126
Sukumārī 76; 127
Sumāgadhī 125
Sunkośī 61; 64; 65
Suprabhā 113; 127
Suprayogā 127
Suranadī 77

Surasā 127
Surathā 57; 127
Surkhab 75
Surkhan 142
Sursooty 114
Suruli 74
Susartu 87; 121; 128; 135
Suṣomā 125; 128
Sutlej 8; 10; 11; 19; 101; 114; 120; 122; 148; 149
Sūtpalāvatī 128
Śutudri 10; 118; 128; 148
Suvāmā 128
Suvarṇarekhā 100
Suveṇā 146
Suveṇu 113; 128
Suwan 128
Svacchodā 2
Śvetyā 87; 121; 128; 129; 135
Śvetyāvarī 128
Swat 45; 75; 129
Syandikā 129
Śyenī 129

T

Tagdumbash 124
Talperu 51
Tamasā 44; 129
Tāmasī 129
Tamba Kosī 64
Tambar 64; 65
Tamir 125
Tamour 62
Tāmrā 64; 130
Tāmraparṇī 130; 131; 138
Tāmravarṇā 130
Tāmravarṇī 131
Tāmravatī 130
Tamur 80
Tanshkand Daria 125
Tapatī 132
Tāpī 132; 133; 143
Tāptī 98; 102; 132
Tarim 124
Tawa 97
Tawi 11; 101
Teesta 134
Tel 82
Temur 96
Tendoni 97
Tikkirā 7; 19
Tilbeh 65
Tiliyā 135
Tirthan 8; 149
Tirumanimattar 69
Tista 61; 106
Tribhāgā 105; 107; 134
Tridivā 134
Trisāmā 105; 107; 134
Trisrotā 12; 61
Trisrotasī 134
Triyāmā 105; 107; 135
Tṛṣṭāmā 121; 135
Tṛṣṭāmayā 87
Tṛtīyā 135
Tsango 19; 21
Tochi 74
Tons 25; 44; 85; 102; 104; 130; 145; 156
Tuṅgā 72; 135; 136; 137
Tuṅgabhadrā 72; 76; 135-138; 143; 145; 146
Tuṅgaveṇā 138

U

Uhl 8; 149
Uniar 11
Unner 96
UpaJalā 55
Uri 97
Uruñjirā 148
Uśīrā 138

Utpalāvatī 138
Uttangan 156

V

Vadhūsarā 138
Vaghur 133
Vaigā 139; 146
Vaigai 73; 74; 139
Vaihāyasī 139
Vaingaṅgā 143
Vaitaraṇī 18; 29; 139; 140
Vākī 134
Vakhsh 142
Valkinī 109
Vāluvāhinī 141
Vaṁśadharā 107; 141
Vaṁśadhāriṇī 141
Vaṁśakarā 141
Vaṁśavarā 141
Vanch 142
Vaṅkṣu 53; 106; 142
Vañjulā 56; 86; 141; 142
Varā 142
Varadā 137; 142; 143
Varaṇā 10; 44; 142; 143; 144
Varṇā 72; 73; 146
Varṇāśā 100; 144
Varuṇā 144
Vasaukasārā 144
Vāsiṣṭhī 145
Vāsiṣṭhī Godāvarī 45; 50; 145
Vasvokasārā 37
Vatrak 153
Veda 71; 146
Vedagaṅgā 72
Vedasmṛti 145
Vedaśruti 129; 145
Vedatrayī 145
Vedavatī 137; 138; 145; 146
Vegavāhinī 146
Vegavatī 73; 139; 146
Vel 16
Veṇā 70; 73; 146
Veṇṇā 73; 146; 147
Vennar 69
Veṇumatī 147
Veṇvā 73; 147
Veṇyā 70; 146
Vetha 152
Vetramatī 109
Vetravatī 147; 153
Vettara 69
Vilolā 153
Vimalodā 113
Vipāś 8; 119
Vipāśā 8; 147; 148
Virajā 149
Vīriṇī 149
Virupa 81
Viśālā 113; 149
Viśalyā 97; 150
Vishav 152
Viṣṇupadī 35; 77
Viśvāmitrā 60; 150
Vitastā 86; 120; 121; 150; 151; 152
Vraja 67
Vrataghnī 152
Vṛddhā Gaṅgā 49
Vṛṣabhā 153
Vṛṣabhaṅginī 153
Vṛtraghnī 153
Vypar 138
Vygi 139; 146

W

Waingaṅgā 50; 143;; 146
Wakhan Darya 142
Wān 51
Wana Toi 52
Wardha 50; 143; 146
Wira 73
Wunna 143

Y

Yakṣu 142
Yamunā 6; 12; 14; 23; 24; 25; 28; 38; 44; 55; 58; 59; 85; 89; 95; 102; 104; 111; 114; 115; 121; 126; 127; 141; 147; 149; 153; 154; 155; 156
Yarkand 14; 124
Yazzulam 142
Yenna 71; 73
Yerla 72

Z

Zaskar 122
Zhob 52

INDEX OF TĪRTHAS & TEMPLES

A

Ādiraṅgam 68
Agastyāśram 92
Agni-tīrtha 109; 155
Ahalyā-tīrtha 48; 92
Akhaṇḍeśvara 103
Akolla 92
Alandi 16; 54
Aṁbarīśvara 133
Amoghākṣī Devī 148
Aṅgirasa-tīrtha 92
Anantaraṅgam 68
Anaraka-tīrtha 92; 155
Anasūyā temple 91
Apsareśa-tīrtha 92
Aṣṭasaubhāgya-tīrtha 103
Aśva-tīrtha 39; 48; 62; 92
Aśvakrānta-tīrtha 20
Aśvī-tīrtha 21; 133
Auśanasa-tīrtha 116
Avaidhavya-tīrtha 103
Avimukta-tīrtha 39; 123
Ayodhyā 14; 15; 25; 53; 60; 77; 117

B

Badarikāśrama 4
Badarīnātha 4; 5; 116
Baḍavā temple 12
Bāṇa tīrtha 48; 92
Bhadrācalam 48
Bhadrakarṇa tīrtha 92
Bhadreśvaratīrtha 92
Bhāskara-kṣetra 137
Bhīmāśaṅkara 15; 17
Bhīmeśvara-tīrtha 92
Bhṛgutuṅga-tīrtha 31
Bhū Devī 131
Bhūteśvara 39
Bilvaka-tīrtha 48
Brahma-tīrtha 39; 48; 92
Brahmeśvara-liṅga 92
Bṛhadīśvara temple 69

C

Camasodbheda 115; 116
Cambay 83
Candra-tīrtha 40; 92
Carmākhya-tīrtha 40
Changadeva 132
Chidambaram 68; 69
Citrāṅgadeśvara 40

D

Dakṣiṇa Kāśī 131
Daṇḍāraṇya 48
Darbheśvara-tīrtha 133
Daśāśvamedhika-tīrtha 40; 48; 92
Daurvāsika-tīrtha 40
Dehu 54
Devahṛda 72
Devaprayāga 4;5
Deva-tīrtha 92
Deveśa-tīrtha 40

Devī-tīrtha 40; 109
Dhanyapur 103
Dhāreśvara 133
Dharmapṛṣṭha 86
Dhautapāpā 93
Dhūtapāpā 93
Dūdheśvara 109
Dvaitavana 116

G

Galiteśvara 133
Gandharva-tīrtha 40; 116
Gaṇeśvara-tīrtha 93
Gaṅgādvāra 40; 44; 48
Gaṅgā-Sāgara-Saṅgama 40
Gaṅgāvāhaka-tīrtha 90
Gaṅgeśvara-tīrtha 40; 93
Gaṅgotrī 44; 114
Gargasrota-tīrtha 116
Gaurī-tīrtha 40
Gautameśvara 93; 133
Go-tīrtha 93; 109
Govardhana tīrtha 48
Guhāraṇya-kṣetra 136
Gupteśvara-tīrtha 133

H

Haṁsa-tīrtha 93
Haṁsaprapatana-tīrtha 40
Haridvāra 40; 44

J

Jambukeśvara 40; 69
Jamunotrī 114
Jāpeśvara-tīrtha 40
Jaratkāreśvara 133
Jñāna-tīrtha 40
Joshimaṭha 4
Jyotirliṅga 15; 46; 91; 123

K

Kāla-tīrtha 41
Kālakeśvara-tīrtha 41
Kālañjara-tīrtha 41
Kālīmaṭha 85
Kallolakeśvara 93
Kalyāṇ-tīrtha 131
Kāma-tīrtha 93
Kāmākhyā Devī 20
Kāmarūpa 20
Kanaka-Durgā 71
Kanakhala 41; 48; 88; 93
Kāñcipuram 139; 146
Kāntāreśvara 133
Kanyā-tīrtha 93
Kanyākumārī 131
Kapālamocana 41
Kapāleśvara 48
Kapila-tīrtha 41; 49; 93
Kardamila 111
Karhad-kṣetra 71
Karṇaprayāga 4;5
Kāśī 41; 123
Kāśī Viśvanātha 131
Kāṭeśvara-tīrtha 133
Kedār-tīrtha 128
Kedāranātha 86
Khadga-tīrtha 109
Khadgadhareśvara 109
Khambhat 83; 94
Kokamukha 65
Kośeśvara 5
Koṭeśvara temple 103
Koṭi-tīrtha 49; 93; 103
Kṛttivāseśvara-tīrtha 41
Kubjāmra-tīrtha 41
Kumbheśvara Mahādeva 91
Kurujāṅgala 55
Kurukṣetra9; 54; 55; 56; 88; 102; 116; 132
Kuśa-tīrtha 93
Kuśāvarta-tīrtha 41; 48; 49
Kuṭṭaleśvara 131

L

Lachmanjhūlā 44
Lakṣmaṇa-kuṇḍa 49
Liṅgī-Janārdana 93

M

Madhuvana-tīrtha 155
Madurai 73; 139; 146
Madhyaraṅgam 68
Mahādeva 71
Mahī-Sāgara-Saṅgama 83
Maṇikarṇa-tīrtha 41
Maṇikarṇeśvara 20
Manohara-tīrtha 93
Mānuṣa-tīrtha 7
Mātṛ-tīrtha 49; 93
Mātṛbhūteśvara 69
Mukteśvara-tīrtha 133

N

Nāga-tīrtha 41; 49
Nāgadhanvana 116
Nāgeśvara 133
Nakulīśvara 41
Nandaprayāga 5
Nandī-tīrtha 93
Nārada-tīrtha 93
Narasiṁha temple 17
Nārāyaṇa temple 41; 68
Nashik 49
Naṭarāja temple 69
Nau-bandhana-tīrtha 152
Nīlakaṇṭha 109

O

Okhīmaṭha 85
Oṅkāranātha 91

P

Paṁpā-kṣetra 136
Pañcanad-Tīrtha 121
Pañcavaṭī 46; 49
Pandharpur 16; 23
Pāpanāśana 130; 131
Pehoa 9; 114; 115
Phalgu 104
Piṅgaleśvara 94
Piśācamocana 41
Pitāmaha-tīrtha 41; 93
Pitṛtīrtha 101
Plakṣa Praśravaṇa 114; 116
Prabhāsa 114; 116
Prājāpatya-tīrtha 41
Pravarā-saṅgama 49; 51; 105
Prayāga 10; 38; 42; 44; 115; 121; 144; 154; 155; 156
Pṛthūdaka 9; 10; 28; 99; 114
Puṣkara-tīrtha 116
Puṣkaraī 94

R

Rājahmundry 49
Rāmakuṇḍa 49
Rāma-temple 48
Rāmeśvara-liṅga 132
Rāmeśvara-tīrtha 133
Ṛṇa-tīrtha 94
Ṛṇapramocana-tīrtha 155
Rudraprayāga 4; 5; 85

S

Śakra-tīrtha 94
Śakreśvara-tīrtha 42
Sākṣa Gopāla 15
Śalagrāma-tīrtha 31
Sālivatīśvara 131
Saṅgameśvara-tīrtha 42; 94; 109
Śanī temple 91
Śaṅkara temple 131
Śaṅkha-tīrtha 116
Sapta-sāgara-yātrā 48
Sapta-sārasvata-tīrtha 116
Sargabindu-tīrtha 94
Saubhāgya-tīrtha 103
Sāvitrī-tīrtha 94
Sītākuṇḍa 49

Śivapurī 91
Śivasamudram 68
Śivodbheda 115
Somanatha 114
Soma-tīrtha 49; 56; 94; 109; 116
Śrī Devī 131
Śrīkakulam 78
Śriṅgerī 72; 136
Śrīraṅgama 68; 69
Śriraṅgapattanam 68
Śrīsailam 71
Śrī-tīrtha 42; 71
Śivavaikuṇṭham 131
Stambha-tīrtha 83; 94
Subhūmika 116
Subramaṇya 131
Śūkara-kṣetra 152
Śukla-tīrtha 91;92
Śukra-tīrtha 94
Śūlabheda 94
Śūrpaṇeśvara 91
Svāmī-tīrtha 76
Svargadvāra 42
Svayaṁbhūliṅga 131

T

Tāpī-sāgara-saṅgama 132; 133
Tāpeśvara-tīrtha 94
Tapovana-tīrtha 49
Thanjavur 69
Tridaśeśvara Mahādeva 18
Triveṇī 26; 30; 44; 64; 65; 115
Tryaṁbaka 46; 49; 50; 94
Tryaṁbakeśvara 46; 48

U

Ujjayinī 12; 122; 123; 124
Umā-tīrtha 103
Umāhaka-tīrtha 94
Uttara-tīrtha 42

V

Vāhneya-tīrtha 42
Vaidyanātha 60
Vañjarā-saṅgama 49
Varadarāja temple 131
Varāha-kṣetra 65
Vārāṇasī 10; 44; 129; 142; 144
Vaṭeśvara-tīrtha 94
Vidyādhareśvara 42
Vikīrṇa tīrtha 109
Vinaśana 114; 115; 116
Vipra-tīrtha 49
Virāṭanagarī 71
Viṣṇu-tīrtha 49; 94
Viṣṇuprayāga 4; 5
Viśvarūpa-tīrtha 42
Viṭhobā temple 16
Vṛṣa-tīrtha 26
Vṛṣadhvaja-tīrtha 42
Vṛṣotsarga tīrtha 94
Vyāghreśvara-tīrtha 42

W

Wāī 71

Y

Yama-tīrtha 42; 95
Yodhipur 94

GENERAL INDEX

A

Abu mt. 108; 144
Acehoda lake 1; 2
Ādiśeṣa 68
Agastya 66; 67; 122; 130
Agastya Malai 131
Aghora 50
Agni 32; 77
Agniṣṭoma 7; 9; 28; 56; 89; 112; 113; 115; 125; 150
Agniṣvātas 1
Aja 118
Akhaṇḍa 103
Akṣayaloka 80
Alambuṣā 113
Altin Tag 125
Alvars 131
Alexander 152
Āmalaka 66; 67
Amarakaṇṭaka 60; 80; 91; 95; 126; 150
Amāvasu 1
Amāvāsyā 2; 38
Ananta Nāga 151
Anasūyā 91
Andhaka 83; 90; 123
Aṅga 85
Aṅgiras 55
Aral Sea 142
Aravalli 78; 83; 115
Arbuda 108
Ārjīka 8
Arṇa 117
Ārṣṭaṣeṇa 12
Arundhatī 117
Aruṇodā 124
Āryāvarta 28
Ashoka 123
Aśvakrānta 21
Aśvamedha 20; 27; 32; 33; 61; 64; 86; 112
Aśvamukhas 12
Aśvattha 63
Aśvins 46
Atirātra 9; 28; 113
Atri 48; 55; 91
Avabhṛtha-bath 117
Avantis 12; 76; 123
Avimukta 123

B

Baba Budan mt. 146
Baḍavāmukhas 12
Baladeva 123
Bal Chukki 68
Bali 55
Bandarpunch 155
Banhal Pass 151
Barabangahal 3
Bara Lacha 11; 23
Baramula 152
Bastar-hills 80
Betul Plateau 143

Bhadal 3
Bhadrāśva 36; 124
Bhagīratha 33; 36; 37; 49
Bhagīratha Kharak 4
Bhāṇḍīra-vaṭa 154
Bhandar Plateau 130
Bharadvāja 14; 48
Bhārgavas 55
Bharata 25; 53; 60; 76
Bharata-āśrama 65
Bhartṛharī 123
Bhasmācala 20
Bhasmakūṭa 20
Bhils 83
Bhīmaratha 15
Bhīṣma 5; 35; 56
Bhṛgu 92; 138
Bhṛgukacha (= Broach) 92
Bhūdhara 27
Bhūdhara 27
Bhūloka 2
Bindusara 33
Bisal lake 79
Brahmā 19; 27; 33; 34; 47; 58; 66; 70; 77; 79; 113; 114; 123; 127; 136; 139; 143; 144
Brahmagiri 47; 48; 50; 65; 66;68
Brahmahatyā 9; 10; 76; 113
Brahmakuṇḍa 20
Brahmaloka 5; 27; 33; 89; 149
Brāhmaṇācchaṅśina-śastra 6
Brahmāṇḍakaṭāha 35
Brahmapurī 36
Bṛhaspati 6; 46; 71
Brindāvana 68
Buddha 123
Bunderpunch 58
Bungall mt. 101

C

Caitraratha 2; 35; 124
Candraprabha mt. 1;2
Candraprabha lake 56
Cardomon hills 74
Chamb 3;4
Candra Droṇa 146
Chaukhamba 4
Chāyā 132
Chilka 81
Chotanagpur hills 18; 25
Citrakūṭa 25; 85; 102
Citrāṅgada 2
Citrratha 1; 25; 117
Cyavana 138

D

Dadhīci 109; 113
Dakṣa 16; 22; 40 128; 140
Danta hills 116
Danu 27
Dardi Water Fall 96
Daśa-harā 37
Dāśarājña-war 101
Daśaratha 117; 129
Devavrata 35
Dhanbar 108
Dharma 139
Dhauldhar range 149
Dhulkhed 16
Dhundu 27
Diti 135
Divodāsa 112
Draupadī 59
Drupada 59
Durgā 151
Durjaya 59
Dvādaśī-vrata 3
Dvaitavana 18
Dvāpara 2
Dvijapriya 149

E

Eocene Sea 15

Everest 65

F

Falls Point 81

G

Gādhi 62; 63; 64
Gagan Chukki Fall 68
Gaja-grāha-yuddha 26; 125
Gandhamādana 4; 12; 19; 36; 55
Gandharvas 4; 52; 89
Gandhi-sāgar 24
Gaṇeśa 47; 67
Gaṅgāmūla 136; 137
Gaṅgāvataraṇa 33
Garo hills 21
Garuḍa 151
Gautama 47; 48; 49; 55
Gavilgarh hills 102
Gaya 103; 104; 149
Girikā 126
Girnar hills 126
Girnar hills 100
Gonche lake 2
Govardhana 154
Govinda-ghat 5
Guha 136; 137
Guhyakas 1; 2
Gulf of Mannar 130; 131

H

Haihayas 63
Hairaṇvat 53
Hampi 136; 137
Haṁsa 80
Hanumān 155
Hara 144
Haridvar hills 138
Harihara 136; 137
Harivarṣa 19
Hemakūṭa 7; 36; 57
Hemaśṛṅga 78
Himādri 54; 57
Himālayas 1; 3; 12; 13; 14; 20; 23; 26; 27; 28; 29; 32; 36; 44; 52; 53; 54; 58; 61; 64-67; 80; 97; 106; 114; 118; 123; 129; 153; 155
Himavat 4; 21; 23; 25; 36; 106; 111; 117; 119; 121; 135; 138; 147; 150
Hindu 121
Hindukush 74; 75; 107; 129
Hindusthana 121
Hirakund Dam 82
Hiraṇyākṣa 135

I

Ikṣvāku 33
Ilāvarta 55
India 121
Indra 6; 9; 17; 27; 32; 49; 50; 52; 55; 67; 109; 111; 113; 117; 148
Indradyumna 82
Indraloka 110
Indus 121
Īśāna 50

J

Jahnu 37
Jalodbhava 150; 151
Jamadagni 20; 48; 63; 112;
Jambudvīpa 55
Jamunotrī 155
Janaka 54
Janārdana 3; 21; 154
Janpao-range 24
Jarudhi mt. 19
Jayā 47
Jñansambandhara 68
Jñāneśvara Sant 16; 54

K

Kabir 91
Kabira-Vaḍa 91; 92

Klailāsa 1; 2; 19; 20; 21; 47; 66; 67; 117; 121; 123; 130
Kaimur hills 130
Kaiṭabha 20
Kalahandi hills 78
Kalinda mt. 58; 156
Kāliya 154
Kalki 21
Kalmāśapāda 119
Kāmadeva 20
Kāmadhenu 24; 103; 109
Kamban 68
Kaṇva 84; 105
Kanyā 71
Kapila 32; 40; 60
Kapiñjala 60
Kapisthala 55
Karakoram-range 121
Karkul lake 124
Karṇa 11
Kaśyapa 27; 48; 135
Kauśika 55; 64
Kauśikāśrama 64
Kauṭilya 77
Kavera 66
Kayal 130
Kedāranātha 85
Kekaya 25; 53; 60; 77
Ketumāla 36; 37
Kiṇkara 119
Kodarma Plateau 111
Kokri Bardi Hill 123
Kolāhala mt 126
Kolis 83
Kongys Tso lake 2
Korkai 130
Kośala 109
Koynā Devī 72
Krauñca 99
Krauñca-vadha 129
Kṛṣṇa 20; 37; 59; 100; 123; 154
Kṛṣṇarāja-sāgara 68; 69
Kṛītikās 77
Kṣīrasāgara 103
Kubera 49
Kumaon hills 117; 118
Kumārila 150
Kumbhamelā 49; 124
Kumbhaparva 38
Kuntī 11
Kuru 132
Kurus 6; 36
Kuśadhvaja 54
Kuśapriya 84
Kuśika 62; 64
Kuttalam Fall 131
Kuvalayārūḍha 95

L

Lahul 11
Lakṣmaṇa 46; 49
Lakṣmī 35; 113
Laṅkā 48; 155
Lauhityās 78
Likhita 13
Lohal 4
Lohīt 20
Lola 144
Lopāmudrā 66; 67; 79; 122
Lop Nor 125

M

Madhu 20
Madras 3; 53
Magadha 85
Mahabaleshwar 70; 146
Mahābhadra 36
Mahābhiṣa 33; 34
Mahadev hills 143
Mahādevī 31
Mahākāla 123

Mahākāla-vana 123
Mahākānana 123
Mahatma Gandhi 109
Mahendra mt. 77; 87; 105; 107; 123; 134;135; 141
Maheśvara 27
Mahī 82
Mahiṣāsura 99
Mahīvāsa 82
Maikala 95; 111; 125
Makarasaṅkrānti 38; 40
Malaya 73; 105; 128; 130; 131; 138
Malla-dvādaśī 154
Mallikārjuna 71
Mālyavān 37
Mānasa 36; 78
Mānasarovara 19; 117; 120
Mandāra hills 19; 110
Mandhar Water Fall 96
Māndhātā 89; 91
Mandla hills 96
Maṇibhadra 1; 2
Manu 74; 149
Marco Polo 130
Marusthalī 79
Maruts 6
Marwar hill 83
Matināra 112
Matsya 151
Matsyāvatāra 74; 151
Matsyopākhyāna 149
Mehad lake 83
Mehwas 82
Mekala-Kanyakā 91
Mekala range 90
Mewar hills 108
Menakā 84
Menā 32
Meru 2; 4; 32; 35; 36; 37; 47; 55; 56; 110; 124; 125; 142
Merumandara 55; 56
Mishmi hills 19
Mora hills 104
Mūlatāpī 132

N

Nabhasya 7
Nāgas 89; 90
Nāgaloka 115
Nāgārjuna-sāgara 73
Nāgodbheda 115
Nāhuṣas 112
Naimiṣāraṇya 29; 59
Nala 98
Namuci 9; 52
Nandana 4; 36
Nadīkuṇḍa 108
Nārāyaṇa 68; 71
Nau 151
Nīlācala 20
Nīlagiris 131
Nīlanāga 151
Nīrā 17
Niṣadha 98

P

Palni hills 139
Pamir 106; 124; 142
Pañcagauḍa 45
Pañcameśvara 54
Pāṇḍavas 18; 71
Pāṇḍinātha hill 20
Paṇis 31; 107
Paraśurāma 19; 20; 63; 139
Parāśara 2; 154
Pāriyātra mt.3; 12; 22; 23; 26; 76; 78; 82; 84; 98; 100; 120; 122; 144; 145; 147; 152; 153
Pārvatī 16; 20; 47; 58; 61; 123; 124; 130; 140; 151
Pātālaloka 32; 33
Pāṭaliputra 126

Patar plateau 24
Pirpanjal 8; 148; 151
Pitāmaha lake 75
Pitṛs 1; 2; 7; 31; 39; 103
Pitṛloka 2; 139
Pitṛvrata 56
Plakṣa tree 112
Prabhāsa 112
Pradyota 123
Prāgjyotiṣa 20
Prahlāda 18; 59; 77; 84
Prajāpati 30
Pralaya 90
Pratīpa 34
Proṣṭhapadī-Aṣṭakā 2
Pulastya 5; 56
Puloma 138
Pulomā 138; 139
Punasa Dam 96
Pūrṇakumbha 38
Puru 112; 152
Purukutsa 89
Purūrauas 3; 53
Puṣkalāvatī 75
Puṣkara (Pushkara) 49; 79; 127; 133
Puṣpagiri 75; 105
Putreṣṭi 117

Q

Qala Punj 142

R

Rādhā 37
Rāhu 51
Rājānaka 17
Rājasūya 56; 62; 64;
Rākṣasa-tāla 120
Rāma 46; 48; 49; 132; 138; 140; 145
Rantideva 23
Rāvaṇa 46; 120; 131
Ṛcīka 62; 63
Reṇukā 63
Rohtang pass 8; 148
Ṛkṣa mt. 6; 14; 25; 26; 56; 60; 70; 80; 85; 86; 90; 91; 98; 102; 104; 110; 122; 125; 126; 127; 129; 132; 134; 139; 141; 149; 150
Ṛṣyaśṛṅga 64
Rudra 53
Rudraloka 89; 150
Rudra-Sarovara 124
Rukmakavaca 125
Rūpadhara 3

S

Sābarmati Ashram 109
Sadyojāta 50
Sagara 32; 33
Sagaropākhyāna 32
Sagar plateau 26
Sahya mt. 7; 15; 29; 65; 67; 70; 73; 86; 107; 127; 135; 141; 146; 147
Sahyādri 16; 17; 46; 54; 66; 67
Sahasradhārā Fall 96
Śailodā lake 110
Śakti 119; 154
Śakuntalā 84
Śālagrāma 30
Śālaveya hill 111
Salt sea 36
Sambaka mt. 19
Śaṁbhu 117
Samudra-manthana 51
Saṁvaraṇa 132
Sandīpanī 123
Sanglakh range 75
Sañjīvanī 99
Sañjñā 153
Śaṅkarācārya 136

Śaṅkha 13
Śaṅkhacakra-gadādhara 95
Śaṅkhakūṭa mt 36
Saṅkrānti 38
Śaṅkukarṇa 16
Santals 26
Śantanu 2; 19; 34; 35
Santopantha 4
Śāradāmbā 138
Saramā 107
Sārasvata 113
Sārasvata-loka 113
Sarpa lake 57
Satīdesh 151
Satīsara 151
Satpura 96; 132
Satyavatī 2; 62; 63; 64
Satya-yuga 91
Sāvitrī-forest 36
Shinkai-Ohnat mt. 52
Shippila 120
Siddhas 7
Siṁha 46
Sindha 121
Śipra lake 123
Sirmur hills 28; 114
Śītā 46; 49; 140
Śītānta mt. 36
Śītoda lake 36
Śiva 15; 16; 20; 32; 33; 36; 37; 47; 50; 58; 61; 67; 70; 77; 83; 88; 90; 91; 99; 103; 120; 123; 124; 130; 136; 137; 140; 143; 144; 150
Siwalik hills 44; 58; 114; 138; 156
Skanda 32; 60; 75; 77; 83; 99
Soma 5; 6; 8; 51
Somaloka 23
Somapās 89
Somapatha-lokas 1
Śravaṇakumāra 117
Śrāvastī 117
Śrī 71, 111
Śrīkaṇṭha 154
Śṛṅgavān 37; 110
Śrīnivāsa 68
Śrīpati 95
Śrīvatsāṅka 95
Śrutāyudha 100
Sthāṇeśvara 126
Subramaṇya range 75
Sudāmā 123
Sudāsa 119
Sudyumna 13
Śukadeva 91
Sukeśī 144
Śukrācārya 27
Śuktimat mt. 70; 74-77; 85; 99; 108; 127; 134; 141
Sumanas 89
Sumati 32
Sundarbans 44
Suparśva mt. 36; 125
Surabhi 24
Surange La mt. 2
Surapadma 67
Sur Lake 81
Śūrpaṇakhā 49
Sūryaloka 29; 59
Svarga 33
Svargaloka 27; 32
Svarakṣu mt. 36
Śvetagiri 128
Śyāmāka 7
Śyāvāśva 17

T

Talakāverī 68
Tāmraliptaka 122
Taṁsu 112
Tāraka 83; 99

Tatpuruṣa 50
Tant-Gari 3
Tenkāśī 131
Thokchan 2
Tripurāsura 15
Triśaṅku 60
Triśikha 36
Tukārāma Sant 16; 54
Tulasī 35

U

Udārāṅga 95
Udaya mt. 77
Udayana 123
Uddālaka 86
Udumbara 63
Umā 32; 90; 151
Uparicara 126
Urvaśī 20; 59
Urvaśīkuṇḍa 20
Uśanas 99
Uṣas 148
Uśīnara 55
Uśīragiri 138
Uttara Kurus 14
Utathya 114

V

Vaḍavānala 114
Vadhraśva Ṛṣi 112
Vaibhāga 36
Vaidehaka 151
Vaitaraṇī-vrata 140
Vājapeya 29; 33; 146
Vajra 109
Vālmīki 129
Vāmadeva 50
Vāmana 3; 27; 35; 47; 77
Varadamūla hill 137; 143
Varāha 135; 138; 151
Varāhamūla 152
Varāha-parvata 136; 137
Varāhāvatāra 65; 151
Varuṇa 62; 100; 114
Varuṇodā lake 35; 124
Varushand hills 74
Vasanta-pañcamī 38
Vāsavadattā 123
Vasiṣṭtha 9; 34; 48; 108; 112; 117; 119; 154
Vasu 2
Vasus 34; 124; 126
Vāsuki 151
Vatsa 123
Vāyu 38
Verang Fountain 151
Verinag 152
Vicitravīrya 2
Victoria lake 142
Videha 109
Vidyānagara 137
Vijayanagara 137
Vikramāditya 123
Vindhyas 2; 6; 24; 29; 67; 74; 76;80; 83; 91; 95; 96; 98; 100; 102; 107; 110; 127; 141; 146; 147; 149
Vindhyapada 132
Vipula mt. 36
Vīra 95
Vīrabhadra 16
Virocana 55
Viṣṇu 16; 27; 30; 35; 38; 47; 51; 53; 66; 70; 77; 80; 84; 89; 90; 95; 99; 103; 113; 117; 125; 135; 136; 137; 143; 149; 150; 151; 152; 154
Viṣṇu-loka 30; 154
Viṣṇumāyā 66; 67
Viśvāmitra 9; 48; 62; 63; 64; 84; 108; 119; 148
Vitastā-pūjā 151

Vivasvān 132
Vṛṣabha mt. 36; 153
Vṛtra 5; 6; 109; 111
Vyāsa 91

W

Warkaris 16; 54
Wular lake 152

Y

Yakṣas 1; 2; 117
Yama 140; 153; 154
Yogaśāyī 10; 144
Yogasiddhi 26

❖❖❖❖